THE
DOCTORS
OF THE
CHURCH

THE
DOCTORS
OF THE
CHURCH

THIRTY-THREE MEN AND WOMEN WHO SHAPED CHRISTIANITY

BERNARD McGINN

A Crossroad Book
The Crossroad Publishing Company
New York

The Crossroad Publishing Company
370 Lexington Avenue, New York, NY 10017

Cover art and interior illustrations by Bro. Michael O'Neill McGrath, osfs

Printed in the United States of America

Library of Congress Cataloging-in-Publication Data
McGinn, Bernard, 1937-
    The doctors of the church : thirty-three men and women who shaped
Christianity / by Bernard McGinn.
        p. cm.
    Includes bibliographical references.
    ISBN 0-8245-1771-7   (pbk.)
    1. Doctors of the church – Biography. 2. Doctors of the church.
I. Title.
BX4669.M25 1999
282'.092'2 – dc21
[B]   99-22090

2   3   4   5   6   7   8   9   10   04   03   02   01   00

To David Tracy,
for almost fifty years, a friend,
colleague, and fellow searcher

Contents

II. MEDIEVAL DOCTORS

III. MODERN DOCTORS

Part Three
WHAT IS THE FUTURE
OF THE DOCTORS OF THE CHURCH?
175

Abbreviations

I. Translation Series

ACW   *Ancient Christian Writers: The Works of the Fathers of the Church in Translation.* Westminster, Md., and New York: Newman Press, 1946–. The series is now being reprinted and continued by Paulist Press.

CWS   *The Classics of Western Spirituality.* New York: Paulist Press, 1978–.

FC   *The Fathers of the Church: A New Translation.* Washington, D.C.: Catholic University of America Press, 1947–.

NPNF   *The Nicene and Post-Nicene Fathers of the Christian Church.* 1st series: 14 vols.; 2d series: 14 vols. The most recent reprint of this collection is Grand Rapids: Eerdmans, 1983

II. Handbooks for the Study of the Fathers and Doctors

Hanson   R. P. C. Hanson. *The Search for the Christian Doctrine of God: The Arian Controversy 318–381.* Edinburgh: T. & T. Clark, 1993.

Huscenot   Jean Huscenot. *Les docteurs de l'Église.* Paris: Médiaspaul, 1997. This is the only other guide to all the doctors of the church known to me. Readers of French can find fairly extensive biographical discussions of each doctor in this work.

Patrology III   Johannes Quasten. *Patrology.* Vol. III. *The Golden Age of Greek Patristic Literature from the Council of Nicaea to the Council of Chalcedon.* Westminster, Md.: Newman Press, 1960.

Patrology IV   Angelo di Bernardino, editor. *Patrology.* Vol. IV. *The Golden Age of Latin Patristic Literature from the Council of Nicaea to the Council of Chalcedon.* Westminster, Md.: Christian Classics, 1986.

Rusch   William G. Rusch. *The Later Latin Fathers.* London: Duckworth, 1977.

Young   Frances M. Young. *From Nicaea to Chalcedon: A Guide to the Literature and Its Background.* Philadelphia: Fortress Press, 1983.

PREFACE

WHO COULD FAIL to be impressed upon entering St. Peter's basilica? Whether we are seeing it for the first time or for the hundred and first, no other Christian edifice makes as dramatic an impact. Approaching St. Peter's through the embrace of the vast colonnaded square designed by the master artist of the Baroque Gian Lorenzo Bernini, the visitor climbs a series of low steps to pass through the bronze doors into the church's immense interior. Marble altars and mosaics, the golden-coffered ceiling and chromatic floor lead the tourist or pilgrim on to the central focus of the basilica — the main altar and great bronze baldacchino, or canopy, that mark the burial place of Peter. Impressive as this site, the *confessio Petri*, is, St. Peter's has a second and further center of attention. The baldacchino (constructed by Bernini between 1626 and 1633) is designed to frame an even more fantastic object that dominates the rear wall of the basilica. This is the *cathedra Petri*, the world's largest reliquary, designed and built by Bernini and his workshop between 1657 and 1666. As his son, Domenico, once said: "The two works, the square and the *cathedra* are, as it were, beginning and end of the magnificence of that great church, and the eye is as much infatuated at the beginning on entering the square as at the end on seeing the *cathedra*."

Since at least the thirteenth century an ancient wooden chair had been venerated as the throne on which the apostle and traditionally first bishop of Rome once taught. As the new basilica neared completion, Pope Alexander VII decided that this relic should be enshrined in a manner befitting its importance as the symbol of the teaching authority of the Petrine see. Bernini's concept was to enclose the modest wooden chair in a huge structure of marble, bronze, and stucco under and around a window painted with a dove symbolizing the Holy Spirit, the source of Christian truth. On large marble pillars at the base of the structure he placed four towering bronze figures alive with emotional power and expressivity. They touch, but do not really support, the throne, which appears to hover in the air, as if by divine power. These figures represent four doctors of the church: two in miters for the Western church (Augustine and Ambrose), and two without miters for the Eastern church (Athanasius and John Chrysostom).

The appearance of the four doctors, symbolizing the whole body of the *doctores ecclesiae*, was not a matter of artistic whim. The deeply religious Bernini and his papal patron wished to provide a visual demonstration of the vital link between the doctors of East and West, as well as to emphasize Rome's doctrinal centrality in the post-Reformation period. Although the bishops of Rome did not invent the concept of "doctor of the church," by the end of the sixteenth century they had claimed that there was an unbreakable bond between papal teaching authority and Christendom's most prestigious doctors. To the traditional four doctors of the Western church (Augustine, Ambrose, Jerome, Gregory the Great) and four doctors of the Eastern church (Athanasius, Chrysostom, Basil, Gregory of Nazianzus) sixteenth-century popes added the names of Thomas Aquinas and Bonaventure. After the completion of St. Peter's in the late seventeenth century, eighteenth-century popes began to augment the list of doctors even further. Their successors have continued the practice down to the present day.

On October 19, 1997, in the shadow of the four male doctors so strikingly portrayed in Bernini's *cathedra Petri*, Pope John Paul II declared Thérèse Martin (1873–97), better known as St. Thérèse of Lisieux, a doctor of the church. The crowds that gathered in Rome to participate in this event demonstrated the importance of Thérèse in contemporary Catholicism. The event also testified to the ongoing concern of the contemporary papacy with naming *doctores ecclesiae*. It is no accident that the last three teachers given this official papal recognition were all women — Teresa of Avila and Catherine of Siena in 1970, and now Thérèse of Lisieux. It is slightly ironic to note that in 1967, a scant three years before the declaration of Teresa and Catherine, the article on "Doctor of the Church" in the *New Catholic Encyclopedia* claimed "it would seem that no woman is likely to be named [doctor] because of the link between this title and the teaching office, which is limited to males" (*New Catholic Encyclopedia* 4:939). Despite the resistance of the contemporary papacy to calls for the ordination of women, recent popes have clearly not agreed with the claim that the teaching office, even in its most exalted forms, is limited to males. If Bernini were brought back to life and commissioned to do a new version of the *cathedra*, he might well be advised to use two men and two women to symbolize the august body of thirty-three official *doctores ecclesiae*.

There have been 265 popes in the history of the Catholic Church, yet only 33 doctors (only two were bishops of Rome!). Although for the last four centuries it is only the Roman popes who have been interested in adding new names to the list of doctors, recent popes have not used their power of nomination to aggrandize the papacy by adding more of their predecessors. Since the modern explosion of additions to the ranks of the doctors, which has more than tripled the number since 1700, only one pope, Leo I (declared a doctor in 1754), has made the list — and few would disagree with this belated recognition of a teacher revered in both Eastern and Western Christianity. A survey of the new doctors shows that the bishops of Rome have continued to think of "doctor" as an ecumenical denomination, involving both Eastern and Western Christendom. More strikingly, in the past thirty years they have also come to see it as not limited to male teachers who enjoyed the power of holy orders.

But who are the doctors of the church and why are they significant? While Orthodox Christianity continues to revere some patristic teachers as *hierarchs* (the Eastern Christian equivalent of *doctor ecclesiae*), modern Orthodoxy has not been interested in extending the number of doctors. Protestant Christians have, on the whole, been even less concerned with the doctors. Why has Roman Catholicism been so intent on naming and honoring doctors? Do they really play any role in contemporary Catholicism aside from an honorific one? How does one get to be a doctor of the church? Why did these thirty-three men and women among the thousands of Christian teachers over almost two millennia make the cut? To turn from the past to the future, is it likely that there will be more doctors officially proclaimed in the new millennium? The recent papal declaration of Thérèse of Lisieux, capping the unprecedented admission of three women to what had been an exclusively male club, prompts such questions and forms the genesis of this book.

In what follows I will try to provide a brief introduction to the *what*, the *who*, and the possible *why* of thirty-three men and women doctors of the church who have shaped Christianity. I write both as a Roman Catholic and as a student of historical theology. As a Catholic, I believe that the doctors do play a significant role in the life of the church, one that should be taken in as ecumenical and inclusive a fashion as possible. As a historical theologian, I have spent three decades reading and teaching the doctors of the church (admittedly some much more than others). To have the opportunity to present the full range of the doctors of the church to a broad readership is both inviting and intimidating. The task is attractive because many of the doctors are not well known to contemporary readers; but it is also intimidating, since even lengthy books on each of the doctors would be insufficient to plumb the depths of their teaching. What will be given here, then, is only an introduction, a brief handbook. Its purpose is to clarify what a *doctor ecclesiae* is and to emphasize that actually *reading* the doctors themselves is far more rewarding than reading about them.

I have structured the book around three questions: What is a doctor of the church? Who are the doctors of the church? How should we conceive of the future role of the doctors of the church? The first section will examine the development of the concept of *doctor ecclesiae* and the role that doctors have played in the life of the church. The second, and longest, section will give short summaries of the lives and teachings of each of the thirty-three current doctors, emphasizing what is central to their contribution to the history of Christian faith. These introductions are meant as prolegomena or invitations to begin reading the doctors themselves, so each treatment will include a short bibliography listing essential works in translation and some helpful studies in English of the doctor's life and thought. Finally, the brief third section is more experimental — a look at what the future of the list of doctors might bring us.

When I was first asked to consider writing this book by my friend Michael Leach, I was immediately conscious of my limitations in writing about *all* the doctors of the church with anything like adequacy. Though I have taught and written about many of these doctors, others were figures I had read only sporadically, and some not at all. This is why the writing of this book has proven to be so rich an experience for me personally. As I've had the opportunity to reread great books of these masters, or to take up, for the first time, things I always wanted to read, I've come to a deeper appreciation of why all the doctors of the church remain such rich resources for the flourishing of Christian life and thought. Although their writings are not always easy reading, and although their lives and contentions may be distant from us, these are figures who are not just week-end celebrities, but inspirations for the ages.

•

Every book is more than the product of the person who writes it. This book would never have existed if Michael Leach had not suggested it. In shaping its progress, I owe thanks both to the staff at Crossroad, and (as usual) to my wife, Patricia, a kind, but never indulgent, reader.

BERNARD McGINN

Chicago, December 1998

Part One

WHAT IS
A DOCTOR
OF THE CHURCH?

*In medio ecclesiae aperuit os ejus; et implevit eum Dominus spiritus
sapientiae et intellectus.*

(In the midst of the church he opened his mouth; and the Lord filled
him with the spirit of wisdom and understanding.)

THIS PASSAGE from Sirach 15:5 begins the Introit, or entrance chant,
of the mass for doctors of the church (though the masculine language now needs revising). Also distinctive of the liturgical honor
given to this restricted group of thirty-three persons representing almost two
millennia of Christian teaching is the antiphon sung at the Vespers of the
feasts of doctors: "O most excellent doctor, light of holy church, Saint N.,
lover of God's law. Beseech God's Son in our behalf." These texts from the
church's worship remind us that the position of a doctor is not something just
for the classroom or for learned discussion, but that the doctors speak "in the
midst of the church" and therefore *to* the whole church. To understand their
distinctive role in Christianity, we need a brief survey of how the concept of
doctor ecclesiae originated and developed.

The passing on of spiritual wisdom is among the earliest specialized tasks
of human communities. Almost all religions have some form of teaching authority, though often of a diffuse character. In the world religions that span
many peoples and geographical areas, responsibility for teaching the tradition is usually the prerogative of highly trained elites that have grown and
changed over centuries. Christianity provides an excellent example.

The Jesus movement was born in the midst of the vibrant and diverse
world of late Second Temple Judaism, a world which featured many kinds of

religious teachers. In the gospels Jesus is often addressed as *rabbi,* or teacher
(e.g., Matt. 26:25, Mark 9:4, John 1:38). His special teaching role is emphasized by one saying attributed to him that cautions his followers against
taking on the title: "You, however, must not allow yourselves to be called
rabbi, since you have only one master, and you are all brothers" (Matt. 23:8).
A similar view is reflected in John 13:13, where Christ explicitly accepts for
himself the titles "teacher" and "lord" (*didaskalos/kurios*) from the disciples.
"Rabbi" occurs most often in the gospel of John, the same gospel in which
Jesus promises his followers another counselor and protector to teach them
after he departs: "The Paraclete, the Holy Spirit, whom the Father will send
in my name, will teach you everything and remind you of all that I have said"
(John 14:26). If we take the message of John's gospel seriously, *the* doctor of
the church is always the Spirit sent in Jesus' name to the community of love
symbolized by those gathered in the upper room at the Last Supper. All subsequent teaching is rooted in the Holy Spirit as the living inner source of the
instruction delivered to humanity through Jesus Christ, the Incarnate Word.

The development of titles and terms expressing positions of leadership
and teaching authority in the early Christian gatherings, or churches (Greek
ekklesiai), is complex and still only partly understood. Preeminence was given
to the apostles (*apostoloi*), the twelve members of Christ's inner circle; but
Paul boldly ascribed the same title to himself on the basis of the appearance of
the Risen Jesus to him, commissioning his preaching to the Gentiles (1 Cor.
15:1–11). The term "bishop" (*episkopos,* literally "overseer") appears in the
New Testament, where it seems to be used interchangeably with "priest"
(*presbyteros;* e.g., Acts 20:17 and 28, Phil. 1:1; see also Didache 15.1–2). Despite the presence of such community leaders from the beginning, it is clear
from the Pauline epistles (the earliest Christian documents), as well as from
other sources, that it was the Holy Spirit acting within the community who
remained the essential source of Christian truth. In 1 Corinthians 12, for example, Paul discusses the various gifts of the Spirit given to the members of
that *ekklesia* — including wisdom (*sophia*), knowledge (*gnosis*), and prophecy
(*propheteia*) — and proclaims, "We were baptized into one body in a single
Spirit, Jews as well as Greeks, slaves as well as free men, and we were all
given the same Spirit to drink" (1 Cor. 12:13). All Christians, he says, have
received the Holy Spirit as a pledge in their hearts (2 Cor. 1:22); in another epistle he warns the church at Thessalonika, "Do not stifle the Spirit
or despise the gift of prophecy with contempt; test everything and hold on to
what is good" (1 Thess. 5:19–20).

Leadership in teaching, in worship, and in administration continued to de-
velop in Christianity. By the early second century, the letters of Ignatius of
Antioch provide evidence that in some Christian churches a clear distinction
had emerged between the single bishop understood as the central institutional and doctrinal authority and the priests and deacons who assisted him
in various ways. Ignatius speaks of the bishop as the "purpose," "mind," or

perhaps "mouthpiece" (*gnome*), of Christ, just as Christ is the "purpose" of the Father (Ephesians 3.2). In his Letter to the Smyrnaeans he says: "You must all follow the bishop as Jesus Christ followed the Father, and follow the presbytery as the apostles; respect the deacons as the commandment of God. Let no one do anything that has to do with the church without the bishop" (Smyrn. 8.1).

The great struggles over the definition of what it meant to be a Christian during the course of the second century, debates carried on both externally with Rabbinic Judaism and the Roman political and religious world as well as internally among competing understandings of what constituted proper Christianity, brought to the fore the power of the bishops as the true expositors of Christian faith and the leaders of the community. Ever since, at least in the older Christian denominations, bishops have been seen as holding the most authoritative official teaching position in the church. Any doctrine that would disagree with that of the bishops, especially as expressed in collegial fashion (from the second century on bishops began to hold regional meetings, later called synods and councils), could not be described as true or authentic. But bishops did not act alone in teaching and leading their communities. A variety of other officials, mostly male (priests, deacons, catechists, etc.), but sometimes female (e.g., deaconesses), worked with them in instructing and governing each *ekklesia*. This broad penumbra of office indicates that the role of teacher, even as an official title, cannot be restricted to bishops.

More bishops (twenty in all) have been recognized as doctors of the church than any other group. Nevertheless, the nine priests and one deacon who have also been proclaimed doctors demonstrate that the special form of teaching charism the church points to in declaring someone a *doctor ecclesiae* is different from the institutional teaching role of the episcopacy. Furthermore, the recent creation of three women doctors — officially lay persons — shows that the teaching ascribed to doctors is independent of *any* form of ordination to church office. Teresa of Avila, Catherine of Siena, and Thérèse of Lisieux were all members of the laity, nonordained believers who were neither trained to teach nor formally recognized as teachers in their own time. (Indeed, each experienced opposition to her teaching, often from the ordained ecclesiastics of the day.) This fact demonstrates that while the *recognition* of someone as a doctor of the church is an act of ecclesiastical authority *from above*, so to speak (by pope or, as we shall see, possibly by an ecumenical council), the charism or grace that constitutes a person as a doctor arises from *within*, that is, from the gift of the Holy Spirit, the teacher of all Christ's followers. This position was clearly expressed by Pope Paul VI in the homily he delivered in 1970 declaring Teresa of Avila as the first woman doctor. Paul begins, "We have conferred, or better, we have *recognized* the title doctor of the church for Saint Teresa of Jesus" (*Acta Apostolicae Sedis* 62 [1970]: 590).

If a doctor can be a bishop but by no means need be, we must inquire more closely about the meaning of the Latin word *doctor* to understand what the difference between "ordained" teacher and officially recognized "charismatic" teacher means. *Doctrina* in Latin signifies the act of teaching, instructing, or training of any kind, so a *doctor* is a person who teaches anything (in classical Latin this included athletic instructors and animal trainers). Nevertheless, the pagan Romans mostly used *doctor* to indicate the higher forms of teaching, as when Cicero spoke of Plato as a *doctor* (*Tusculan Disputations* 1.20). Christians soon appropriated the word to describe the task of all those who conveyed the message of salvation to others. The earliest uses occur in the first major writer of Latin Christianity, Tertullian, a layman from North Africa. His *Objection against Heretics* (c. 200) uses *doctor* both to refer to priests and also to indicate how all Christian teachers depend ultimately on the Holy Spirit: "If the apostles themselves, who were appointed as doctors to the nations, were to follow the Paraclete as their doctor, how much more room was there for us in the saying 'Seek and you shall find' (Matt. 7:7) — we to whom teaching comes further down through the apostles, just as the apostles had their teaching through the Holy Spirit" (*Objection* 8). As employed in early Latin Christianity, then, *doctor* was a generic term for all who gave instruction in the faith, though it was primarily used of priests and others who held some official position.

Early Development of the Doctors of the Church

The recognition of Christianity by the emperor Constantine in the early fourth century ushered in a century and a half which saw the conversion of much of the population of the Roman Empire and also the most far-reaching debates over the proper interpretation of Christian faith since the second century. The disputes concerning the formulation of belief in the Trinity (the Arian controversy), as well as the correct way of proclaiming Jesus Christ as both God and man (the christological controversies), led to a series of large meetings of bishops to hammer out the creeds that were accepted as dogmas, or defined declarations, of the faith. These meetings, held at Nicaea in 325, at Constantinople in 381, at Ephesus in 431, and at Chalcedon in 451, were recognized as "ecumenical" (i.e., universal) councils and have remained the touchstones of orthodox Christianity ever since (see Appendix II).

The disputes of the fourth and fifth centuries also brought to the fore some of the greatest teachers of the early church. Most were bishops who were actively engaged in the heated polemics of the day, attacking the heresies, or errors, they saw around them (see Appendix I for a list). In the Greek East, Athanasius, Gregory of Nazianzus, and Basil fought against the Arians, who did not admit the full divinity of the Logos; later Cyril of Alexandria, who was both masterly theologian and crafty politician, combatted false views about the nature of Christ. Western bishops, like Hilary, Ambrose, and Augustine, also attacked the Arians, as well as a series of heresies not found in the East, such as the claims associated with the monk Pelagius that salvation depended in large part on human free will. The role of these church leaders in the doctrinal disputes of the period c. 315–450, the second major stage in the shaping of Christian orthodoxy, formed the basis for identifying some teachers as doctors of the church in a special sense. Although there had been influential Christian teachers prior to 300 (e.g., Bishop Irenaeus of Lyons in the second century and the catechist and priest Origen in the third century), all those who have thus far been *officially* declared doctors of the church date from the time after Constantine's recognition of Christianity. (A possible factor in this anomaly is that most of the major teachers prior to 300 died as martyrs and the later Latin tradition has resisted mingling the liturgical categories of doctor and martyr.) It is no accident that of the thirty-three doctors no less than thirteen (i.e., 40 percent) were born and died between 300 and 460.

The sense that there were some teachers, mostly bishops, who were particularly noteworthy for their explanation of true belief and opposition to heresy is evident in the earliest uses of the term *doctores ecclesiae* coming from the late patristic period between c. 400 and 600. At the beginning of the fifth century, for example, Rufinus of Aquileia at times used the term *doctor ecclesiae* to translate "teacher" in his translations of the Greek fathers Origen and Eusebius. In his polemical works against the Pelagian bishop Julian of Eclanum, written in the 420s, Augustine of Hippo appealed to the teachings of "the most renowned doctors of the church" (*praedicatissimos ecclesiae doctores*), in one place listing seven names, both Greek and Latin — Irenaeus, Cyprian, Hilary, Ambrose, Gregory of Nazianzus, Basil, and John Chrysostom (*Unfinished Work against Julian* 4). In another late work, *The Gift of Perseverance,* he says, echoing Tertullian: "The apostles and the doctors of the church who followed them and imitated them did both things, that is, they truthfully preached the grace of God (which is not given to us according to our merits) and they taught devout obedience by their saving precepts."

The importance of establishing criteria for orthodoxy is illustrated in the work of the Gallic monk Vincent of Lerins, who about 435 wrote a handbook called *The Warning against the Profane Novelties of All Heretics* designed to distinguish orthodoxy from heresy. Vincent identified the essence of orthodoxy as "what had been believed everywhere, always, and by all" — a much-quoted formula, if not always one easy to apply in concrete cases. Vincent stressed the role of scripture and tradition in determining correct belief and spoke of ecclesiastical writers as "doctors and masters of the churches" in a general way (see *Warning,* chap. 15). Writing about 500 c.e., an Italian monk, Eugippius, was especially concerned with the role of the great teachers as guides to orthodoxy. Eugippius was primarily interested in Augustine, whose reputation as the dominant figure in the West had emerged in the fifth century. In the prefatory letter to his *Excerpts from the Works of St. Augustine* he says: "Who does not know that the blessed bishop Augustine was and is outstanding among the great and esteemed doctors of the Catholic Church?" (*catholicae doctores ecclesiae*). (This dominance of Augustine continues to this day, as is evident from Appendix III, which surveys the use of the *doctores ecclesiae* at the Second Vatican Council and in the recent *Catechism of the Catholic Church.*)

In the era of the collapse of Roman rule in the West, with all the devastating effects this had on education and civil order, church leaders were conscious of the necessity of guaranteeing the preservation of correct doctrine for future generations. The wealthy Roman aristocrat Cassiodorus, who founded a monastery on his estates in southern Italy, composed his *Institutes* about 562 as a guidebook for his monastic school of Christian learning. Building upon Augustine's treatise *On Christian Doctrine,* which laid down the principles of a biblically based education, Cassiodorus established a course of studies that provided the model for medieval monastic schools. It naturally began with the Bible and the various commentaries on scripture, but it also included a chapter on the "Four Accepted Synods," and others devoted to the writings of five Western teachers (Cassiodorus calls them "most learned authors...with whom the ecclesiastical sky shines as if with gleaming stars") — Hilary, Cyprian, Ambrose, Jerome, and, of course, Augustine. A generation later, by the time of Gregory the Great (pope from 590 to 604), there was an emerging sense in the Latin West of the importance of the *doctores ecclesiae*. Gregory himself applied the term *doctores sanctae ecclesiae* to the apostles (*Homilies on the Gospels* 30.7), but also to all teachers who drew "the hidden meanings of the scriptures to common understanding" (*Exposition on First Kings,* bk. 6). Bishop Licinianus of Cartagena in Spain, writing to Gregory to thank him for the copy of the *Pastoral Rule* he had forwarded, praised the pope's book by saying, "The holy ancient fathers, the doctors and defenders of the church, Hilary, Ambrose, Augustine, and Gregory of Nazianzus, bear witness to this superb teaching of yours" (Gregory, *Register of Letters* 1.41a).

By the beginning of the Middle Ages, then, "doctors of the church" was a familiar term to describe authoritative teachers. In the seventh century Isidore of Seville (himself later named a doctor) used a popular analogy to describe their role: "Just as skilled physicians treat the body's varied illnesses with different medicine, there being diverse cures for the varieties of wounds, so too a doctor of the church uses the fitting remedy of teaching for each and all, and will proclaim whatever is needed for each person, according to age, sex, and profession" (*Books of Sentences,* bk. 3). There was, however, still no fixed number of doctors. The standard names most often mentioned were the Latin bishops Cyprian, Hilary, Ambrose, and Augustine, as well as the priest Jerome; but the Greek bishop Gregory of Nazianzus was sometimes joined to them. Gregory the Great was soon added to the list, as Licinianus had suggested in Gregory's own lifetime. The first person to make reference to what subsequently became the standard quartet of Latin fathers/doctors appears to be the Anglo-Saxon monk and polymath Venerable Bede (d. 735), who was to be added to the list of doctors in 1899. Writing to his friend Bishop Acca of Hexham, who had requested a commentary on the gospel of Luke, Bede explained how he had given these four figures pride of place in composing his work: "After I gathered together the works of the fathers, I took great care to examine what was understood in the words of St. Luke and what was expressed by the blessed Ambrose, by Augustine, and then by the most vigilant (as his name implies) Gregory — apostle of our nation — and by Jerome, the interpreter of sacred history, and by the other fathers" (Dedicatory Letter to Acca, *Exposition on the Gospel of Luke*). The emphasis on the number four was symbolically appropriate in the light of the four canonical gospels and the other appearances of four in sacred scripture. About the year 800, a monk named John highlighted this when he referred to, "Ambrose, Augustine, Jerome, and Gregory, who were most learned [*doctissimi*] in both sciences, i.e., divine and human, and who in eloquence were like the four rivers of paradise."

A similar process of creating lists of the church's major teachers was underway in the Byzantine East, though its history is less clear. Eastern Orthodox veneration for the "Holy Fathers" was, if anything, even more powerful than in the West. Three bishops were especially emphasized — Basil of Caesarea, Gregory of Nazianzus, and John Chrysostom, who had been bishop of Constantinople before being ejected from his see. They were often spoken of as the "great ecumenical teachers" (*oikumenikoi megaloi didaskaloi*). The emperor Leo the Wise (886–912) made their feasts obligatory throughout the Byzantine realm, and they were later given a common feast day — January 30, celebrated as the "Feast of the Three Hierarchs." (The enumeration of four Eastern doctors to match the four Western ones by adding Athanasius of Alexandria was a late medieval Western creation.)

An interesting witness to the desire to be true to the major teachers of both the West and the East is to be found in the work of the only Western thinker of the early Middle Ages who, due to his knowledge of Greek, was equally conversant with both sides of Christian tradition. John Scottus Eriugena, the Irish theologian of the ninth century, recognized the real differences between Latin authorities, especially Augustine, and Greek fathers, like Basil, Gregory of Nazianzus, and especially his favorite sources, Gregory of Nyssa, Pseudo-Dionysius, and the seventh-century monk Maximus the Confessor. Eriugena had a strong sense of the "direct communication" of truth from the Word Incarnate, through the apostles and saints, down to the present. His conviction of the inner unity of doctrine, despite so many seeming differences, led him to create a variety of strategies for what he called "contriving a consensus" (*consensum machinari*) among the authoritative teachers.

Doctors of the Church in the Late Medieval and Reformation Eras

The renewal of theology in the West associated with the rise of scholasticism in the twelfth and thirteenth centuries was an important stage both in emphasizing the role of the *doctores ecclesiae* and exploring the kind of authority they enjoyed. The number of doctors remained fluid, though a certain priority was given to the fourfold formula. Late in the eleventh century, Berengar of Tours, in his dispute with Lanfranc on the nature of Christ's presence in the Eucharist, appealed to the "authentic writings" of the standard four teachers, Ambrose, Augustine, Jerome, and Gregory. In the mid-twelfth century the German nun Hildegard of Bingen in the sermons she preached to her community on the gospel pericopes referred to "the doctors of the New Testament, such as Gregory, Ambrose, Augustine, and Jerome, and others like them with their teaching." Other lists of the major "fathers" (*patres* and *doctores* were often used interchangeably) came in sixes — either six patristic teachers (Cyprian, Hilary, Ambrose, Jerome, Augustine, Gregory), or the usual four with the medieval additions of Isidore of Seville and Bede. In the thirteenth century we find a variety of lists. The Franciscan teacher Bonaventure, for example, mentions twelve doctors (six Latin and six Greek) to parallel the twelve patriarchs of the book of Genesis (*Collations on the Hexaemeron* 16.26).

An important aspect of the creation of the scholastic method of theology, reflected in Peter Abelard's noted handbook *Sic et Non (Yes and No)*, was the necessity for working out ways to find agreement among, or to harmonize, differing positions in the views of inherited "authorities" (*auctoritates*), that is, the texts of the major patristic authors. The scholastics distinguished between the *authentica*, the inherited teachings of the councils and church fathers, and the *magistralia*, the positions of the modern masters of theology (*magistri*). Both groups could be called "doctors," at least in the general sense of someone who shared in the task of communicating the faith to others.

The teaching of Thomas Aquinas (1224–74) about the nature of what he called *sacra doctrina* and the role of *doctor ecclesiae* provides a good illustration of how *doctor* came to be understood as an analogous term, i.e., one shared in to some extent by all who hold the Christian faith, but which is especially identified with a few preeminent teachers. In his great *Summa of Theology (Summa theologiae)* the Dominican theologian identified the subject of the book as *sacra doctrina* (not theology as such) and spoke of the need for a "doctor of Catholic truth" to instruct both advanced students and beginners. (Thomas preferred the term "sacred doctrine" over theology because it emphasized the active task of teaching and being taught.) All believers need sacred doctrine in order to be saved because all must be taught by God about the saving mysteries that surpass human comprehension. Some, in turn, are themselves called upon to share in that teaching role through God's grace and ecclesiastical approbation (an authorization Thomas restricted to males).

Aquinas emphasized that Christ is always the primary *doctor ecclesiae* (e.g., *Commentary on Peter Lombard's Sentences*, bk. 3, 12.3). On the basis of his distinction between "saving grace" (*gratia gratum faciens*) and "special, or charismatic, grace" (*gratia gratis data*), which is given to communicate spiritual teaching to the church, he insisted that Christ, as "the first and main doctor of faith," possesses the fullness of all teaching grace (*Summa* IIIa.7.7; 42.4). In his *Commentary on the Gospel of John* Aquinas showed how Christ's unique teaching role resides in his full equality with the Father (chap. 1, lecture 11) and comprises the two main aspects of all teaching — "instructing the devout and refuting adversaries" (chap. 8, lecture 1). Aquinas's stress on Christ as *the* doctor of the church did not exclude the action of the Holy Spirit: "The Son hands doctrine over to us, since he is the Word; but the Holy Spirit makes us able to receive it" (chap. 14, lecture 6). No external word of any doctor avails unless the Holy Spirit, who can inspire the minds of even untutored Christians with the "highest wisdom and eloquence in an instant" (*Summa against the Gentiles* 1.6), provides understanding from within.

Aquinas often discussed how the grace of *doctor* is communicated by Christ to his followers. As befits his careful distinction between the realms of natural and supernatural knowledge, Thomas's understanding of the role of human doctors is expressed in two contexts. The first is his view of what it means to be a doctor or teacher (*magister*) in general, an issue he takes up especially in his *Disputed Questions on Truth* 11.1. The second is the scattered remarks he makes about the role of the special Christian teachers called "doctors" (Thomas does not provide any single summary treatment).

Aquinas's consideration of the human teacher in *On Truth* begins by citing an objection taken from Matthew 23:8, namely, that no human can teach, but only God. He argues, to the contrary, that humans can share in the activity of teaching, because all knowing is the actualization of the potential for understanding found in the "primary conceptions of the mind." Thomas says, "When the mind is led from these universal conceptions to actually knowing particular things which formerly were known only in potency and as it were in general, then someone is said to gain scientific understanding" (*scientia*). This comes about in one of two ways: either "discovery" (*inventio*), when natural reason finds unknown things on its own; or "instruction" (*disciplina*) when reason receives external help, as in the case of teaching. Therefore, "a person can truly be said to be a real doctor, both teaching truth and illuminating the mind, not as if he gives light to reason, but as helping the light of reason along to perfect understanding through the things he proposes from without."

Thomas discusses the special form of teaching that consists in cooperating with the interior illuminating action of the Holy Spirit primarily in his treatise on grace in the first half of the second book of the *Summa* (especially Ia-IIae.111.4; cf. *Commentary on 1 Corinthians* chap. 12, lesson 2). Special, or charismatic, graces are given to some humans to help others in the path to salvation (Ia-IIae.111.1). Thomas defends Paul's enumeration of these graces in 1 Corinthians 12:4–11, explaining that three categories of graces are necessary for external teaching or persuading someone concerning "divine matters that are above reason." The first category comprises full knowledge of divine things, something Thomas sees as indicated by the three graces first mentioned by Paul (1 Cor. 12:8–9a): (a) the certainty of the doctor's faith; (b) the "word of wisdom," that is, the ability to derive the essential conclusions from belief; and (c) the "word of science," or the knowledge of human matters that allows the doctor to find appropriate examples for his teaching. In order to function as a doctor of supernatural teaching, two further kinds of grace are necessary — first, a person must be able to confirm or prove what he says in a miraculous way (Thomas says the charisms mentioned in 1 Cor. 12:9b–10a are examples of this); and second, he must be able to convey his knowledge to his audience in a fitting manner by the "forms of tongues and interpretation of statements" that Paul mentions in verse 10b. It is doubtful that the Dominican meant that all *doctores ecclesiae* need to be miracle-workers, though he doubtless thought that many had been. All doctors do, however, share in charismatic graces that exceed ordinary human gifts.

Thomas Aquinas has no set terminology or standard list of teachers or doctors, because this would not fit with his fluid and analogous understanding of the term. All Christians are both "taught" and called upon to be in some way "teachers." Theologians (called *magistri, doctores,* or *doctores sacrae scripturae*) have a professional obligation to convey true teaching, and Thomas has several discussions of their status (e.g., *Quodlibetal Questions* 5.12). Nevertheless, he recognizes that since the times of the apostles (whom he often calls the "doctors of faith" or "doctors of the whole world") a small number of Christians have been called in a special way to cooperate with the Holy Spirit in instructing others. He terms these "holy doctors" (*sacri doctores/sancti doctores*) and "doctors of the church" (*doctores ecclesiae*) interchangeably.

The authority that Aquinas gives to the doctors of the church is a secondary one, rooted not in themselves but in scripture and the church. As a "science," *sacra doctrina* argues necessarily and properly from the biblical text and uses "the authoritative texts of others, the doctors of the church, in arguing from these proper authorities, but in a probable way" (*Summa* Ia.1.8, ad 2). Hence, in upholding that it is wrong to baptize Jewish infants if their parents are unwilling, Thomas recognizes that this was condoned by some patristic doctors, but "because the teaching of catholic doctors has its authority from the church, we must abide by the custom of the church more than the authority of Augustine, or Jerome, or any doctor" (*Quodlibetal Questions* 4.2) — still an important principle for the understanding of the authority of doctors of the church. Aquinas also admits that the *doctores ecclesiae* sometimes disagree and can even be in error on things that have not yet been determined by supreme teaching authority. In the preface to his treatise

Against the Errors of the Greeks, he even allows for a form of development of doctrine. Heresies provide the occasion for "the holy doctors of the church to treat matters of faith with greater circumspection in order to eliminate errors that have arisen." The less cautious statements of the ancient doctors, prior to the rise of heresies, then, "are not to be condemned or rejected, but neither should they be continued; explain them reverently" (see also *Disputed Questions on God's Power* 9. 8. ad 2). The lists of "ancient doctors" to whom Thomas extends his hermeneutic of reverence are varied, though they almost always include both Greek and Latin fathers. Given the attacks on the mendicants like Thomas for "usurping" teaching positions in the universities, he is especially fond of citing how many of the doctors of the church were monks or other religious — Gregory of Nazianzus, John of Damascus, Jerome, Augustine, Basil, Chrysostom, "and many others" (*Against Those Who Attack the Worship of God and the Religious Life*, chap. 2). Thomas Aquinas, then, had a very "catholic," or broad, notion of doctor, embracing many patristic figures. It is interesting to observe, however, that in one place his representative list includes exactly the quartet enshrined four centuries later in Bernini's *cathedra Petri*: Athanasius and Basil for the Greeks, and Ambrose and Augustine for the Latins (*Against the Deadly Teaching of Those Who Restrain People from Entering the Religious Life*, chap. 16).

Although Thomas Aquinas and other scholastic theologians used the term *doctor ecclesiae* in a broad analogical way, the fourfold formula of Latin doctors continued to grow in popularity in the thirteenth century. This strength of this inherited formula received further support from a shift in the process of making saints. In the patristic period and early Middle Ages saint-making had largely been an affair of local churches, monasteries, and often popular acclaim. During the course of the twelfth and thirteenth centuries the reformed papacy gradually acquired universal jurisdiction over the mechanism of declaring who would be raised to the altars (see Kenneth L. Woodward, *Making Saints* [New York: Touchstone, 1996]). In 1234 Gregory IX published a decree, later incorporated in canon law, which finalized this development. As a part of papal jurisdiction over all forms of sanctity, Pope Boniface VIII issued a decree in 1298 (entitled "Gloriosus Deus") which, for the first time, gave official papal recognition to the by-now traditional four Latin doctors: Gregory (listed first because of his papal status), Augustine, Ambrose, and Jerome. In this document Boniface put the four doctors on the same level as the twelve apostles and four evangelists, decreeing that each member of these groups should be honored with the celebration of the "double class" feast day throughout the entire church. He praised the *doctores ecclesiae* in the extravagant rhetoric of the time:

> The brilliant and salvific writings of these doctors illumine the church,
> are adorned by virtues, and informed by right living. Through them, as
> if through shining and burning lamps placed on a candelabrum in the

Lord's house, dark errors are put to flight and the day star irradiates the body of the whole church. Under the influence of a downpour of celestial grace, their fruitful eloquence unlocks the mysteries of scripture, solves knotty problems, casts light upon obscurities, and settles doubts. The whole breadth of the church glows brightly with their profound and glorious statements, like brilliant gems. Lifted up by the singular eloquence of their words, the church flashes forth in a more glorious way.

Lex orandi, lex credendi — The rule of prayer is the rule of belief. The recognition of the four Latin doctors as pillars of the faith of the church, equal to the apostles and evangelists in the liturgical calender, marked a decisive stage in the evolution of the concept of *doctor ecclesiae* in Latin Christendom. After this, the four often appear in late medieval art, holding books as emblems of their teaching authority. Nevertheless, the cooperation of both Eastern and Western doctors in "instructing the devout and refuting heretics" was never forgotten. Nor did the declaration of the "famous four" Latins preclude the possibility of more recent teachers being also described as *doctores ecclesiae*. For example, when the Dominican artist Fra Angelico painted scenes from the life of St. Lawrence in the private chapel of Pope Nicholas V in the Vatican palace (1447–49), he included eight doctors in the decoration — the four standard Latins, along with Pope Leo the Great, two Greeks (Chrysostom and Athanasius), and also his fellow Dominican Thomas Aquinas.

The development of the list of doctors of the church beyond the standard enumeration of four "official" Latin doctors and four more-or-less official Eastern doctors was the fruit of the era of religious divisions and polemics that began in the sixteenth century. Many of the Reformers who broke with Rome had both deep knowledge of and high respect for the fathers and doctors of Christian tradition, but the Reformers' emphasis on the role of "scripture alone" (*sola scriptura*) as the criterion of faith tended to give these fathers and doctors a less evident role in Reformation Christianity than they had enjoyed in medieval Catholicism. The popes, especially after the lengthy Council of Trent (1545–63), which reasserted papal authority and reorganized late medieval Christianity into modern Roman Catholicism, worked assiduously to strengthen their claim to determine real sanctity and proclaim true teaching and authentic teachers. Thus, modern papal proclamations of new *doctores ecclesiae,* both from the broad list of ancient doctors recognized in the medieval period, as well as from newer teachers, were in part the product of the competition between various forms of Western Christianity. Still, the fact that the popes have continued to include Eastern doctors, as well as the unprecedented recent creation of female doctors, shows that the popes think of doctors as important for all Christians.

If the naming of new doctors has been influenced by the large-scale politics of the papacy's opposition to Reformation Christianity, we should not be surprised that the list of new doctors has also been shaped by forms of smaller-scale politics, especially the competition between various religious orders of the Catholic Church. Today even believers are ready to admit — and sometimes to be amused by — the politics that is an inescapable aspect of the life of the church. (It's just that believers do not think that it is *all* politics.)

The first new doctor to be given official papal recognition by the inclusion of his feast as the double feast of a *doctor ecclesiae* in the new edition of the Roman Breviary (prayerbook for clergy) was Thomas Aquinas. This was done in 1568 by Pius V (1566–72), one of only two popes declared saints in the past five centuries. Not surprisingly, Pius was an austere Dominican who implemented the decrees of Trent and signified his unyielding opposition to Reformation Christianity most notably by his excommunication of Queen Elizabeth I in 1570. Pius's admiration for his confrere was also expressed through his sponsorship of a new edition of the works of the great Dominican theologian. (The importance of Thomas Aquinas's teaching in post-Tridentine Catholicism down to the present time is evident from a glance at the statistics in Appendix III.)

The next declaration of a new doctor was by Sixtus V (1585–90), who had been Pius's confessor and like him was an energetic reformer. Sixtus, a Franciscan professor of theology at the Roman University before his election, showed his scholarly interests by founding the Vatican Press and beginning a new edition of the Latin Vulgate Bible. Pope Sixtus named Aquinas's great Franciscan contemporary, Bonaventure of Bagnorea, as a doctor in 1588. Both of the mendicant orders, the mainstays of late medieval theology, now could boast of having a *doctor ecclesiae* in their ranks. In terms of the scope and profundity of their immense writings, as well as the impact they have had both then and now, few Christian teachers can be said to be more deserving of the honor. Sixtus also extended the liturgical rank of a double feast to the by-now canonical four Greek doctors — Athanasius, Basil, Gregory of Nazianzus, and John Chrysostom.

Doctors in the Modern Age

It is curious that no pope exercised the prerogative of naming a *doctor ecclesiae* for the next 132 years — the longest such span in modern times. Perhaps the preoccupation with the religious and political tensions of the seventeenth century, the era of the wars of religion, distracted a series of popes who were great patrons of the arts but scarcely noted theologians. The revival of additions to the list of doctors in the early eighteenth century coincided with a renewed interest in naming saints and the creation of the official rules that govern saint-making and doctor-declaring down to our own time.

Three popes of the early eighteenth century added Latin authors to the list of doctors in the space of less than a decade. Anselm of Canterbury was declared a doctor by Clement XI in 1720. This was followed in close succession by Innocent XIII's declaration of Isidore of Seville in 1722, and Benedict XIII's nomination in 1729 of the relatively obscure patristic figure Peter Chrysologus. (Benedict, who canonized a large number of saints, was himself named Peter — Pietro Francesco Orsini.)

Shortly after this intense burst of declarations, an important scholarly study summarized past practice and laid down the broad rules for the future naming of saints, as well as *doctores ecclesiae*. Between 1734 and 1738 Prospero Lambertini, archbishop of Bologna, published his *The Beatification of Servants of God and the Canonization of the Blessed,* four large volumes which still remain the most thorough consideration of the process of canonization. Lambertini had served in the curia under all three of the popes just mentioned; he was also destined to ascend the papal throne in 1740 as Benedict XIV. Born in 1675, Lambertini arrived at the papal court about 1700 and was named *promotor fidei,* or "Devil's Advocate," in 1709, an office he held for twenty years. (The Devil's Advocate is the popular name for the member of the Congregation of the Causes of Saints whose duty was to make a critical examination of the lives and miracles of all those whose causes had been introduced for beatification and eventual canonization. The office was eliminated in 1983.) Building on this experience, as well as other service in the curia, the scholarly Lambertini decided to compose his own reflections on the process of saint-making. As he put it in writing to a friend: "I could have turned to more pleasurable studies to which I was naturally prone by reason of my lively character, but I felt within me that I was called by religion itself to work for its glorification" (see Ludwig von Pastor, *History of the Popes* 35:25). Book 1 of Lambertini's massive work deals with the history of canonization; the second and third books treat the stages in the process, while book 4 concerns the miracles necessary for being canonized and liturgical questions about the cult of the saints. In the second book Lambertini takes up the subsidiary issue of doctors of the church, specifying three conditions necessary for someone to be declared a *doctor ecclesiae* — eminent teaching (*eminens doctrina*), outstanding sanctity (*insignis vitae sanctitas*), and official declaration by the church (*ecclesiae declaratio*). Lambertini allowed that such ecclesiastical declaration could be given either by the pope or by a general council (see bk. 2, chaps. 11–12). Although no council has thus far made such a declaration, the possibility remains an important option, one of considerable ecumenical significance.

Lambertini's description of the procedure for investigating causes of beatification and canonization was both a summary of a process that had been developing since the twelfth century and a clarification and standardization for future ages. His stringent observations governed saint-making down to the major changes introduced under John Paul II in 1983. (John Paul has canonized more saints than all other twentieth-century popes combined.) But the learned archbishop did not try to set down exact rules for the declaration of *doctores ecclesiae*, both because no clear procedures had been established in the past, and (more importantly) the condition that doctors need to be saints, even if not papally canonized, guaranteed that their teaching and example would at least not be harmful. Like Thomas Aquinas, Lambertini noted that when a saint is declared a *doctor ecclesiae* this does not mean that every aspect of what he (or now she) taught has been approved, but merely that their general teaching has been recognized as possessing eminent value. Scripture and the teaching of the universal church (the "ordinary magisterium," as Catholic theologians term it) are the norm. Aquinas himself is a good example of this important distinction, since he opposed the Immaculate Conception (the teaching that Mary was born without original sin) — a dogma defined by Pius IX in 1854.

Without any fixed procedure, and with the "escape clause" that papally declared doctors of the church are *general* models of eminent teaching who may be mistaken in some details, the subsequent story of declarations of doctors after the publication of Lambertini's treatise is somewhat obscure, at least in the sense that it is often difficult to determine *why* and *how* a particular Christian saint was declared a doctor. Famous theologians, as well as some relatively obscure ones, have been named. Powerful religious orders have successfully pushed the causes of some of their favorite sons (and more recently daughters). Papal favor for a particular cause doubtless has played a large role, but it is often difficult to know how important this has been in individual cases. The popes have usually adopted a simplified form of the process used in canonization. In this model a document called a *positio* exploring the teaching of the candidate is drawn up and is then given a judicial hearing before a panel appointed by the Congregation of Sacred Rites, which oversees the church's liturgical life and is empowered to assign the liturgy for a doctor to a particular saint. If the panel judges favorably, the pope then often consults with the cardinals concerning the advisability of the nomination, but final acceptance of the cause is a matter of papal prerogative. In a number of cases, popes seem to have used much simplified forms of consultation in advancing the cause of a doctor. The "paper trails" for a number of cases are quite murky and have not been given detailed historical investigation.

When Prospero Lambertini became pope he may well have been trying to give an example to his successors in naming his illustrious predecessor Leo the Great a doctor in 1754. Leo's name had often been found in ancient lists of *doctores ecclesiae,* so Pope Benedict may have been hinting that only established patristic teachers should be considered doctors. But papal prerogative was too strong and the role of ongoing later teachers too powerful for Catholic Christianity to restrict the line of declared doctors to teachers of the patristic age.

The nineteenth-century additions to the list of doctors included more medieval figures than patristic. In 1828 Leo XII named the eleventh-century monk Peter Damian, and Bernard of Clairvaux was declared a doctor by Pius VIII in 1830. Pius IX, the central figure of the nineteenth-century papacy, especially for his role in the declaration of papal infallibility at the First Vatican Council in 1870, confirmed older traditions of doctor-naming by advancing Hilary of Poitiers in 1851 (as we have seen, Hilary was mentioned in many of the early lists). But Pius also broke with precedent in declaring two relatively recent saints doctors during the later years of his pontificate. A brief consideration of these two postmedieval figures reveals something about the politics of doctor-making, as well as the variety of procedures adopted.

Alphonsus de Liguori, the founder of the Redemptorist order and a noted moral theologian, died in 1787 and was canonized in 1839 by Pius's predecessor, Gregory XVI (a pope so opposed to modernity that he refused to allow railroads in the papal states). Alphonsus's sane, middle-of-the-road moral teaching, however, was not without its opponents, especially among the Jesuits. In 1866, at the behest of the Redemptorist order, which had gathered a large list of names of supporting bishops, Pius IX opened the case of whether Alphonsus should be declared a doctor. In large part, the Redemptorist initiative was undertaken in response to the Jesuit professor of moral theology at the Roman College (now the Gregorian University) Antonio Ballerini, who had attacked Alphonsus in 1863. The case was treated very much like a cause for canonization. A large collection of documents (the *positio*) was gathered and a judicial process begun. Alphonsus's cause was argued before two panels appointed by the Congregation of Rites, with a *postulator* defending the case and a *promotor fidei* ("Devil's Advocate") arguing against it. The pope was doubtless favorable because, despite a divided vote, the case was passed on to the cardinals resident at the curia. The cardinals voted in its favor in March 1871, and Pius IX was happy to accept the decree of the Congregation of Rites proclaiming Alphonsus de Liguori a *doctor ecclesiae* issued on March 23, 1871.

If Alphonsus de Liguori's case was a contentious one, involving both papal policy and opposed religious orders, the second modern saint Pius advanced to the status of doctor illustrates a less controversial and therefore more informal mode of procedure. St. Francis de Sales, the seventeenth-century bishop, preacher, and spiritual writer, had long been one of the most widely read and appreciated Catholic teachers among both clergy and laity. The stimulus for naming Francis a doctor seems to have originated from the pope himself and not to have required the elaborate proceedings of Alphonsus's case. Pius recognized Francis de Sales as a *doctor ecclesiae* in 1877.

Pius IX's successor, Pope Leo XIII (1878–1903), created no less than four doctors. In contrast to Pius, Leo was open, at least in a relative sense, to the great social and scientific changes of the nineteenth century. His encouragement of modern biblical studies and opening of the Vatican archives to research (1893), as well as his encyclical on social questions (*Rerum novarum* of 1891), were signs of a cautious change in papal policy — though not one to be followed by his successor, Pius X. Leo was also greatly concerned with Christian unity, as is shown by his letter *Praeclara gratulationis* of 1894, invit-

ing both Protestants and Orthodox, especially the independent churches of
the East, to return to union with Rome. This may help explain his naming
of three Eastern Fathers as doctors of the church in 1883: Cyril of Jerusalem,
Cyril of Alexandria, and John of Damascus. Late in his long pontificate Leo
also declared the Venerable Bede a doctor in 1899.

Nineteenth-century popes added nine names to the list of doctors; their
twentieth-century successors have outdone them with ten thus far. The list
is an untraditional and even unusual one, not only in its inclusion of women,
but also for its nomination of some relatively obscure names in the history of
Christian thought. Benedict XV, the pope at the time of the World War I,
kept alive Leo XIII's initiative concerning Eastern doctors by adding the
name of Ephrem, the greatest teacher of the Syriac church, in 1920. Benedict's declaration emphasized once again that the role of doctors is a charism
for the entire church — not just the Latin West and the Byzantine East.

Pius XI (1922–39), a scholar, librarian, and former professor of dogma, tied
with Leo XIII by naming four doctors, all Western teachers and members of
religious orders. Pius was also an innovator in his practice of combining canonization with declaration of doctoral status. The first person he honored was
St. Peter Canisius, the Jesuit preacher and writer of catechisms, whose work
was indispensable to the success of the Counter Reformation in sixteenth-
century Germany. Peter was canonized and "doctored" at the same time in
1925. Pius followed this by naming the first Carmelite doctor in 1926, the
great mystical teacher St. John of the Cross. In 1930 he canonized the Jesuit theologian Robert Bellarmine and the next year added him to the list
of doctors, so the Jesuits now had the glory of two *doctores*. Shortly thereafter (December 6, 1931), Pius took the unusual step of declaring a second
Dominican, Albert the Great, the teacher of Thomas Aquinas, as a doctor.
Albert had been beatified in 1622, but had not been formally canonized, despite the appeals of German bishops in 1872 and 1927. Pius's declaration had
the effect of canonizing Albert while making him a doctor.

The later years of Pius XI's pontificate were overshadowed by the gather-
ing clouds of war, and no more doctors were named. His successor, Pius XII
(1939–58), ascended the *cathedra Petri* on March 12, 1939, the eve of World
War II. Soon after the victory over Nazism, Pius named his only doctor in
1946. This was the early Franciscan teacher, St. Anthony of Padua, whose
surviving works are relatively popular sermons rather than theological treatises. Now the Franciscans could rest happy that they had equaled the
Dominicans and Jesuits with two doctors apiece.

Given Pius XII's interest in theological questions, as evidenced in his
encyclical *Humani Generis* and in the definition of the doctrine of the Assumption of Mary (both in 1950), it is surprising that he did not nominate
more doctors during his busy pontificate (he made no less than thirty-three
saints). The role of papal prerogative in doctor-making is evident in the case
of St. Lawrence of Brindisi, which was introduced under Pius XII, but only

completed by his successor Pope John XXIII (1958–63). Lawrence, canonized in 1881, was a member of the Capuchin branch of the Franciscans. It was at their request that Pius XII allowed his cause to be introduced to the Congregation of Rites, and at first all proceeded smoothly. In November 1950 the cardinals approved the congregation's decision that Lawrence was worthy to be declared a doctor; but Pius, for reasons of his own, refused his assent. The mysterious delay was apparently too well-known to be left without comment. In the Apostolic Letter of March 19, 1959, in which Pope John finally declared Lawrence a *doctor ecclesiae,* it is noted with a brief and, given Pope John's subtle wit, wry comment: "Our Predecessor, due to the importance of the matter, delayed revealing his mind [on it] in order to implore a greater abundance of divine aid in making such a weighty decision" (*Acta Apostolicae Sedis* 51 [1959]: 461).

The most recent innovation in the history of the *doctores ecclesiae* has been the naming of three female doctors. Given how much has been written about the pontificate of Paul VI (1963–78), it is odd that there has been little discussion of his initiative in elevating the first two women to the status of doctor, Catherine of Siena and Teresa of Avila. (Major biographies of Paul either do not mention these declarations, or treat them in a few lines.) On September 27, 1970, Paul preached a sermon in St. Peter's declaring Teresa a doctor (for the text, see *Acta Apostolicae Sedis* 62 [1970]: 590–96). Though the homily says nothing about the process used in the case, it does contain a defense of the unprecedented naming of a female doctor (something that Thomas Aquinas did not think possible). Pope Paul praises Teresa's teaching as based on "the extraordinary action of the Holy Spirit" and as reflecting "the secrets of prayer." Then he raises the question as to whether the naming of a female doctor violates Paul's precept, "Women are to remain quiet in the assemblies" (1 Cor. 14:34). Not at all, says the pope. The title of doctor is not connected to the hierarchical function of the magisterium. Through baptism, women participate in the common priesthood of all the faithful. "In such profession of faith," he continues, "many women have arrived at great heights, even to the point where their words and their writings have become lights and guides for their brethren." These brief but pregnant words reflect the transformation of attitudes that was begun with the Second Vatican Council and that still, though sometimes painfully, is progressing in the Catholic Church.

A week later, on October 4, Pope Paul preached another sermon, this time announcing Catherine of Siena as a doctor. Paul no longer needed to defend making a woman doctor. Instead, he emphasized the traditional understanding of *doctor ecclesiae* as a recipient of special graces for the good of the church, citing the apostle to the Gentiles at length. He also underlined Catherine's support of the papacy and her concern for a reform of the church conducted according to papal lines, even to the extent of hailing the Dominican tertiary as "anticipating not only the teaching, but the very language of the Second Vatican Council" (*Acta Apostolicae Sedis* 62 [1970]: 676).

Given the precedent set by Paul VI, the declaration of St. Thérèse of Lisieux as the third woman doctor by John Paul II on October 19, 1997, was scarcely a surprise (1997 was the centenary of Thérèse's death). What is surprising is that Pope John Paul, the greatest saint-maker in history (280 canonizations to date!), has not declared more *doctores ecclesiae*. The pope's motivation for naming Thérèse to this status is evident both in his apostolic letter issued for the event and especially in the homily he delivered in St. Peter's for the occasion. October 19 was World Mission Sunday and Thérèse, although she never left her enclosed Carmelite house in Lisieux, had been declared patroness of the missions in 1929 because of her dedication to spreading the faith in foreign lands. Pope John Paul, who has made worldwide missionization the prime goal of the Catholic Church in the new millennium, hailed the "Little Flower" as exemplary of the missionary mandate of all the baptized. Missionizing is based upon teaching, so John Paul highlighted Thérèse's "Little Way" as exemplary of the essentials of belief, based as they are in "the profound truth of love as the center and heart of the church." For John Paul, the Carmelite nun's love-centered teaching is the answer to the rationalism, materialism, and hedonism of the modern world. As a *doctor ecclesiae* she has become a "reference point" for our understanding of revealed truth. In clarifying the nature of her status, the pope employed an original threefold division of forms of ecclesiastical teaching, distinguishing the "contemplative study to which theologians are called," the "magisterium of pastors," and the "profound understanding of spiritual things given to saints." He concludes that "not by chance does the church choose only saints to be distinguished with the title of doctor." The homilies of Paul VI and John Paul II form a good summary of the contemporary, more inclusive, but not radically new Catholic understanding of the role of doctors in the life of the church.

There can be no question that Pope John Paul was pleased to be able to declare Thérèse a doctor (he had visited her shrine in 1980). Was he, one wonders, the initiator of the cause? Surely the Carmelite order, which had orchestrated Thérèse's rapid canonization with great efficiency in the early twentieth century, must have played a role. We can also note that the addition of two women gives the Carmelites three doctors over all, to equal the three each for the Dominicans and Franciscans. (This may suggest that the next doctor will be a Jesuit.) The procedure followed in this most recent declaration was not detailed by the pope, though his apostolic letter speaks generally of responding to the wishes of "very many faithful throughout the world" and a "great number" of bishops, as well as consultation with both the Congregation for the Causes of the Saints and the Congregation for the Doctrine of the Faith (formerly the Holy Office). We know that it involved, as usual, getting the advice of the cardinals too. The Little Flower enjoys a large and enthusiastic following in many parts of the Catholic world, so the "grassroots" aspect of the cause must have been quite significant. According to one story making the rounds, an American auxiliary bishop with a lifelong devotion to Thérèse convinced a well-known American cardinal to approach the pope on the question of the possibility of declaring the saint a doctor. With the pope's approval, the American cardinal canvassed the other members of the Sacred College for their views and then sent on only the replies that were favorable to Rome, where the case was taken from there. As the Romans say of such stories, "Se non è vero, è ben trovato," which can be roughly translated as, "Even if it isn't true, it will be often repeated."

The early lists of the doctors were diverse and open-ended, just as the process of saint-making was for the first millennium of Christian history. As a result of the Great Reform Movement of the late eleventh and early twelfth centuries, the papacy became the arbiter of doctrine in a more centralized and juridical way than ever before. This new position led to papal claims over the *official* naming of saints and declaration of doctors that have become ever stronger since the thirteenth century. For the past four centuries at least, a doctor of the church is a person that the pope has officially recognized as possessing the sanctity of life and eminence of teaching that deserve public liturgical celebration. What has become increasingly obvious, especially through the recent naming of women as doctors, is that the teaching charism specific to doctors is not tied to hierarchical position or ordination. It is, as Thomas Aquinas understood and as recent popes have emphasized, a "miracle" of grace.

In concluding this brief historical sketch, we can return to my initial question, "What is a doctor of the church?" In the broadest understanding of the term, all baptized Christians, under the inspiration of the Holy Spirit, are called to be doctors insofar as they believe and teach the faith by word and example to the best of their ability. But the restricted, proper meaning of the title *doctor ecclesiae,* as the term developed over many centuries, was first employed to describe the ordained, hierarchical teachers of the fourth and fifth centuries whose explanations and defenses of the faith were seen as criteria for orthodox, or correct, belief. Paradoxically, many of these doctors made statements that, in the words of Thomas Aquinas cited above, need to be "explained reverently," rather than literally defended as totally adequate statements of Christian belief.

So, in conclusion, we may ask some difficult questions: Is orthodoxy nothing more than a historical construct? Are the doctors of the church accidents of history — mostly bishops rewarded for being on the winning side? There are no easy *historical* answers to these questions. This book is written from the perspective of a Catholic theologian who believes that however unusual and "political" the institutional decisions made about some of those who have been given the title of *doctor ecclesiae,* doctors are still vital for the church's teaching and the progress of theology. It is not within the purview of theologians to decide who should or should not be recognized as doctors, because any theologian's judgments are individual, and because the doctors serve a wider and much longer-lived constituency than most theologians can hope for. We need to remember that not even the popes *make* doctors. As Pope Paul VI reminded us, the popes do not create doctors; they recognize what the Holy Spirit alone can give and has given to many men and women in the history of the church.

Part Two

WHO ARE THE DOCTORS OF THE CHURCH? A BRIEF SURVEY

I. PATRISTIC DOCTORS

I

ATHANASIUS
OF ALEXANDRIA
(C. 300–373)

FEAST: MAY 2

I N THE YEAR 361, Athanasius, the anti-Arian patriarch of Alexandria, had been on the run for five years, hiding among the monks of upper Egypt from the wrath of the pro-Arian emperor. One evening as he was in a small boat on the Nile, headed for a safe house, he heard the sound of an imperial galley approaching behind him. In the darkness, the soldiers hailed him: "Have you seen Athanasius?" "Sure I have," he responded. "Is he far from here?" "No, he's not far off. Row hard!" The galley started to beat its way south, while Athanasius quietly turned around. During Athanasius's long patriarchate (328–73) he spent no less than five periods in exile for his staunch support of the Nicene, or Orthodox, position on the theology of the Trinity — almost sixteen years in all. This steadfast witness won him the title "Father of Orthodoxy" and helps explain his profound influence in both Eastern and Western Christianity. Although Athanasius was intransigent and sometimes even violent in his reaction to error, his dedication to the vocation of bishop as teacher and pastoral leader won him strong support among his followers.

Athanasius was born in Alexandria, perhaps of a mixed family, since he was familiar with both Greek and Coptic. He was a deacon of bishop Alexander and served as his secretary at the Council of Nicaea in 325, the meeting that condemned Arius's teaching that the Second Person of the Trinity was not fully equal to and coeternal with the Father. Athanasius succeeded Alexander in 328 and was immediately confronted with the two issues that marked his forty-five-year rule as leader of the Egyptian church: the Melitian schism and the Arian heresy.

The Melitian schism was primarily a local issue. Melitius was a bishop who had broken with the see of Alexandria over the readmission of Christians who had lapsed during Diocletian's persecution. The Council of Nicaea sought a compromise that recognized the legitimacy of the Melitian bishops, but ordered them to return to obedience to Alexandria. The Melitians resisted and allied themselves with pro-Arian bishops of the East in their ongoing struggle against Athanasius. The new patriarch turned for support to the monastic movement that had proliferated in Egypt since the end of the third century, enlisting the patronage of the most famous of the ascetics, Antony (c. 250–356), whose *Life* he composed shortly after the old monk's death.

Athanasius's greatness rests in his unremitting opposition to Arius and his sympathizers. More than anyone else, the patriarch of Alexandria was responsible for working out the theological defense of the Nicene formula that the Son was "of the same substance" (*homoousios*) as the Father. He did so at great personal cost over many decades. Most of the bishops of the East, if not sympathizers with Arius himself, were unhappy with Nicaea and wanted to summon a new council that would work out a compromise solution. In the interests of ecclesiastical and political harmony, the emperors often sided with them. Hence Athanasius's many exiles. During the first of these, when he was banished to Trier in the West between 335 and 337, Athanasius had the opportunity to complete two treatises that he had been working on for some years, *Against the Pagans* and *On the Incarnation of the Word of God*. The latter is one of the doctor's most impressive writings. As the modern Christian apologist C. S. Lewis put it, "only a master mind could...have written so deeply on such a subject with such classical simplicity."

In 337 Athanasius was returned to Alexandria as a hero — even the aged Antony left the desert and came to the city to welcome him and preach Nicene orthodoxy (*Life of Antony*, chaps. 69–71). From 339 to 346 Athanasius was exiled once again, this time to Rome where he forged close ties with the pro-Nicene Roman bishop. During this period Athanasius probably worked on the first and second of his *Orations against the Arians,* the most important of his many writings against the heretics. A change in imperial politics enabled him to return to his see for a decade and continue his writings against the opponents of Nicaea, composing his large *Apology against the Arians* and his *Letter on the Decrees of Nicaea*. In 356 Athanasius was exiled for a third time by the Eastern emperor Constantius, but he fled instead to the monks in the Egyptian deserts and continued his pastoral activity and attacks against the Arians. He defended his actions in such treatises as the *Apology to Constantius* and the *Letter about his Flight*. During this time he also seems to have composed another of his important works on the theology of the Trinity, the *Letters to Bishop Serapion on the Divinity of the Holy Spirit*. At the death of Constantius, Athanasius returned to Alexandria, only once more to be exiled under the brief reign of the pagan emperor Julian. Finally, he was exiled a fifth time (366–67) under Jovian. During the final, more peaceful, years of his long patriarchate, the redoubtable champion of orthodoxy continued to prepare the ground for the triumph of the Nicene party that was realized at the First Council of Constantinople in 381. Athanasius did not live to see it, dying in 373.

Athanasius's teaching testifies to a fundamental, but often forgotten, truth of early Christianity, namely, that trinitarian doctrine is inseparable from the proper understanding of the person and work of Christ. The eternal mystery of the Trinity is revealed in and through the salvific life of the God-Man. Hence, the patriarch of Alexandria based his theological vision not on a cosmological framework in the manner of an Origen, but on the historical revelation of the life of Jesus as preached and lived in the church. In this sense, Athanasius's theology, even at its most subtle and insightful points, is always catechetical in its fundamental perspective.

This outlook is well illustrated in the brief treatise *On the Incarnation of the Word of God*. The work falls into three parts: (1) a consideration of the motive for the Incarnation — Athanasius's *Cur Deus Homo?*, or *Why the God-Man?*; (2) the role of the mysteries of Christ's death and resurrection in the economy of salvation; and (3) a refutation of the objections of the Jews and pagans to the Incarnation. Sin, the patriarch argued, brought death and corruption into the world, but God was not willing to allow humanity made in his image to perish. In order to re-create his image in mankind, God needed to do away with death and corruption. "Therefore, he assumed a human body in order that death might once and for all be destroyed and that humans might be renewed according to the Image [i.e., the Son]" (chap. 13). (In accordance with older forms of Christology, Athanasius stressed the Word's taking on of flesh and body, though he never denied a human soul in Christ, as did some of his followers who were subsequently condemned.) Like Bernard of Clairvaux after him, the patriarch argued that the Word had to take on a sensible nature in order to attract those who existed only on the level of sense knowledge. "There were thus two things the Savior did for us by becoming man. He banished death from us and made us anew; and, invisible and imperceptible as he is in himself, he became visible through his works and revealed himself as the Word of the Father, the Ruler and King of the whole creation" (chap. 16). Christ's death on the cross ("the very center of our faith," as Athanasius calls it) in the paradoxical logic of salvation was actually the death of death and corruption; his rising on the third day is the manifestation and beginning of the new life in which all believers share. Athanasius's proof for the resurrection is not set in the past, but in the present: How can a dead person effect the deeds we see Christ doing every day in the lives of those who follow him? The goal of the whole process is divinization (*theopoiesis*): "He assumed humanity that we might become God" (chap. 54).

The scriptures reveal that only a Word who is fully equal to the Father can be a Word that saves. On this basis, the patriarch constructed his refutation of the Arian position. This is most readily available in the three books of his *Orations against the Arians*. The first book is a defense of the Nicene position on the eternity and full equality of the Son with the Father. The second and third books discuss the scriptural passages on which the Arians based their view of the Son's inferiority, showing the insufficiency of heretical exegesis. In these books Athanasius makes major strides towards clarifying the logic of the trinitarian "grammar" that was being worked out in the fourth century. Especially important is his recognition of the difference between what later came to be called "proper" and "common" attributes, that is, those proper to each Person and those common to all three Persons insofar as they are denominations of the divine nature. In *Against the Arians* 3.4 he puts the distinction this way: "Thus, since they are one and the Godhead itself is one, the same things are predicated of the Son as of the Father, except the title 'Father': for instance, 'God,' . . . 'All-sovereign,' . . . 'Lord,' . . . 'Light.' "

Athanasius's support of early monasticism is also important for judging his role in the history of Christianity. His *Life of Antony* written a year after the aged hermit's death and rapidly translated into several languages was a best-seller that spread the fame of the new spiritual movement around the Mediterranean world. For more than a millennium, hagiography was to be one of the most popular forms of literature, and Athanasius's life of his friend was one of the premier models of the genre. Though rarely historical by modern standards, saints' lives give us important windows opening out onto the faith and practice (at least in an ideal way) of Christians of the past. Meant to be read as sources of inspiration and even entertainment, in the hands of a master like Athanasius or Bonaventure they also reveal deep theological insights. In recounting the hermit's life, Athanasius once again demonstrates his christocentric vision of the world when he says, in concluding his account of Antony's temptation by the devil: "This was Antony's first triumph over the devil — or rather, the first triumph of the Savior in Antony" (chap. 7).

Reading Athanasius

Almost all of Athanasius (including some spurious works) can be found in *St. Athanasius: Select Works and Letters*, NPNF, 2d series, vol. 4. There are also a number of more modern and readable translations. Begin with the *Life of Antony*, CWS 16, his most accessible work, but be sure to read *On the Incarnation of the Word of God* and the *Orations against the Arians* to appreciate the core of his theology.

Bibliography

F. L. Cross. *The Study of St. Athanasius.* Oxford: Oxford University Press, 1945.

Aloys Grillmeier. *Christ in the Christian Tradition: From the Apostolic Age to Chalcedon.* New York: Sheed and Ward, 1965. See the treatment of Athanasius on pp. 193–213.

Hanson, chaps. 9 and 14. A detailed account of Athanasius's reputation and thought.

Alvyn Petersen. *Athanasius.* Ridgefield, Conn.: Morehouse Publishing, 1995. A good short introduction.

Thomas F. Torrance. "Athanasius: A Study in the Foundations of Classical Theology." In *Theology in Reconciliation.* Grand Rapids: Eerdmans, 1975, pp. 215–66.

Young, 65–83. A good brief account.

2

EPHREM THE SYRIAN

(C. 309–73)

FEAST: JUNE 9

I N THE SUMMER of 363, in the city of Nisibis in northern Mesopotamia, a melancholy scene unfolded. The pagan emperor Julian the Apostate, who had initiated new persecutions of the Christian church, had been slain in battle with the Persians on June 26. His successor Jovian had made a humiliating peace, which ceded five provinces, as well as Nisibis, to Persian rule. The defeated Roman army with Julian's embalmed body was now camped outside Nisibis on its way back to Tarsus. The deacon and catechist of Nisibis, Ephrem, viewing the body of the hated Julian and the Persian flag flying over his city, composed the following hymnic meditation on divine judgment:

> There I saw a disgraceful sight:
> The standard of the captor set up on the tower,
> The corpse of the persecutor laid in a coffin. . . .
> I went right up, my brothers, to the coffin of the filthy one,
> And I stood over him and derided his paganism,
> And said, "Is this indeed he who exalted himself
> Against the Living Name and forgot that he is dust?"

(Hymns against Julian 3.3–4)

Not much is known of the life of Ephrem, the only doctor of the church from the non-Byzantine East. Later hagiographic tradition portrayed him as a monk and ascetic, but he was not a monk in the traditions of the Greek East or Latin West. Ephrem was closely connected with the proto-monastic asceticism of the early Syrian church. Many of his hymns were written to be sung by the "Daughters of the Covenant," female virgins living in small groups who served the local community. The evidence of Ephrem's many poems and treatises shows him as a faithful servant of the bishops of his native Nisibis and a stern opponent of the many heresies that flourished in this crossroads of the East. Ephrem was born of Christian parents and received early training under Bishop Jacob, who built the first church at Nisibis and attended the Council of Nicaea. Jacob is also said to have appointed Ephrem as the head of the Christian school at Nisibis. During his three decades or more of service to a succession of bishops at Nisibis, Ephrem composed some of his earliest hymn collections, such as the *Hymns of Paradise,* the *Hymns of Nisibis,* and the anti-Jewish *Hymns on the Paschal Feast.* (Judaism was strong in this area of Mesopotamia and Ephrem often engaged in polemics with Jews.) After the Persian takeover of the city, the Christian population was forced to leave, and Ephrem made his way to the great center of Syriac Christianity at Edessa, where he spent the last decade of his life. Edessa was a cosmopolitan city of learning and of religious diversity. In this environment, the learned Ephrem thrived. Most of his numerous surviving works, both in prose and in poetry, seem to come from this time.

Ephrem is most famous as a poet. Over four hundred of his beautiful hymns still survive. Theodoret of Cyrrhus (d. 466), the last great Antiochene theologian, called him, "the lyre of the Spirit, who daily waters the Syrian nation with streams of grace" (Letter 146). Though he wrote in Syriac, a language close to the Aramaic that was spoken by Jesus and the apostles, Ephrem's poems and treatises were translated into many languages, and he was known to Western writers, like Jerome. Many later works were pseudonymously ascribed to him, and it is only in recent decades that scholars have come to general agreement about which writings are really his. The deacon's poetic works fall into two groups: the *madrase,* or hymns, which take a wide variety of forms based on syllabic patterns, and the more regular metrical homilies called *memre.* The *madrase* have been grouped under various headings: *On Faith, On Fasting, On Virginity, Against Heresies, On the Nativity, On the Church, On Holy Week,* as well as the collections mentioned above. Six volumes of *memre* have been edited, but it is difficult to determine which are genuine.

Most of Ephrem's prose works are scriptural commentaries; according to tradition he commented on every book of the Bible. The only one that survives in complete form in the original Syriac is the *Commentary on Genesis,* but many are known through translations into Armenian, including his famous *Commentary on the Diatesseron* (the Syriac harmonized version of the four gospels). Ephrem also wrote polemical treatises, such as his *Prose Refutations of Mani, Marcion, and Bardaisan,* and highly rhetorical compositions like *The Homily on Our Lord* and the *Letter to Publius,* a meditation on the Last

Judgment. In both prose and poetry he is considered the most accomplished author of the Syriac tradition.

The ecumenical character of early Christianity has been increasingly recognized in recent decades. The gospel was acculturated not only into the Greek-speaking world of the eastern Mediterranean, but also rapidly into the Latin-speaking West and the Syriac world of the Middle East, which in many ways was the closest to the Jewish roots of the first Christians. (This fact helps explain the frequent strained relations between Jews and Christians in Syria.) The Syriac expression of Christian belief and practice cannot be measured by the philosophical and rhetorical categories common to Greeks and Romans. Syriac spirituality, as Roberta Bondi notes, was characterized by its individualism, its fierce asceticism, and especially by its strongly symbolic forms of expression, based both on scripture and on the symbols of the natural world. Ephrem is a master at the expression of this symbolic worldview, utilizing a wealth of natural symbols (the pearl, the mirror, the harp, the olive — to name but a few), as well as a rich typology of the images and figures of the Old and New Testaments. In the twentieth of his *Hymns on Virginity*, Ephrem reflects on the function of symbolism as a way to God:

> O Laborer whose symbols were gathered,
> Who is a reservoir of all symbols!
> In every place, if you look, his symbol is there,
> And when you read, you will find his types.
> For by him were created all creatures,
> And he engraved his symbols upon his possessions.
> When he created the world,
> He gazed at it and adorned it with his images.
> Streams of his symbols opened, flowed, and poured forth
> His symbols upon his members.

The final three hymns of this collection (nos. 28–30) form an admirable summary of the deacon's symbolic theology. Both nature and scripture are filled with "symbols" (Syriac *raze'*, which can also mean "mysteries") that function as prisms through which God makes himself known. Here Ephrem speaks of the "three harps of God" — the Old Testament, the New Testament, and nature itself. All three are meant to sound together harmoniously, but some people do not listen to this harmony (Jews use only the first harp, while Manichaeans and Marcionites despise the "harp of creation"). Christ is master artist who brings out the full and saving melody of all three instruments (*On Virginity* 29.1–2):

> The Word of the Most High came down and put on
> A weak body with hands,
> And he took two harps
> In his right and left hands.

The third he set up before himself
To be a witness to the other two,
For the middle harp taught
That their Lord is playing them.
He played, and that third harp
Was harmonious and completed the other two.

Like the works of all the fourth-century doctors, Ephrem's writings center on the salvific action of the God-Man. Though he was a representative of Nicene orthodoxy and opponent of the Arians, we do not find any of the language of *homoousios* and other Greek technical terms in his Christology. Rather, Ephrem poetically visualizes the mystery by which the Only Begotten of the Father left the hidden realm of divinity to take on the human condition and free us from sin and evil. In his first hymn, *On the Nativity*, for example, he takes an axiom common to almost all the fourth-century doctors, but puts it in his own poetic way: "The Deity imprinted itself on humanity, so that humanity might also be cut into the seal of the Deity." Ephrem is a powerful witness to the centrality of the doctrine of divinization in early Christian thought: "The Most High knew that Adam wanted to become a god, so he sent his Son who put him on in order to grant him his desire" (*Hymns of Nisibis* 69.12). The Syriac doctor's concrete and symbol-filled theology of Christ also had an important place for the Eucharist, which he hymned as life-giving medicine that makes the eschatological kingdom present in our midst. Equally notable is Ephrem's well-developed Mariology, which he expressed in a rich typological manner, weaving together many symbols of Mary to express her role in the history of salvation. In another place in the *Hymns on the Nativity* (11.6–7), we read:

A wonder is your mother: the Lord entered her
And became a servant; he entered able to speak
And he became silent in her; he entered her thundering
And his voice grew silent; he entered shepherd of all;
A lamb he became in her; he emerged bleating.
The womb of your mother overthrew the orders.

Syriac Christianity, in fact, delighted in the use of female imagery, often referring to the Holy Spirit in feminine terms, a practice also found in Ephrem. Hence, the ideal of the virginal Christian as "Bride of Christ," the inner meaning of the Song of Songs as the *magna carta* of Christian mysticism, was not foreign to Ephrem. In his *Hymn of Faith* 14.5, he expresses this with a power equal to that of Bernard and the other great bridal mystics:

The soul is your bride, the body your bridal chamber,
Your guests are the senses and the thoughts.
And if a single body is a wedding feast for you,
How great is your banquet for the whole church!

Reading Ephrem

Growing interest in early Syriac Christianity has led to the appearance of good new translations of Ephrem's works with informative introductions. Especially recommended are the following three: *St. Ephrem the Syrian: Hymns on Paradise*, trans. Sebastian Brock (Crestwood, N.Y.: St. Vladimir's Seminary Press, 1990); *Ephrem the Syrian: Hymns*, trans. Kathleen McVey, CWS 66, containing the hymn collections *On the Nativity*, *Against Julian*, and *On Virginity and on the Symbols of the Lord*; and *St. Ephrem the Syrian: Selected Prose Works*, trans. Edward G. Matthews, Jr., and Joseph P. Amar, ed. Kathleen McVey, FC 91, which translates the important Genesis commentary.

Bibliography

Along with the introductions in the above works see:

Sebastian Brock. *The Luminous Eye: The Spiritual World Vision of St. Ephrem*. Kalamazoo, Mich.: Cistercian Publications, 1992. The best guide to Ephrem.

Roberta C. Bondi. "Christianity and Cultural Diversity. I. The Spirituality of Syriac-speaking Christians." *Christian Spirituality: Origins to the Twelfth Century*. Ed. Bernard McGinn, John Meyendorff, and Jean Leclercq. New York: Crossroad, 1986, 152–61. A useful brief introduction.

Robert Murray. *Symbols of Church and Kingdom: A Study of Early Syriac Tradition*. Cambridge: Cambridge University Press, 1975. A classic work.

3

HILARY OF POITIERS
(C. 312–67)

FEAST: JANUARY 13

I N 353 a young Roman army officer named Martin experienced a conversion after giving half his cloak away to a beggar who revealed
himself in a dream as Christ. Two years later, Martin was able to leave
the army to devote himself more fully to Christ. His biographer, Sulpicius
Severus, records that "he sought out the holy Hilary, bishop of Poitiers, a
man well known at that time for his proven faithfulness in the things of God"
(*Life of Martin*, chap. 5). Hilary ordained Martin exorcist. Some years later,
after the bishop's return from exile, Martin rejoined Hilary and, at his recom-
mendation, set out to form the first monastery in Roman Gaul at Ligugé (five
miles from Poitiers). Hilary's faithfulness in the things of God is evident in
his support of nascent Western monasticism, and especially in his leadership
of Latin opposition to Arianism. He was the earliest Western bishop to enter
the fray in the question that helped define the orthodox development of the
fourth century; he was also the first important Christian thinker from Gaul.

   Although doubts have been cast on the historicity of the intellectual autobiography set at the beginning of his major work, *The Trinity* (bk. 1.1–14),
this account of Hilary's "most ardent desire of comprehending and knowing"
God that eventually led him to the ministry of the priesthood and preaching
to others rings true to the aspirations of the great fourth-century leaders of
the church. Hilary was born in Poitiers, apparently from an aristocratic family, given his excellent education in the Latin classics. He has the unique
distinction of being the only doctor of the church who is known to have
been married and a father — clerical celibacy was the exception rather than

the rule among clergy in his time. He became bishop of his native city about 353, and shortly thereafter wrote his *Commentary on Matthew*, a pastoral exegesis of much of the gospel, stressing the Old Testament's prophetic and typological relation to the New. This work demonstrates the bishop's wide acquaintance with earlier Latin Christian thinkers, especially Tertullian.

Hilary first gained clear awareness of the Arian threat about 355 as a result of pro-Arian synods held at Arles and Milan. Like his colleague Athanasius in the East, he strenuously resisted the Arianizing policies of the emperor Constantius, as we can see in such writings as his *Book against Valens and Ursacius*. For this he was exiled to Phrygia in Asia Minor in the autumn of 356. While in the East, Hilary collaborated with pro-Nicene bishops and gained some acquaintance with Greek theology (the extent of this is still disputed). It was also during this exile that he began work on his major treatise, the twelve books entitled *The Trinity*, which he appears to have originally called *On Faith*. This defense of the eternity and full equality, or "consubstantiality" (*homoousios*), of the Son with the Father (see especially bk. 4.4–7), was the first important Western treatise on the Nicene declaration of faith. Indeed, no Eastern writer thus far had attempted so comprehensive a treatment of the biblical basis and arguments for the orthodox position. Hilary also wrote a treatise titled *The Synods* to help bridge the gap between the strict "Homoousians" of the West and the "Homoi-ousians," or Semi-Arians, of the East, who were anti-Arian but suspicious of the Nicene formula (see Appendix 1).

In 360 Hilary was allowed to return to Gaul and promptly resumed his activities against the Western Arians. In 364 he unsuccessfully tried to depose Maxentius, the Arian bishop of Milan, against whom he subsequently wrote a polemic work. Nevertheless, the bishop of Poitiers also worked to win back moderate bishops who hesitated over what trinitarian formulas were accurate. Not all of Hilary's writings concerned doctrinal disputes, as his lengthy *Treatise on the Psalms*, which survives only in part, and his introduction to the christological interpretation of the Bible, the *Treatise of the Mysteries*, show. Hilary died in 367, when the tide was already turning against Arianism, especially in the West.

Hilary appears to have gained some knowledge of Origen during his exile, but his biblical exegesis and theology of the Trinity are primarily his own creation. Although his thought does not rank with the Latin doctors of the generation immediately following him — Ambrose, Augustine, and Jerome — his status as a pioneer has not been given sufficient recognition. As in the case of some of the other *doctores ecclesiae* who are little read today, we need to try to appreciate why his witness to the church's tradition is still significant for contemporary faith.

Hilary, along with Athanasius, is among the oldest of the teachers officially declared *doctor ecclesiae*. In the case of the bishop of Poitiers, we find a good example of a theologian who had the courage to take up the pressing issues of his day even when he realized that there was much that remained to be worked out. He was willing to learn on the job, as we might say today, and even to risk making mistakes because his situation demanded action and boldness. Theologians, even doctors of the church, as Thomas Aquinas and others remind us, are far from infallible. Insofar as they are "of the church," however, both then and now they deserve benign, if never uncritical, appreciation. Hilary's contributions to the development of trinitarian theology were important, but so were his failures — if only to remind us of how imperfect every form of theology really is. Hilary did not need the reminder. He was always conscious of the insufficiency of human words in the face of the mystery of God: "The perfection of learning is to know God in such a way that, although you realize he is not unknown, you know that he may not be described. We must believe in him, understand him, adore him, and by such actions we shall make him known" (*The Trinity* 2.7; cf. *The Synods*, chap. 65).

Hilary's theology of the Trinity rests upon the faith and practice of the church, specifically on the Risen Christ's command to baptize "in the name of the Father, and of the Son, and of the Holy Spirit" (Matt. 29:19; cf. *The Trinity* 2.1). In books 2–4 of his *magnum opus* he is concerned with the general relation between the Father and the Son and a demonstration of the full divinity of the Second Person. Books 4–7 refute Arian theology on the basis of texts drawn from both the Old and the New Testaments, while books 8–12 constitute a second refutation of Arian biblical interpretation, arguing that Hilary's work is a compilation, fusing several different treatises together. The bishop's insistence on the eternal generation of the Son and his attempts to avoid any language subordinating the Son to the Father were important steps forward in the creation of Latin trinitarian theology. He was also conscious of the necessity of avoiding the opposing error — the Sabellianism that confused the three persons into complete identity. Hilary therefore insisted that in God there is a "oneness of substance or nature" (*unitas substantiae*), but not a "union of person" (*unio personae*) — "The Father and the Son are the one and true God, but by nature not by Person" (*The Trinity* 5.10). Nevertheless, Hilary's terminology regarding the mystery, particularly the words to be used to speak of God as three, was imprecise and often confusing (e.g., he deliberately avoided speaking of the Holy Spirit as a Person). Hilary's theology shows other failings, at least by the standards of later orthodoxy. For example, in defending the divinity of the Incarnate Word, he used expressions that at times negate the reality of the humanity of the Savior, reducing Christ's human sufferings to a mere "appearance" of pain (see *The Trinity* 10 passim). Comparable problems can be seen in Hilary's contemporary in the Eastern church, Athanasius, who could not understand the importance of the God-Man's need to possess a human soul so that redemption would be the reward of the whole human person. Once again, we are reminded that the doctors of the church are models for later believers in the depth of their commitment to expressing the truth of the faith, not in all the transitory details of their own formulations.

Reading Hilary

Most of Hilary's works are available in *St. Hilary of Poitiers: Select Works*, NPNF, 2d series, vol. 9. A better translation of his greatest work is *Saint Hilary of Poitiers: The Trinity*, trans. Stephen McKenna, FC 25.

Bibliography

There is little in English.

C. F. A. Borchardt. *Hilary of Poitiers' Role in the Arian Struggle*. The Hague: Nijhoff, 1966.

J. E. Emmenegger. *The Functions of Faith and Reason in the Theology of Saint Hilary of Poitiers*. Washington, D.C.: Catholic University, 1947.

Hanson, chap. 15. The most recent review of Hilary's life and thought.

Patrology IV, 33–61. A good survey of Hilary's theology.

4

CYRIL OF JERUSALEM
(C. 313–86)

FEAST: MARCH 18

I N SEPTEMBER of the year 335 bishops from all over the East converged on Jerusalem by imperial order to take part in the consecration of the great new basilica, called the Martyrium, or Church of the Holy Sepulchre, that Constantine had ordered built at Golgotha. The lengthy address that Eusebius, Constantine's court theologian, gave for the occasion, probably on September 13, still survives. Praising both emperor and building in fulsome terms, Eusebius concludes: "It is reasonable that you have heeded these manifest proofs of the Savior's power and have displayed to all men, believers and unbelievers alike, a house of prayer as a trophy of his victory over death, a holy temple of a holy God, and splendid and great offerings to the immortal life and the divine kingdom" (*Tricennial Orations,* chap. 18). The ceremony also enthroned the new bishop of the city, Maximus, accompanied by his young deacon, Cyril, who was to succeed him as bishop in 348. Preaching in this same basilica shortly after his installation, Cyril reminded his audience of catechumens, "He who on this holy Golgotha saved the robber for one hour of faith, will also himself effectively save you for believing" (*Catechetical Lectures* 5.10).

Cyril was born into a Christian family probably at Caesarea about 313. He may have been a protégé of Eusebius, though his theology of the Trinity differed from that of the bishop of Caesarea. Ordained deacon sometime before 335, Cyril was priested in the early 340s. The details of his long reign as patriarch of Jerusalem (c. 348–86) need not concern us here. Like all the episcopal leaders of the time, his career was much involved with the struggles over the proper understanding of the Trinity. Cyril was resolutely opposed to the Arian claims about the inferiority and temporal generation of the Son, but he was not a supporter of Athanasius either. Like Athanasius, however, he was several times exiled from his see due to faction fights, both those of the Arian controversy and of other quarrels characteristic of his contentious era. Whatever the shortcomings of some of his early teaching on the Trinity, Cyril's orthodox intentions were recognized late in life by the First Council of Constantinople, which expressly supported him against rival candidates to his see.

While Cyril is an interesting witness to the developing trinitarian orthodoxy of the mid-fourth century, his primary contribution to theology is to be found in the picture he provides of the general catechetical teaching of Christianity at the time of the conversion of the Roman Empire. Cyril may also be described as the great liturgical *doctor ecclesiae*, given the fact that under his episcopacy Jerusalem was developing the elaborate liturgy that made such an impression on the flocks of pilgrims to the Holy Land. The export of this liturgy, or at least elements of it, to other Christian centers was of central importance in the liturgical history of the church.

Cyril's writings are not extensive. Aside from a letter to Emperor Constantius reporting the appearance of a miraculous cross of light over Jerusalem on May 7, 351, and a single homily, his fame rests on the *Catechetical Lectures*, which he gave most probably about 350. These twenty-four discourses, taken down in shorthand by one of his listeners in the church of the Holy Sepulchre, fall into three parts: a *procatechesis*, or introductory address; eighteen lectures given to the candidates for baptism; and five mystagogical catecheses addressed to the newly baptized during Easter week. The final five have sometimes been ascribed to Cyril's successor, Bishop John of Jerusalem (386–417), but it is likely that John merely reworked materials reflecting Cyril's preaching.

The *Catechetical Lectures* provide the most complete picture we possess of the instruction given to catechumens in the fourth century. No other document of the time gives us the same feeling of actually being present in the congregation as the bishop instructs the new members of his flock, making frequent reference to details of their daily lives. Cyril is a sane and sober guide to the faith. Despite the controversies raging at the time, he does not go into disputed questions or condemn different persons and parties in the church. He prefers to lay out the essentials of belief in the context of the liturgical life of the community.

The richly rhetorical *procatechesis* invites "those being enlightened" (*photizomenoi*) to persevere in the sacred preparation for baptism that they have undertaken. (Cyril insists throughout on the secret nature of the truths that are being handed over — the *disciplina arcani* of the early church was still in force.) The first lecture deals with the temper of mind necessary for those on the path to enlightenment: freedom from earthly cares, forgiveness of enemies, and daily reading of the Bible. The second talk treats of penance and remission of sins, as well as the devil, the adversary the *photizomenoi* encounter on the path. Lectures 3, 4, and 5 deal respectively with baptism, the ten essential dogmas, and the nature of faith. The following twelve lectures provide a detailed explanation of the creed of the church of Jerusalem, which is close to the document later approved at First Constantinople in 381. Along with a rich treatment of the eternity of the Word and the Incarnation, as might be expected, Cyril is unusual in his early emphasis on the full divinity of the Holy Spirit (see, e.g., Lectures 4.16, 16.4, and 17.5). Also interesting is the extended treatment of the last things, especially the attention given to the Antichrist, in Lecture 16 — an illustration of how important eschatology remained in the era of the triumph of Christianity. The mystagogical catecheses (Lectures 19–23) provide further analyses of the three sacraments that the neophytes had received at the Easter Vigil. Lectures 19–20 concern baptism; Lecture 21 treats confirmation, and Lectures 22–23 discuss the Eucharist and the liturgy. In all his addresses Cyril's stress is upon the saving faith brought to us by the God-Man. For example, in treating the famous text from Exodus 33:13, in which Moses asked to see God's face, he concludes: "The Lord replied, 'No man shall see my face and live' (Exod. 33:20). This was the reason that, since no one can behold the face of Godhead and live, the Lord took to himself a human face that we can look upon and live" (*Catechetical Lecture* 10.7).

Reading Cyril

There is a full translation of the *Catechetical Lectures* in *St. Cyril of Jerusalem: Catechetical Lectures*, NPNF, 2d series, vol. 7. The partial translation of William Telfer in *Cyril of Jerusalem and Nemesius of Emesa* (Philadelphia: Westminster, 1955) contains a good introduction.

Bibliography

Aside from Telfer's introduction, there are brief treatments in:

Hanson, 398–413.
Patrology III, 362–77.
Young, 124–33.

5

Basil of
Caesarea
(c. 330–79)

I N THE YEAR 355 a young man from an aristocratic Christian family in
Cappadocia of Asia Minor returned to his ancestral estates after five
years of schooling in Athens. Basil was quite stuck up about his education, but still unsure what to do next with his life. According to the account
written by one of his younger brothers, Gregory (later bishop of Nyssa), it was
his elder sister Macrina who straightened the young man out and put him on
track to become the most influential of all the Greek bishops of the fourth
century. As Gregory's *Life of Macrina* put it, Basil "was excessively puffed up
by his rhetorical abilities and disdainful of all great reputations, and considered himself better than the leading men of the district. But Macrina took
him over and lured him so quickly to the goal of philosophy [i.e., Christian
teaching] that he withdrew from worldly show...and went over to this life
full of labors for one's own hands to perform." Big sister as savior.

Basil was the senior figure among the three late fourth-century leaders of
Eastern Christianity known as the Cappadocian Fathers. Two of the three —
Basil and his best friend, Gregory of Nazianzus, are listed among the doctors of the church. Although Basil's younger brother, Gregory of Nyssa, is
not officially a doctor, he made equally great contributions to the history of
Christian thought. It has often been said that Eastern Christianity never had
a figure like Augustine, that is, one teacher and doctor of such scope and
depth of thought that his theology marked everything that came after him.
This may be true, but it is no less true to say that the Cappadocian Fathers as
a group (older contemporaries of the bishop of Hippo) are as central to the

Eastern Orthodox tradition as Augustine has been to the Latin West. Perhaps the only other time when the history of Christianity has seen a similar group of stellar teachers may have been at the University of Paris in the mid-thirteenth century when Albert the Great, his pupil Thomas Aquinas, and their contemporary Bonaventure were all at work.

Basil was born about 330 in Caesarea into a remarkable Christian family. The pious and learned Macrina ("the fourth Cappadocian," as Jaroslav Pelikan terms her) later formed a community of religious women. A brother Naucratios lived a hermit's life; Gregory, though a married professor of rhetoric, eventually became a bishop at Basil's prodding. The youngest brother, Peter, was bishop of Sebaste. When, under Macrina's tutelage, Basil finally decided to devote himself to God, the results were astonishing. He was baptized in 356, and his contributions to so many aspects of Christian life and practice over the less than quarter-century of his remaining life make it difficult to think of him as one person. Like many of the major episcopal leaders of the fourth century, Basil was a forceful, sometimes even domineering, personality. Bishops were political figures, and Basil would not have been successful unless he was willing to immerse himself in the politics of his age.

While his older contemporary, Athanasius, was a patron and publicist of monasticism, Basil was a monastic leader. After his baptism, he took a trip to the monastic sites in Egypt and elsewhere in the East. Fired with enthusiasm, he founded a monastic community on his ancestral estates at Annesi in 357. It was for this community that he composed the two rules, the *Longer Rules* and the *Shorter Rules*, which, after later redactions, still govern the life of the coenobitical monasteries of Eastern Christianity. Basil emphasized the need for community as the proper context within which the monk was to live out the New Testament ethics of humility, obedience, and mutual love. During this time, he and Gregory of Nazianzus also compiled the first *Philokalia*, a spiritual anthology culled from the works of Origen. Basil's monastic period was not to last long. In 364, Eusebius, the bishop of Caesarea, ordained him priest, and for the next few years Eusebius greatly depended on his well-educated and well-connected presbyter to help run the diocese. In 370 Basil succeeded Eusebius and served a bishop of Caesarea until his death in 379.

In these last fifteen years of his life as abbot and bishop Basil emerged as the leader of the Orthodox forces in the East, taking up the role that had long been held by Athanasius. In evaluating his contribution, it is important to recognize how the struggle over the correct teaching regarding the Trinity had evolved over the forty years since the Council of Nicaea. For the Cappadocians, like the staunch Niceans of the Western church (e.g., Hilary of Poitiers and Ambrose of Milan), the creed formulated at Nicaea in 325 was the bottom line — the authentic faith of the church. Any individual or later synod that rejected it or attempted to water it down was automatically anathema. Nevertheless, the Cappadocians were not as fixated on the term *homoousios* (i.e., "of the same substance") as they have been portrayed. They recognized that many of the bishops who preferred to speak of the Son's relation to the Father as "similar according to substance" (*homoios kat'ousian*) were saying much the same thing as what Nicaea had intended. Basil, like others, sought to win over the bishops who occupied this middle ground and thus achieve a consensus. He did this through the creation of a theology of the Trinity that clarified the basic vocabulary for speaking of God-as-One and God-as-Three. Basil was also one of the first to analyze the full equality of the Holy Spirit with the other "two" named in Christian formulas of faith.

The opponents of Basil and his friends and followers in the 360s and 370s were not Arius (long dead) or the first generation of those who denied the eternity and equality of the Son with the Father. The other side were those today called "Neo-Arians," that is, figures like Eunomius, a bishop of Cyzicus in Asia Minor, who tried to work out a philosophical defense of God's simplicity that excluded the Son and the Holy Spirit from true divinity. Another group vigorously combatted by Basil were the "Fighters-against-the-Spirit" (*Pneumatomachi*), the name given to those who rejected the divinity of the Holy Spirit. (These were also called "Macedonians" after the Arian bishop Macedonius of Constantinople who died about 362.)

The principal doctrinal writings of Basil relating to the Arian controversy consist of three books *Against Eunomius* (364), the important treatise *On the Holy Spirit* (374–75), and some brief writings, such as the treatise *On Faith*. In these works Basil initiated the theological program of the Cappadocian Fathers that became an essential building-block of the orthodox consensus of both the Eastern and Western churches. Basil and the other Cappadocians were better trained in philosophy (especially Neoplatonism) than Athanasius or Hilary, but they always utilized their philosophical tools within the framework of a Christian conviction regarding the transcendental difference between the God of the Bible and the world he had freely created. God is not the ultimate reality *within* the cosmic framework, as pagan philosophers taught, but is eternally and wholly independent of it. This transformation of philosophical categories is evident throughout the thought of Basil and the other Cappadocians. To cite just one illustration, Basil insisted that in the process of creation there are not "three ultimate principles [*hypostases*]" (the title of Plotinus's *Ennead* 5.1), but "one ultimate Beginning of all existent things, creating through the Son and perfecting in the Spirit" (*On the Holy Spirit* 16.38). The three Persons of the Trinity did not act as hierarchically differentiated principles in the manner of Plotinus's three *hypostases*, but as the Christian God who is both three and one.

Unlike Origen (from whom they took much in some areas), the Cappadocians insisted on the infinity and immeasurable perfection of the unknowable Creator who revealed himself in scripture. Although created minds could never grasp him (as Eunomius held), let alone become "bored" with him (Origen's explanation for the fall of angels and other spirits), God had revealed the mystery of his inner trinitarian life in the Bible. The fundamental task of *theologia* (i.e., that part of doctrine that dealt directly with God) was to work out the proper language for expressing the trinitarian truth about God found in the church's confession of faith. Basil's greatest contribution to this ongoing work of constructing the edifice of trinitarian theology was to utilize the term *hypostasis* (and sometimes *prosopon*) to indicate the reality of the three — Father, Son, and Holy Spirit — as distinguished from the substance, essence, or nature (*ousia/physis*) of the divine unity. This was an important advance in clarity, especially because Nicaea had confusingly equated *hypostasis* and *ousia*. "It is indispensable," Basil said (Letter 210), "to have a clear understanding that just as he who fails to confess the community of the essence or substance falls into polytheism, so too he who refuses to grant the distinction of the *hypostases* is carried away into Judaism." Henceforth, the formula "one substance and three hypostases" (*mia ousia, tres hypostaseis*) was to be the touchstone of orthodoxy. Against Eunomius Basil also argued that the term "ungenerated" is not equivalent to "uncreated." The former is an *epinoia*, or characteristic of the Father (i.e., a proper attribute), whereas the latter is a common attribute of all three divine Persons.

Basil's writings against the Neo-Arians, central to the reaffirmation of Nicaea declared at the First Council of Constantinople in 381, constitute the primary reason why the bishop of Caesarea has always been hailed as one of the greatest of the *doctores ecclesiae*. But these works do not exhaust the breadth of his contributions. Basil was a great pastoral bishop, whose innovations, especially his foundations of hospitals for the poor, were important for the future. He also took a keen interest in education, penning a treatise entitled *Admonitions to Young Men on the Profitable Use of Pagan Literature*. The bishop was also a redoubtable exegete. His *Homilies on the Hexaemeron*, probably given in the late 370s, were groundbreaking in their attention to the "literal" meaning of the creation account, though this literal meaning (like Augustine's) primarily concerned the philosophical truths revealed in the creation account. This text reveals how much the well-educated Basil had absorbed of ancient philosophy during his school days at Athens, and yet how decisively he broke with pagan cosmology. Basil was also a liturgical pioneer, though it is hard to say how much of the "Liturgy of Basil" found in the Eastern Church to this day is really his. This human dynamo left over 350 letters, which provide us with detailed information about his life and many of the controversies in which he was engaged. It is hard to believe that Basil, justly called "the Great," was less than fifty when he died.

Reading Basil

In many ways, Basil's *Homilies on the Hexaemeron* are the best entry into his thought. The nine homilies can be found in *Saint Basil: Exegetic Homilies*, trans. Agnes Clare Way, FC 46. Basil's doctrinal writings on the Trinity, especially the treatise on the

Holy Spirit and the writings against Eunomius, are translated in *Saint Basil of Caesarea: Selected Writings* (NPNF, 2d series, vol. 8). For Basil's monastic rules, see *Basil of Caesarea: Ascetical Writings*, trans. M. Monica Wagner, FC 9.

Bibliography

Paul J. Fedwick, ed. *Basil of Caesarea: Christian, Humanist, Ascetic.* 2 vols. Toronto: PIMS, 1981. A rich collection of essays.

Paul J. Fedwick. *The Church and the Charisma of Leadership in Basil of Caesarea.* Toronto: PIMS, 1979.

Robert C. Gregg. *Consolation Philosophy: Greek and Christian Paideia in Basil and the Two Gregories.* Patristic Monographs 8. Cambridge, Mass., 1975.

Hanson, chap. 21. A good survey of the Cappadocians.

Jaroslav Pelikan. *Christianity and Classical Culture: The Metamorphosis of Natural Theology in the Christian Encounter with Hellenism.* New Haven: Yale University Press, 1993. Important recent study of the Cappadocians and their use of classical philosophy in the service of Christian thought.

Young, chap. 3. A helpful account of the three Cappadocians.

6

GREGORY OF NAZIANZUS

(C. 330–90)

FEAST: JANUARY 2

HE TIME: May 381. The place: Constantinople, the capital of the Roman Empire. Emperor Theodosius has summoned a meeting of bishops to reaffirm the creed declared at Nicaea fifty-six years earlier. In Constantinople theological argument over the relationship between the Son and the Father is not the preserve of clerics and scholars, but the passion of all. Gregory of Nyssa, who was present at the Council, says, "In this city if you ask anyone for change, he will discuss with you whether the Son is begotten or unbegotten. If you ask about the quality of the bread, you will get the response, 'The Father is greater, the Son is less.' If you say that you want a bath, you will be told that 'there was nothing before the Son was created'" (*On the Divinity of the Son and Holy Spirit*). The head of the orthodox bishops at this First Council of Constantinople, however, is an unlikely figure. He is Gregory, born in Nazianzus in Cappadocia and bishop of the small town of Sisara. Two years before, the retiring Gregory had been called to take up the leadership of the small Orthodox community in the capital, long a stronghold of parties opposed to Nicaea. His superb preaching of the orthodox position, however, had attracted large crowds and dramatically strengthened the Nicene camp. Now their theology is about to triumph under his leadership.

In the history of Eastern Christianity, only three writers have been awarded the title of "theologian": the Evangelist John; Gregory of Nazianzus; and Symeon ("The New Theologian"), a monk of Constantinople at the turn of the first millennium. To many Western Christians the special status accorded to Gregory may seem a bit strange. Much of his life was lived in the shadow of his powerful friend Basil of Caesarea, a man he deeply loved and respected, but toward whose imperious actions he also expressed ambivalent feelings. Despite his rhetorical gifts, Gregory was only an occasional writer. His orations (i.e., sermons), poems, and letters display a superb knowledge of the Bible, but he wrote no biblical commentaries. Although he exercised a decisive role in ecclesiastical and dogmatic history late in life, he was not an ecclesiastical politician in the sense that Athanasius and Basil were. With his ambivalences about power and his equally complex attitude toward the tensions between monastic retreat and active service, Gregory is a figure whose personal anxieties are instructive precisely because they mirror the ambiguities of his age.

Gregory was born about 330, the son of Gregory the Elder, bishop and wealthy landowner of Nazianzus. (The rapid transition from a married clergy to a celibate one, largely a result of the triumph of the monastic ideal, is evident in the lives of many of the fourth-century doctors.) As a youth he became close friends with Basil, also a scion of the landed class. Together they went to study at Athens in the 350s. Gregory stayed on in this great educational center, and it was probably at Athens that he was baptized at about 359. Shortly thereafter he returned to Cappadocia, where he spent some time with Basil in the monastic community established by his friend at Annesi. While Basil apparently found it easy to abandon his monastic life to take up episcopal service, Gregory was never able to be quite as much a monk, or quite as effective a bishop, as his friend and idol.

About 361 the elder Gregory compelled his son to accept ordination; this was so much against his will that he fled to Basil for advice. After consideration, he composed his *Apology for His Flight* (c. 362), a treatise on the obligations of the priesthood that both justified his initial flight from sacerdotal responsibilities and explained why he now was ready to accept them. Gregory's problems with clerical responsibilities were just beginning. In 371 Basil maneuvered him into becoming bishop of Sisara — a see he never occupied. While Gregory made his complaints known in writing, Basil's highhanded action did not create a real break between the two friends. Basil died in 379, and Gregory preached his funeral oration.

It was only during the last years of his life that Gregory unexpectedly emerged as the public champion of the Cappadocian position and a major theological voice. Gregory's retirement into monastic retreat was interrupted by the ascent to the imperial throne of the orthodox emperor Theodosius in 379. Under the Arian-sympathizing emperors the Nicene congregation in the Eastern capital of Constantinople had been reduced to a handful, but with new confidence this community now invited Gregory to assume its leadership. Although he served as patriarch of Constantinople for less than three years, Gregory's preaching in this position, as well as his activity as organizer of the synod (the First Council of Constantinople) that reaffirmed the creed

of Nicaea, provided the ground for his title of "Gregory the Theologian," as
well as his recognition as a doctor of the church. Gregory, however, was not
made for political in-fighting in the same way as Basil. When his transfer from
the see of Sisara to Constantinople was challenged at the synod, Gregory used
the attack as an excuse to retire to the half-monastic and half-philosophical
leisure which had always attracted him. Here he composed the fascinating
autobiographical poem *On His Life*. During this time Gregory also combatted
the views of Apollinaris of Laodicea (d. 390), a follower of Athanasius who
had denied the reality of the human soul of Christ. Not old, but clearly worn
out and often cranky, Gregory died about 390.

If Basil can be said to be the most influential of the Cappadocian Fathers
due to his powerful personality, and Gregory of Nyssa is increasingly recognized as the most subtle and original mind of the three, we can say that
Gregory of Nazianzus was the most gifted communicator of the group — the
master of a style of preaching as remarkable for its rhetoric as it was for its
clear expression of doctrine. Although Gregory left about 400 poems, including a number on doctrinal topics, as well as 245 letters, it is primarily his 45
orations that have given him his place in the history of Christian thought.
Most of these date from his brief time in Constantinople. Among them the
five *Theological Orations* (Orations 27–31 of the collection) preached in 380
represent the mature fruit of the Cappadocian teaching on the Trinity.

The *Theological Orations* form a mini-treatise defending Nicene faith
against the Eunomians and those who denied the divinity of the Holy Spirit.
In the first sermon Gregory introduces his topic, arguing that only a person
who lives a life of prayer and devotion can rightly "philosophize" about God.
The second oration emphasizes the divine unknowability, a topic to be more
richly developed by Gregory of Nyssa in the following years. Gregory shows
that though we cannot know *what* God is, his creation clearly reveals *that*
he is (Oration 28.5ff.). In the third and fourth Orations Gregory reaches the
heart of the struggles that had racked Christianity for the five decades since
Nicaea, namely, the relationship of the Son to the Father. In the third sermon
he defends the unity of the divine *monarchia* and the eternity of the beget-
ting of the co-equal Word from the Father. Especially important is the way
in which the bishop distinguishes between the relative and absolute terms
used of God, as well as those that are conditioned and unconditioned. In the
fourth Oration Gregory takes up the proper interpretation of the scriptural
texts that seem to suggest the Word's inferiority to the Father, concluding
with a discussion of the importance of distinguishing the common, proper,
and assumed names predicated of Jesus Christ, the Word made flesh. Finally,
the fifth and longest sermon develops Basil's attack on those who denied the
full divinity of the Holy Spirit. Here Gregory advances the case for a progression in the understanding of the divinity of the Spirit (Oration 31.26–29),
arguing that since the Holy Spirit is the source of our divinization, the Spirit
must be consubstantial with Father and Son. Gregory summarizes Cappado-

cian *theologia* with admirable brevity: "The Godhead is, to speak concisely, undivided in three separate Persons.... When we look at the Godhead, or the first cause, or the *monarchia*, that which we conceive is one; but when we look at the Persons in whom the Godhead dwells, and at those who timelessly and with equal glory have their being from the first cause, there are three whom we worship" (Oration 31.14).

Reading Gregory

The central text is the *Theological Orations*. A good translation with introduction can be found in *Christology of the Later Fathers*, edited by Edward Roche Hardy in collaboration with Cyril C. Richardson (Philadelphia: Westminster Press, 1954), pp. 128–214. A selection of other works by Gregory is available in *St. Gregory Nazianzen, Archbishop of Constantinople: Select Orations, Sermons, Letters*, NPNF, 2d series, vol. 7.

Bibliography

Rosemary Radford Ruether. *Gregory of Nazianzus: Rhetor and Philosopher.* Oxford: Oxford University Press, 1969. The most important study in English.

D. F. Winslow. *The Dynamics of Salvation.* Cambridge, Mass.: Harvard University Press, 1979.

7

AMBROSE
OF MILAN

(339–97)

FEAST: DECEMBER 7

THE EARLIEST LIFE of Ambrose, written by his secretary Paulinus, tells the following story. A few days before the bishop's death in 397, Paulinus was taking down Ambrose's dictation, "when suddenly a flame, shaped like a short shield, spread over his head and little by little entered in through his mouth, like someone entering his own house. His face became white as snow, but afterwards his features resumed their usual appearance" (*Life of Ambrose* chap. 42). Paulinus was convinced that this dramatic vision was a manifestation of the Holy Spirit entering Ambrose, the inspired teacher, preacher, and exegete.

Ambrose was born into the high Roman nobility in Trier and grew up in Rome. His family was Christian, but, like many at the time, he was not baptized until an unusual event made it necessary. While serving as imperial prefect of Milan in 374, the quarreling parties of Orthodox and Arian Christians chose him bishop by acclamation due to his noble rank and reputation for justice. Ambrose the catechumen was then baptized and ascended to one of the most important sees in the Western church. Although the new bishop had little theological education, under the guidance of the learned priest Simplicianus he rapidly achieved mastery, not only of the Bible and Greek fathers (especially Origen), but also of Neoplatonic philosophy and the writings of Philo, the great Jewish exegete. Ambrose himself admitted, "I began to teach what I had not myself learnt. I had to be learning and teaching at the same time" (*On Duties* 1.4).

For the remainder of his life the astute and strong-willed Ambrose was the most powerful bishop in the Western Empire, battling Arians and pagans, maneuvering through the minefields of imperial politics, and even excommunicating Emperor Theodosius when he felt it necessary — "The Emperor is within the Church, not above the Church," as he put it (*Sermon against Auxentius*). (Ambrose's treatment of the Jews, however, shows a less savory aspect of his political involvements.) But it is not the political Ambrose, reflected in his letters and some of his treatises, that marks his greatest impact on the church; it is rather Ambrose the preacher and biblical interpreter. Though he was trained as a lawyer and administrator, Ambrose's career as a bishop showed him to be both an effective preacher and also a theologian whose originality has been underestimated due to his dependence on Greek thought.

It is difficult to date many of the bishop's writings or to detect major evolution in his thought. Most of his exegetical works (twenty treatises) were revised versions of sermons. Although his longest commentary is his *Exposition on the Gospel according to Luke,* all his other biblical works deal with the Old Testament. Ambrose was a master of spiritual exegesis, as Augustine, whom Ambrose baptized in 387, testifies. The most important of the Old Testament commentaries deal with creation, *The Hexaemeron* (nine sermons, making considerable use of Basil), and with the psalms (two works treating thirteen psalms). Some of Ambrose's moral and dogmatic works (fifteen treatises) were also based on homilies; others were called forth by the disputes and issues of the day. In addition, the bishop left ninety-one letters, some special sermons, and a disputed number of hymns (Ambrose was a pioneer in introducing hymnody into the Western liturgy).

Ambrose's dogmatic works, such as *On Faith to the Emperor Gratian* and *On the Holy Spirit,* center on demonstrating the full divinity of the Son and the Holy Spirit against the Arians. The bishop was also concerned with unpacking the meaning of the liturgy and sacraments, as two collections of homilies he gave to the newly baptized demonstrate: *On the Mysteries* and *On the Sacraments.* Ambrose's greatest contribution, however, rests in his teaching about the practice of the Christian faith, that is, in the areas of what would later be called moral and mystical theology. He saw the life of virtue and deeper experience of God as necessary parts of one continuous process of appropriating the grace offered us by Christ through the church.

Ambrose's treatise *On Duties* has been called the first comprehensive survey of Christian ethics. Though modeled on Cicero's famous treatise of the same name, the bishop co-opts elements of Stoic moral theory to show the superiority of the Christian way of life based on knowledge of the true God and lived in the hope of heavenly reward. *On Duties* uses the exemplary figures of the Old and the New Testaments as models, and many of the bishop's treatises on the Old Testament allegorize the patriarchs and other biblical figures to provide a typology of the Christian life. However, it was a book that Ambrose never wrote an actual commentary on — but one that plays a major role in many of his works — that provides the key to understanding his teaching on the life to which all Christians are called. That book is the Song of Songs, the hymn of Christ's love for the church and for the soul. Like Origen before him, Ambrose saw the Song of Songs as superior to all the songs of the Bible because it reveals that "our charity is Christ" (*Caritas itaque nostra Christus*).

The role of the Song's message of love is evident in Ambrose's treatises *On Isaac or the Soul*, *On Death as a Good*, and *On the Mysteries*, as well as in his works on virginity, such as *On Virgins*. These books demonstrate that Ambrose should be considered the first great mystical theologian of the West, one who always insisted on the ecclesial character of mystical contact with God. It is only in and through the church, that is, in the sacramental life begun in baptism and nourished through the Eucharist, that we can experience the love of Christ the Divine Bridegroom. Though Ambrose insists that the marriage with Christ revealed in the Song of Songs is begun for all Christians in the sacrament of baptism, he taught that the fullness of this bond is realized in the life of the consecrated virgins who are signs in this fallen world of the bodily integrity to be given to all the saved at the time of the resurrection of the body.

In describing the ascent of the soul to God, Ambrose made considerable use of elements drawn from Platonic mysticism, especially from Philo and Plotinus, such as the need for journeying within, the stages of ascent, the theme of mystical intoxication, and the divine birth that takes place in the soul. Nevertheless, he transformed these aspects of pagan thought by incorporating them within an overarching mysticism of love based on the Song of Songs. The treatise *On Isaac*, for example, interprets the patriarch Isaac as the soul on the road to purification, a soul who is also identical with the Bride of the Song. In *On Isaac* 6.50 Ambrose summarizes this message by sketching out four stages in spiritual progression found in the Song. "First, impatient with love and not bearing the delays of the Word, she [the soul] asked that she might receive kisses (Song 1:2), and she deserved to see the Beloved and was led into the King's bedchamber (Song 1:4)." (Since this treatise on the mystical life was probably a series of homilies given to the newly baptized, we can interpret this stage as the loving union with God found in the initiatory sacrament itself.) The second stage in the path to God, says the bishop, is when the Word departs from the soul, though his absence is not for long (see Song 2:8). This pattern of presence followed by absence is meant to inspire the soul to call the Divine Lover back by repeated prayers, so that she can be drawn even closer to him (Song 3:1–4). This is the third stage, the purification of life by which we prepare ourselves for the fourth stage, in which the Word awakens the soul from sleep as he passes by (Song 5:2–6). "And," Ambrose says, "she went forth at his word, and finally through wounds — the wounds of love — she found and she held the One she sought so as not to lose him." Though the perfection of this embrace can only be found in heaven, Ambrose believed that all Christians are called to share in the bridal love revealed in the Bible.

Reading Ambrose

Ambrose's contribution to mysticism, as suggested above, is most readily seen in the exegetical treatises, *On Isaac or the Soul* and *On Death as a Good*, both available in *Saint Ambrose: Seven Exegetical Works,* trans. Michael McHugh, FC 65. Of his five treatises on virginity, the most important is the first, *On Virgins,* which he wrote in 377 for his sister Marcellina. The two brief liturgical and sacramental treatises should also not be missed. A fuller picture of the doctrinal and moral teaching of the bishop would include *On Duties, The Hexaemeron,* and *On the Faith to Gratian.* Most of the treatises can be found in *St. Ambrose: Principal Works,* NPNF, 2d series, vol. 10.

Bibliography

Much of the best literature about Ambrose is in languages other than English.

Peter Brown. *The Body and Society: Men, Women, and Sexual Renunciation in Early Christianity.* New York: Columbia University Press, 1988, chap. 17. A fine treatment of Ambrose's view of virginity.

Bernard McGinn. *The Foundations of Mysticism: Origins to the Fifth Century.* New York: Crossroad, 1991, 202–16. A consideration of Ambrose's contribution to Western mysticism.

Neil B. McLynn. *Ambrose of Milan: Church and Court in a Christian Capital.* Berkeley and Los Angeles: University of California Press, 1994. The best recent account of Ambrose's episcopacy and political involvements.

Patrology IV, chap. 3. A full account of Ambrose's writings.

Boniface Ramsey. *Ambrose.* London and New York: Routledge, 1997. A good recent survey of Ambrose's life and works, including a selection of texts.

8

JOHN CHRYSOSTOM
(345–407)

FEAST: SEPTEMBER 13

O
NE DAY in early October of 403 the great capital city of Constantinople was all astir. In an unforeseen turn of events, the popular
patriarch John, a preacher so eloquent that he was later known
as "Golden-Mouth" (i.e., Chrysostom), recently exiled because of the false
accusations of his enemies, had now been recalled by imperial order. Accompanied by thirty bishops and a vast crowd of citizens singing psalms and
carrying candles, he processed through the city to the Church of the Holy
Apostles, where he delivered an impromptu address, repeating the same text
from the book of Job that he had used when he went into exile: "'Blessed
be God' (Job 1:21), who allowed me to go into exile; blessed also be God,
who has ordered me to return." This incident from the tumultuous years of
John's patriarchate captures the inner spirit of one of the most renowned of
the doctors of the church. Although John's career was intimately bound up
with many struggles, both ecclesiastical and political, the touchstone of his
life was his total trust in God.

John was born in Antioch into a Christian family and received an excellent education under the pagan rhetorician Libanius. He was baptized at
about the age of twenty and took up the ascetic life, first at home, but then
for a number of years (372–78) among the monks who lived on Mt. Silpios
above Antioch. His severe asceticism, however, ruined his health, and he was
compelled to return to the city, where he became first a deacon and then a
priest in 386, assisting the orthodox bishops Melitius and then Flavian. John's
ordination launched him on his life's task, that of the preacher par excel-

lence. John appears to have preached extemporaneously, as is shown by the informality and asides often found in his homilies, but his masterly command of language, evident in his clarity and his eloquence, the depth of his insight into scripture, as well as a certain populism of his style of address, gave him a large and fervent following both in Antioch and later in Constantinople. Though John wrote many treatises on topics both doctrinal and topical (the best known is his work entitled *The Priesthood* from c. 390), it is primarily for his hundreds of homilies, most of them in the form of extensive commentaries on the major books of the Old and the New Testaments, that he has been justly hailed as a great *doctor ecclesiae*, both in his own day and down through the centuries.

Many of John's sermon collections reflect the controversies and events of the day. Among his earlier homilies, for example, there is a group called *On the Incomprehensibility of God,* preached against the extreme Arian followers of Eunomius who claimed to have full knowledge of the divinity. Another series is known as *Against the Judaizers,* that is, it is directed against Christians who were attracted to the Judaism that was an active presence in Antioch. His *Homilies on the Statues* reflect a crisis in 387 when rioters had overturned images of the emperor and occasioned imperial punishment of the city. But John was first and foremost a biblical expositor. His dozen years of preaching at Antioch produced sixty-seven homilies on Genesis, fifty-eight on Psalms, eighty-eight on the gospel of John, and no less than ninety on Matthew, as well as smaller collections on other biblical books. However, John's major love among the biblical authors was always Paul. He left a large series of sermons devoted to the apostle's epistles (over two hundred homilies in all), as well as a commentary on Galatians originally given as a group of sermons. In addition, John preached seven homilies, *In Praise of Saint Paul,* which constitute one of the most illuminating introductions to the apostle to the Gentiles ever penned. In the first of his *Homilies on Romans,* the greatest of his Pauline expositions, John testifies to his love for Paul in the following words: "As I keep hearing the epistles of the blessed Paul read, and that twice every week, and often three or four times, whenever we are celebrating the memorials of the holy martyrs, I gladly enjoy that spiritual trumpet and become roused and warmed with desire at recognizing a voice so dear to me; and I seem to fancy him all but present to my sight and to behold him talking to me."

In 398 John was unexpectedly promoted to the see of Constantinople as its twelfth bishop. Here he was plunged into the intricate politics of the imperial court of Emperor Arcadius and his powerful wife, Eudoxia. John was certainly not without political skills; he often used the popularity of his preaching to further his own positions and programs. He was also capable of acting in tactless and even authoritarian ways that garnered him a reputation for ill temper. Nevertheless, John was fundamentally not a politician, but a pastor who sought to serve the interests of the church and to give practical moral instruction to his flock.

The mismatch between the man and the position meant that John's five years as patriarch were filled with controversy. Though he continued to preach often, especially on his beloved Paul, as well as on the Acts of the Apostles (fifty-five homilies), much of his energy was taken up with political maneuvering. Eventually John's enemies, led by the unscrupulous patriarch Theophilus of Alexandria, had him condemned by a packed synod of his ecclesiastical enemies in September of 403, the event that led to his first exile. John's triumphant return, noted above, was short-lived. Enraged over sermons that she thought critical of her, Eudoxia orchestrated a second exile in the spring of 404. John was first sent off to a mountain town in southern Turkey, but in early 407 he was ordered removed to a remote village on the Black Sea. For three months the aged and infirm patriarch was dragged across Asia Minor until he died on the road.

It is difficult for modern readers to appreciate the effect of John's teaching, tied as it is to the rhetoric of an ancient style of preaching that often seems long-winded to us. John, as distinct from the contemporary Cappadocian Fathers, was not a speculative thinker who made notable contributions to better understanding of the doctrine of the Trinity or the constitution of the God-Man. Trained under Diodore of Tarsus, the foremost exegete of the Antiochene School, John was a practical teacher who sought to reveal the doctrinal, moral, and spiritual meaning of the biblical text for his audience. Although the Antiochenes paid attention to the authorial intention and historical context of the biblical books and tended to avoid excessive allegorization, their exegesis, as shown in John's sermons, was still far from modern historical-critical readings in its stress on the spiritual application of the text to everyday life. We read John Chrysostom not to find the most penetrating arguments against heretics, or to discover original insights into doctrinal developments, but rather as a window on the Christian world of antiquity. The "Golden-Mouth" presents us with the concrete actuality of Christian life in a world still half-pagan. He is anxious to give his flock the sound doctrine that will enable them to avoid the different forms of heresy and error they meet everyday, but he is even more concerned to provide them with moral instruction, both positive (especially on asceticism and on prayer and penance) and negative, such as avoiding the dangers of the theater and the games of the arena. At their best, Chrysostom's sermons give us the sense that we are there at the very time when Christian orthodoxy was taking the form that has characterized it down through the centuries.

Reading Chrysostom

Most of Chrysostom's homilies and treatises were translated into English in two nineteenth-century versions: *The Homilies of S. John Chrysostom*, 16 vols. (Parker: Oxford, 1839–52); and *The Works of St. John Chrysostom*, NPNF, 1st series, vols. 9–14. For an appreciation of Chrysostom's preaching and teaching, one might well begin with the sermons *In Praise of Saint Paul,* trans. Thomas Halton (Boston: St. Paul Editions, 1963), and the *Homilies on Romans,* NPNF, 1st series, vol. 11. Some selections from the sermons on John and on Matthew, as well as the homilies *On the Incomprehensible Nature of God* (new translation by Paul Harkins in FC 72), would also give a good insight into the power of John's preaching. Among his treatises, be sure to read *The Priesthood,* of which the best translation is that of W. A. Jurgens (New York: Sheed and Ward, 1955).

Bibliography

J. N. D. Kelly. *Golden Mouth: The Story of John Chrysostom, Ascetic, Preacher, Bishop.* Ithaca, N.Y.: Cornell University Press, 1995. An excellent up-to-date study.
Patrology III, 424–82.
Robert L. Wilken. *Chrysostom and the Jews: Rhetoric and Reality in the Late Fourth Century.* Berkeley and Los Angeles: University of California Press, 1983. An analysis of John's invective against the Jews with rich details on the late fourth-century world.
Young, 143–59. A concise survey.

9

JEROME
(C. 347–420)

FEAST: SEPTEMBER 30

I N HIS LETTER 22, written to his aristocratic friend and patron the Lady Eustochium, Jerome tells the story of what happened to him during Lent of 376 when he was living as a monk in the Syrian desert. The young scholar had already begun his intensive study of the Bible, but he kept getting pulled back to reading the more elegant classical writers he loved so well: Cicero, Plautus, and Vergil. In the midst of a severe fever that threatened his life, suddenly he felt himself caught up before the heavenly judgment seat, where God asked him to state who he was. When he responded that he was a Christian, the Judge thundered: "You're lying; you're a Ciceronian, not a Christian. Where your treasure is, there also is your heart" (Ps. 6:5). Jerome was ordered to be flogged, but as he begged for forgiveness during this beating the celestial court interceded for him and he was allowed to take an oath that if he ever again possessed or read "worldly books" it would be equivalent to denying God. Attesting that the experience was not a dream, he concludes his account: "My shoulders were black and blue and I felt the blows after I awoke from sleep. Afterwards, I read divine books with much greater attention than I had formerly read merely human books" (Letter 22.30). Of course, Jerome didn't keep his oath (as his enemies pointed out with glee); but he did keep his troubled conscience, as well as his unique literary gifts as the world's most famous translator.

Jerome, who was "posthumously promoted" to the rank of cardinal (there were none in his age), was a compulsive translator. Late in life, lamenting the fall of Rome and the death of his friend Paula, he said, "I try to assuage the disgust of my burning spirit by translating" (*aestuantis animi taedium interpretatione digerere conamur*). He was the first great *vir trilinguis:* master of Latin, Greek, and Hebrew. As such, he was in a unique position to undertake the central work of his long and varied life, the translation of the books of the Old and New Testaments that we know today as the "Vulgate," or "common" Latin text of the Bible. Although parts of the older Latin versions of the Bible (the *Vetus Latina*) continued to be used in the liturgy, it was Jerome's version that shaped the history of Western Christianity. Even in the modern era, as newer translations, especially the King James Bible (1611), proliferated, the cultural, religious, and rhetorical role of the Vulgate has remained powerful. In the words of a modern translator, Valery Larbaud: "That the Vulgate is truly a work of genius is confirmed by the qualities we discern there: that solidity, that grandeur, that majestic simplicity of style and expression. . . . What other translator has been able to bring off so colossal an undertaking with so much success, and with consequences so far-reaching in time and in space?"

Jerome was born of a Christian family in Stridon in the Balkans probably in 347 (some hold that he was born as early as 331). He received an excellent education in Rome (c. 360–67) under the grammarian Donatus. Here he was also baptized. In association with his friend Rufinus of Aquileia (with whom he later had a sundering quarrel), he took up a quasi-monastic lifestyle for a few years before setting off for Jerusalem. On the way, however, he decided to live as a hermit at Chalcis near Aleppo (c. 375–77), where he perfected his Greek and began to learn Hebrew. Ill health and conflict with other ascetics around him — Jerome's life is a history of both friendships and conflicts — forced him to leave the desert. He was ordained a priest at Antioch and then spent some time in Constantinople at the time of the great council that saw the triumph of Cappadocian theology. While there, Jerome began his translating efforts. He initially concentrated on putting Greek fathers into Latin, especially Origen, whom he greatly admired at this period.

In 382 Jerome returned to Rome, where he became the secretary of Pope Damasus (d. 384) and served as the spiritual guide for a group of wealthy Roman women who were much taken with the ascetic life. Due to quarrels with Damasus's successor, however, he left Rome and headed once again toward Jerusalem, though he made lengthy stops along the way at Antioch and Alexandria to study with other teachers and biblical scholars. Finally, in 386, he settled in Bethlehem at a double monastery built by his wealthy Roman patrons, Paula and her daughter Eustochium, who had accompanied him on his travels. Here Jerome remained for the last thirty-four years of his life, writing, translating, and often fighting with former friends over issues both personal and doctrinal. After 400, he carried on a lively correspondence with Augustine, as the younger North African bishop sought his advice on biblical and theological matters.

Two doctrinal controversies marked this period of Jerome's life. The first was the Origenist quarrel that erupted in the 390s. Convinced of Origen's errors by Epiphanius and others, Jerome turned against him, stopped his efforts to put the works of the Alexandrian into Latin, and broke with the Origenist bishop of Jerusalem and his former friend Rufinus, who continued his own Origen translation project. In 414 Jerome attacked another former friend, Pelagius, an ascetic who also had once been an advisor to wealthy Romans. In these last years of his life, the aged scholar was much affected by the sack of Rome in 410. Though he had earlier attacked apocalyptic and millenarian ideas, the disillusioned Jerome began to fear that the end of the world was near. Still, he continued to labor with his extensive series of biblical commentaries until his death in 420.

Jerome never consciously set out to make a whole new translation of the Bible. The project began by accident in 382 when Pope Damasus asked him to revise the Old Latin version of the gospels, which he did on the basis of a Greek text (exactly which type is still under debate). Jerome later revised this text, using better manuscripts he found in the East. The rest of the "Vulgate" New Testament was not produced by Jerome, but by someone in his circle, possibly Rufinus the Syrian, or even his enemy Pelagius(!). Jerome's major effort went into his new translation of the Old Testament, done in stages over fifteen years during his time in Palestine. In about 392, he completed a revision of the Psalter based on the Septuagint text found in Origen's *Hexapla* (i.e., "six-fold" edition), which allowed for comparison with the Hebrew. (This edition, later called the "Gallican," because it was used in the Carolingian liturgy, became standard in the Vulgate Bible, despite the fact that Origen did another version directly from the Hebrew.) At about this time, Jerome decided that translating from the Septuagint, even with the help of the *Hexapla*, was not sufficient. Access to God's word, the foundation of Christian belief, demanded going back to the *Hebraica veritas* ("Hebrew truth"). This was a controversial decision; the Septuagint was the "Old Testament of the Church," the version quoted in the New Testament itself. Many, including Augustine, felt uncomfortable with Jerome's choice. Nevertheless, using a version of the Hebrew very close to the standard Masoretic text of today, and consulting with rabbis, Jerome plunged ahead, finishing his version sometime around 406. Jerome did not, however, translate the "deuterocanonical" books like Sirach, Wisdom, and Maccabees, texts that are not in the Hebrew Bible, but that form part of the Christian Bible due to their presence in the Septuagint. The Old Latin versions of these made their way into the Vulgate when all these layers came to be collected into a single manuscript Bible, probably in the sixth century. This standard Bible also included Jerome's important prefaces to the various books of scripture.

Jerome's Vulgate alone would be sufficient for him to have been accorded the title of *doctor ecclesiae*, but he also enriched Latin Christianity through other translations, many commentaries, and some significant doctrinal treatises. Among his other works are homilies, hagiography (three influential lives of desert fathers), and his priceless letters. Jerome translated a good deal of Origen during the period before he turned against the Alexandrian teacher — seventy-eight homilies and some of Origen's minor works. He also produced an expanded version of Eusebius's important *Chronicle*, which was to become the basis for subsequent Latin chronology. But it was primarily in his series of commentaries that Jerome showed himself to be a master of biblical study. His exegesis has been described as eclectic, but this should not lead us to minimize or negate its importance. Under the influence of Origen and the Alexandrians, Jerome recognized the supremacy of the spiritual interpretation of the Bible, but the influence of more sober Antiochene exegesis, and especially his unrivaled knowledge of Hebrew and the topography of the Holy Land, led him to favor a more textual and historical interpretation in his later years. Jerome's exegetical work comes mostly from his Bethlehem period and began with commentaries on four Pauline letters. Most of his later exegesis, with the exception of his *Commentary on Matthew* (c. 398), deals with the Old Testament. Jerome's *Hebrew Questions on Genesis* is a critical examination of textual problems of the Old Latin version, which was instrumental in moving him to begin his own new translation. He was especially concerned with understanding the prophetic writings. His *Commentary on the Minor Prophets* exercised him between 391 and 406. Between 408 and 410 he wrote the eighteen books of his massive *Commentary on Isaiah*. This was followed by the long *Commentary on Ezekiel* (410–15) and by the unfinished *Commentary on Jeremiah*. Jerome's *Commentary on Daniel* (c. 407) was primarily an attack on the pagan Porphyry, who had argued (correctly) that Daniel was a work of the third century B.C.E., not of the sixth century as it pretended.

Jerome was not an original theologian of the stature of the Cappadocians or Augustine. His doctrinal contributions were made in the midst of polemics and are often somewhat one-sided. As a staunch proponent of the ideal of virginity, Jerome wrote letters (e.g., Letter 22) and treatises (e.g., *Against Jovinianum*) that include at times almost pathological attacks on sexuality and marriage. Jerome's polemical writings from the time of the Origenist controversy (e.g., *Against John of Jerusalem*; *Defense against the Book of Rufinus*) show him at his most intemperate. More important are his *On the Perpetual Virginity of the Blessed Mary against Helvidius*, the first Western Marian treatise, and his late *Dialogue against the Pelagians*. However, it is Jerome's correspondence of about 150 letters, some of them really treatises in letter form, that show the man at his best — and sometimes his worst. The letters, precisely because they are so different in style from the Vulgate, prove that Jerome was a great writer before he was a great translator. These missives are alive with personality, engaging in style, and crackling with satiric wit. Among the important topics that Jerome discusses are scriptural interpretation (Letters 20–21), education (Letters 107 and 128), the art of translation (Letter 57), the priesthood (Letter 52), the sack of Rome (Letter 127), the monastic life

(Letters 14, 58, 122, and 125), and, of course, women and the superiority of virginity (Letters 22 and 130).

Reading Jerome

If you understand even the slightest Latin, start your acquaintance with Jerome by reading some chapters of the Vulgate — aloud, as he and his contemporaries would have done. Then read some letters, such as those mentioned above. There are several good English selections: *St. Jerome: Select Letters*, trans. F. A. Wright, Loeb Classical Library (Cambridge: Harvard, 1980); *The Satirical Letters of St. Jerome*, trans. Paul Carroll (Chicago: Regnery, 1956); *The Letters of St. Jerome*, trans. C. C. Mierow and T. C. Lawler, ACW 33. Very few of Jerome's commentaries have been translated, but see *Jerome's Commentary on Daniel*, trans. Gleason L. Archer, Jr. (Grand Rapids: Baker, 1977). For Jerome's doctrinal treatises, see *St. Jerome: Dogmatic and Polemical Works*, trans. John N. Hritzu, FC 53.

Bibliography

Elizabeth A. Clark. *The Origenist Controversy: The Cultural Construction of an Early Christian Debate*. Princeton, N.J.: Princeton University Press, 1992. Helpful for unravelling the intricacies of one of the quarrels that shaped Jerome's later life.

J. N. D. Kelly. *Jerome: His Life, Writings, and Controversies*. New York: Harper and Row, 1975. The most complete account in English.

Valery Larbaud. *An Homage to Jerome: Patron Saint of Translators*. Marlboro, Vt.: Marlboro Press, 1984. Every doctor deserves a tribute as delightful and insightful as this.

A Monument to Saint Jerome: Essays on Some Aspects of His Life, Thought, and Works. Ed. Francis F. X. Murphy. New York: Sheed and Ward, 1952. An old collection, but with many excellent essays.

10

Augustine of Hippo

(354–430)

Feast: August 28

O N AUGUST 28, 430, an elderly bishop lay on his deathbed in the city of Hippo on the southern shore of the Mediterranean. Some weeks before he had ordered four penitential psalms to be written out and hung on the walls of his sickroom so that he could read them continually and weep over his sins. Ten days before he had forbidden all save his doctors to enter his sickroom in order to devote himself totally to prayer. At the end of his life Augustine of Hippo remained true to the spirit of his most read work, the *Confessions*, a theme he had also echoed in the *Retractions*, a list of comments and corrections to ninety-three of his works, which he penned in 428. In this late work he said: "Hence it remains for me to judge myself before my single Master whose judgment of my offenses I desire to escape."

Augustine's lifetime spanned the years of the decline of the Western Roman Empire. When he was born at Thagaste in 354, the empire was still strong and able to cope with enemies without and within. Growing up as a wild youth, he was a young teacher of rhetoric at the time of the first major Gothic invasions and the Roman defeat at Adrianople in 378. But Emperor Theodosius (379–95) made a settlement with the Goths, reunited the empire, put down rebellions, and established Christianity as the state religion. The first quarter century of Augustine's years as convert, priest, and bishop (387–410) were spent in the midst of the warm glow of the "Theodosian Renaissance." The inner weaknesses of the empire, however, were shockingly

65

revealed in the sack of Rome in 410 by the Visigothic leader and sometime Roman general Alaric. The last two decades of Augustine's life were spent in an empire under crisis — political, military, religious. As the dying bishop read the psalms and wept over his sins, barbarian Vandals were besieging his own city.

Augustine is one of those rare figures who both perfectly define an age — in his case Late Antiquity — and yet also surpass their era to become resources for every age. Alfred North Whitehead once described the history of Western philosophy as a series of footnotes to Plato. It would be no less true an exaggeration to say that the history of Western Christian theology is a series of footnotes to Augustine. Augustine wrote on every aspect of Christian belief, and he did so with such originality and skill that he must be ranked among the most influential of all the doctors of the church. Indeed, the very concept of *doctor ecclesiae,* as mentioned in Part I, developed in large part in order to highlight the authority of the bishop's writings.

In his discussion of the meaning of time in the *Confessions* Augustine characterized his life with the words: "I have burst apart [*dissilui*] into times whose order I do not know; my thoughts, the inmost organs of my soul, are torn to pieces by the storms of change, until, purified and melted down by the fire of your love, I will flow back into you" (*Conf.* 11.29). An abiding sense of the torture of temporality is present throughout Augustine's life and writings. But for Augustine, unlike Neoplatonists such as Plotinus, temporality was not just the measure of the fallen soul's imperfection; it was something more positive: the arena in which souls could work out their conversion and return to their Creator. The only way to prevent the sea of temporality and changeability in which we find ourselves from becoming a "region of unlikeness" (*regio dissimilitudinis*), that is, of separation from God, is to surrender ourselves to the fire of divine *caritas* that leads us back up toward the peace and perfect enjoyment (*fruitio*) of eternity. As an even more famous text in the *Confessions* put it: "Late have I loved you, Beauty at once so old and so new; late have I loved you. Behold, you were within, and I outside where I was seeking you and was dashing against the beautiful things you made in my unsightly way. You were with me, and I was not with you" (*Conf.* 10.27).

Augustine's sense of constant change as the hallmark of human existence gives his writings an actuality, a sense of engagement, rare among theologians. Though many of his works are directed to quarrels and issues of the past, much of his preaching, his letters, and many of his treatises speak directly to us today precisely because he himself was so attentive to the ever-changing moment. Augustine's life was a never-ending conversion experience, both mental and spiritual, to an ever deeper awareness of God. Hence, it is not surprising that he changed his views so often during his life. This moving viewpoint means that readers must remain attentive to the various phases of the bishop's life when they try to analyze his teaching on any particular doctrine.

Augustine is an accessible writer with a swift and subtle mind and a remarkable style. During his lifetime he was also a fighter. Although some of
his greatest works, especially his treatise *The Trinity,* were composed out of
the desire for "faith seeking understanding," the description of the task of
theology that he made canonical in the West, much of his immense out-
put was the product of theological controversy. Major struggles against four
sets of opponents were of particular importance in forming his thought and
his role as *doctor ecclesiae:* Manichaeanism; Donatism; Pelagianism; and what
we can call Classicism (i.e., the pagan view of God, world, and history).
His controversies with these opponents were often interconnected, and thus
his responses were made on the basis of a broad, moving front involving a
deepening understanding of many theological issues, especially creation, the
problem of evil, the nature of Adam's fall, the role of grace, the meaning of
freedom in history, and the place of the church — to mention only the most
evident.

Mani (c. 216–76), a Persian visionary, founded a dualistic religion that
competed with Christianity for several centuries. The young Augustine, troubled by the existence of evil in the world and in his own life, was a
Manichaean for a decade before he gradually began to move away from this
materialistic explanation of the problem of evil, first under the influence of
reading Neoplatonic philosophy. Shortly after he was baptized in 387, Augustine undertook a sustained refutation of Manichaeanism over two decades to
purge himself of the errors that had fascinated both himself and his contemporaries. In defending the goodness of creation and the total and temporal
dependence of the world on God's creative decision (largely in five commentaries he wrote on the Genesis creation account), Augustine not only
refuted the Manichaeans, but also took on ancient philosophy, which viewed
the world as a necessary and eternal product of God. In the course of this
struggle Augustine also worked out his approach to the problem of evil, one
that combined two basic elements. The first was a Neoplatonic theodicy emphasizing that evil was not a something, but a privation of good rooted in
the will's freedom; the second was a Pauline emphasis on the pervasiveness
of sin in history due to the inherited fault from Adam. The result was the
Augustinian doctrine of original sin, which he explored in great detail in his
subsequent writings against Pelagius.

Augustine struggled against the Donatists from the time he returned to
Africa from Rome in 391 until his death. Donatism was essentially a debate
about the proper understanding of the church's role in conveying the salvation won by Christ. The party of Donatus (schismatic bishop of Carthage
315–55) held that the sacraments by which Christ's saving grace comes to
us are effective only when given by ministers without sin, implying that the
church must always be the church of the pure and therefore the church of
the few. Augustine argued that the church on earth as the universal instru-
ment of salvation is always a "mixed body" of both good and evil and that

the validity of the sacraments depends, not on the holiness of the minister, but on Christ as the author of the sacraments. In the course of the controversy Augustine laid the foundations for much of the ecclesiology and sacramentology of later Western Christendom. A more dubious contribution of the fight against the Donatists was the theology of persecution he produced after a policy of conciliation had failed: the Donatists were to be "compelled to come in" (Luke 14:23) as an act of what today might be called "tough love."

Augustine was one of the pioneers of Western monasticism, writing a monastic rule for both the priests who lived with him and for a community of women ascetics. Monastic personal asceticism, however, often overemphasized the role of free choice in doing good and avoiding evil, an exaggeration that led Augustine into his third great struggle, that with Pelagius and his followers and sympathizers. Though the controversy involved many aspects of Augustine's late theology, such as the nature of original sin and the necessity of baptism, it centered on three key issues: (1) What is human freedom? (2) How is grace to be understood? and (3) How does divine predestination work? Pelagius, an ascetic from the British Isles, was influential among the Christian aristocrats of Rome. When Augustine first took notice of Pelagius in 412 with his treatise *The Spirit and the Letter* it was in the spirit of friendly correction. He felt that Pelagius had erred in allowing that, with the help of grace, someone could live without sin. Augustine insisted (see 2 Cor. 2:6) that the letter of the law kills, but the grace of the spirit gives life, namely, that we are not justified by our efforts to lead a holy life, but by faith, the free gift of God independent of our merits. Subsequently, it became clear to Augustine that Pelagius's error was more profound. In holding that the fallen will retain the power, however injured and attenuated, to choose between good and evil, Augustine argued (especially in *The Grace of Christ* of 418) that Pelagius had misconstrued the nature of the fall, misunderstood the circumstantial character of freedom, and evacuated the necessity of "the grace of God in our Lord Jesus Christ through which he makes righteous by his justice rather than our own." The implications of the absolute gratuity and necessity of grace and his growing pessimism about fallen human nature led Augustine in his last decade toward a doctrine of double predestination, that is, the teaching that from all eternity the divine decree predestines some to grace and glory and others to damnation. While the main lines of Augustine's teaching on sin, freedom, and grace became standard in the West, Catholic Christianity, beginning with the Council of Orange in 529, stepped back from his late teaching on predestination.

The final struggle which shaped Augustine's thought was one he carried on throughout his life — that with the classical pagan understanding of God, cosmos, humanity, and history. This fight, however, came to a head in 410 when the sack of Rome led pagans to complain that the Christian God was too weak to defend his city. In order to answer this challenge, Augustine composed his *City of God* in twenty-two books between 413 and 426. Here Augustine created a new theology of history by breaking with those Christians who had hailed the conversion of the empire and the intermingling of the destinies of church and empire as manifest signs of providence. (Augustine also attacked the apocalyptic understanding of history, which he felt was equally literal-minded, but pessimistic rather than optimistic about the future.) The bishop "secularized" external history and the Roman Empire. For him these quotidian events were not manifestations of the sacred, but only the sad story of fallen humanity, with no immediate relation to God's ultimate purpose. True history was the inner story of the "two loves [that] built two cities, earthly love of self even unto contempt of God and heavenly love of God unto contempt of self" (*City of God* 14.28). Augustine thought that it was useless to look for progress in the public and external events of history; the meaning of history is the hidden building up of the City of God through the salvific activity of Jesus Christ, the center of history.

Reading Augustine

Reading Augustine is a lifetime task. He wrote well over a hundred works, some of great length, as well as hundreds of letters and sermons. There are many translations of Augustine, so I will not attempt to list individual versions here. The most complete English translation currently available is found in NPNF, 1st series, vols. 1–8. A more complete translation project is now underway: *The Complete Works of Saint Augustine*, John E. Rotelle, general editor (Hyde Park, N.Y.: New City Press, 1996–), planned for forty-six volumes, of which eighteen have now appeared. The best place to begin reading Augustine is the *Confessions*, one of the few works of which one can say that it is as much a literary as it is a theological masterpiece. The *Confessions* is fundamentally a work of theological anthropology, but it touches on all aspects of Augustine's thought. In the vast world of *The City of God* one might well begin by reading books 11–14, describing the origin of the two cities, and then work backward to the early books of polemics against paganism, and finally turn to the later books discussing the course of sacred history and Augustine's view of the last things. Augustine was also the father of Western mystical theology. This is best seen in the homilies he preached to his congregation at Hippo (Augustine believed all Christians were called to a deep consciousness of God's presence). One might begin with his *Homilies on Psalms*, 26, 41, 99, and 119; *Homily on the Gospel of John*, 20; and *Homilies on the First Epistle of John*, 4–5, 7–8, and 10; as well as Letter 147. *The Trinity* is perhaps Augustine's most profound work; a reading of books 8–9 and 14–15 will show why. The bishop's famous handbook on interpreting scripture and preaching, called *On Christian Doctrine*, is another important and influential text; but it would be well to read it along with some examples of his exegesis in practice, such as book 1 of the *Literal Commentary on Genesis* or his treatise *The Lord's Sermon on the Mount*. The bishop's *Enchiridion* of 421 is a late attempt to summarize the essentials of Christian teaching.

Bibliography

Whole libraries have been written about Augustine. Especially recommended are:

Peter Brown. *Augustine of Hippo: A Biography.* Berkeley and Los Angeles: University of California Press, 1967. A superb evocation of Augustine's life and times.

John Burnaby. *Amor Dei: A Study of the Religion of St. Augustine.* London: Hodder & Stoughton, 1938. A classic study of one of Augustine's central themes.

Etienne Gilson. *The Christian Philosophy of St. Augustine.* New York: Random House, 1960. A profound exposition by one of the master historians of philosophy.

Paul Henry. *The Path to Transcendence: From Philosophy to Mysticism in Saint Augustine.* Pittsburgh: Pickwick Press, 1981. An insightful study of the *Confessions.*

Bernard McGinn. *The Foundations of Mysticism: Origins to the Fifth Century.* New York: Crossroad, 1991. Chap. 7 deals with Augustine's mysticism.

R. A. Markus. *Saeculum: History and Society in the Theology of St. Augustine.* Cambridge: Cambridge University Press, 1970. The best book of Augustine's theology of history.

Eugene Teselle. *Augustine the Theologian.* New York: Herder and Herder, 1970. A clear exposition of the development of many of the crucial aspects of Augustine's theology.

Frederick Van der Meer. *Augustine the Bishop: Religion and Society at the Dawn of the Middle Ages.* New York: Sheed and Ward, 1961. Detailed and fascinating.

11

Cyril of
Alexandria
(378–444)

Feast: June 27

J UNE 22, 431, was one of the more exciting days in the history of
Christian doctrine. In the basilica dedicated to Mary in Ephesus (traditionally the city where the Blessed Virgin had died) a group of almost
two hundred bishops had been meeting all day to determine the fate of
Nestorius, the patriarch of Constantinople. Nestorius, though present in the
city, had refused to show his face, protesting that his enemies, especially Cyril
the patriarch of Alexandria, had stacked the house against him by not waiting until John of Antioch and the Syrian bishops arrived. But the assembled
bishops had waited long enough. Cyril read out the creed of Nicaea and a
letter of his own attacking Nestorius's Christology. The bishops unanimously
voted to approve these documents as orthodox and then went on to condemn and depose Nestorius. At the end of the long June day, the crowds,
ardent defenders of Mary as "Mother of God" (a title Nestorius had questioned), greeted the bishops with acclamation and escorted them to their
lodgings with torches and processions.

This dramatic day at the Council of Ephesus, recognized as the third of the
ecumenical, or universal, councils, was the high point of Cyril's public life,
but also a chapter in a long and complex struggle over the proper way to express the gospel faith that Jesus Christ is both God and man. The great work
of the fourth century was the creation of the orthodox theology of the Trinity,
hammered out in the conflicts between the Arians, the "Semi-Arians," and
their orthodox opponents, especially doctors like Athanasius, Basil, Gregory

71

of Nazianzus, and Hilary. Beginning with the late fourth-century disputes over the teaching of Apollinaris of Laodicea, who denied the existence of a human soul in Christ, the christological issue emerged with ever greater force for the next century and more. Two major councils and two doctors of the church played key roles in the development of the dogmatic formulae that tradition enshrined as orthodox — Cyril at Ephesus and Pope Leo I at Chalcedon. The christological debates were, if anything, even fiercer and more difficult than those over the proper faith concerning the Trinity. There were Christians in the East, especially Syria, who never accepted Nestorius's condemnation. They continue to exist to this day — the Nestorian churches of Asia. On the other side, when the Council of Chalcedon in 451 used language that departed from Cyril in aspects of its decisions, some of the late patriarch's more extreme followers refused to recognize the council and thus began the tradition of the Monophysite branches of Christianity still to be found in Egypt, Syria, and Armenia.

Cyril, "the Seal of the Fathers" as Anastasius of Sinai later called him, was born in Alexandria in 378. His uncle, Theophilus, patriarch of the city between 385 and 412, supervised his education and advancement in the clergy. The ancient catechetical school of Alexandria, whose greatest glory was Origen (d. 254), still lived on in the person of the exegete Didymus the Blind (d. 398), under whom Cyril probably studied. Theophilus was a wily, even an unscrupulous, ecclesiastical politician; something of his character and style of episcopacy rubbed off on Cyril, who succeeded him as patriarch. A good number of the fourth- and fifth-century doctors strike us today as intransigent, and sometimes even as immoral, in their political activities. (It was in surveying Cyril's early deeds as bishop that John Henry Newman made the remark that he knew Cyril was a saint, but that nothing obliged him to say that Cyril was a saint in 412.) However, it is only if we insist that the doctors must always be "plaster saints," free from the limitations of their age and personal faults, that these admissions need trouble us unduly.

Aside from establishing his own position against his enemies, the major preoccupation of the first part of Cyril's episcopacy (412–28) was the composition of scriptural commentaries often of great length (seven of the ten volumes of Cyril's works in the Greek patrology are exegetical). The presence of a large Jewish community in Alexandria involved the patriarch in acrimonious disputes with the Jews that are evident in the Old Testament commentaries in which he sought to vindicate Christian possession of the key to the true meaning of the Law. Among these are two works on the Pentateuch and his long *Commentary on Isaiah*. The most important of his biblical works, however, is his masterful *Commentary on John*, directed primarily against the Arians. Cyril also wrote several anti-Arian treatises, deftly mining and organizing the arguments of Athanasius. In these works, as in his later confrontations with Nestorius and his adherents, Cyril argued as the representative of tradition, making skillful use of the "proofs from the fathers." As he once put it, "We follow in all things the views of the holy fathers, but especially those of our blessed and all-renowned father Athanasius" (Letter 39).

In 428 Emperor Theodosius II named an outsider, the Syrian monk Nestorius, as patriarch of Constantinople. Nestorius's theology was rooted in the teaching of the Antiochene theologians, especially Theodore of Mopsuestia (d. 428), and represented a way of trying to express the mystery of the unity and duality in the God-Man different from that found among the Alexandrians. The Alexandrian theologians (and many others) thought of Christ in terms of the Johannine formula of the "Word-taking-flesh" and therefore stressed the unity of the Redeemer. The issue they struggled with was how to be true to the continuing reality of the full humanity of Christ. The Antiochenes, however, thought in terms of a "Word/man" formula that emphasized the fullness of both God and man in Christ, but made it difficult to do full justice to the Savior's unity. Both sides tended to talk past each other in these ongoing debates, which were often as much political as doctrinal. Without the trial and error found on both sides, the development that led to Chalcedon would never have taken place.

While today Nestorius, and especially Theodore of Mopsuestia, are judged more leniently than they were in the past (both for their intentions and for the contributions they made to the ongoing evolution), there is no question that Cyril was a far more penetrating and profound theologian. His Christology was that which the great majority of fifth-century bishops, both of the East and West, felt best expressed the faith of their communities. It was his powerful summation of the meaning of the Incarnation that has ever after been central to the understanding of the redemption wrought by Jesus Christ. We need to remember that Cyril, like the other fathers, was not interested in christological issues for the sake of speculation — the mystery of Christ is the mystery of our redemption. As he put it: "If he conquered as God, then it profits us nothing; but if as man, we conquered in him. He is to us the Second Adam who came down from heaven according to the scriptures" (*Comm. on John* 16.33). The center of Cyril's Christology resides in the *kenosis*, or emptying (see Phil. 2:7–8), by which the preexistent and impassible Logos made himself subject to the conditions and limitations of human existence and thus opened up the path to deification for the human race.

Nestorius's preaching and tactless actions began to evoke protest almost from his arrival in Constantinople. Three particular aspects of his teaching aroused opposition. The first was his claim that Christ, the divine Person of the Word, assumed a human person into the divine nature in the Incarnation, thus suggesting that there were two sons or perhaps even two persons in the God-Man (though Nestorius, like Theodore, used the language of "one person"). The second was the Antiochene penchant for speaking of the Word taking flesh by an act of "will" or "good pleasure." The third, and most objectionable to popular piety, was Nestorius's denial of the traditional title

"Mother of God" (*theotokos*) to Mary, insisting that the term "Mother of Christ" was more appropriate.

Cyril, who had been suspicious of Antiochene theology for some years, immediately began his offensive, writing Nestorius three letters and composing several treatises against him in 430 (e.g., *Five Tomes against Nestorius, On Correct Faith, Twelve Anathemas against Nestorius*). The heart of his case can be seen in the following texts from Cyril's Second Letter, the text approved at Ephesus. Cyril says: "We do not say that the Logos became flesh by having his nature changed, nor for that matter that he was transformed into a complete human being.... On the contrary, we say that in an unspeakable and incomprehensible way, the Logos united to himself, in his hypostasis, flesh enlivened by a rational soul, and in this way became a human being and has been designated 'Son of Man.' He did not become a human being simply by an act of will or 'good pleasure,' any more than he did so by merely taking on a human person." Cyril's identification of the *hypostasis* of the Word as the reality of the unity of the divine and human in Christ was important for later Christology. Unfortunately, he did not make a clear distinction between the terms *hypostasis* and *physis*, so some of his formulations, such as his speaking of "the one incarnate *physis* of the Word" (e.g., Letter 46.2) were not compatible with the dogmatic statement later issued at Chalcedon. With regard to the title of the Blessed Virgin, Cyril issued a direct challenge to Nestorius: "Since the Holy Virgin gave birth after the flesh to God who was united by hypostasis to flesh, therefore we say that she is the *theotokos*."

Cyril's initial victory over Nestorius on June 22 was short-lived. A few days later, the smaller delegation of Antiochene bishops arrived and held their own synod, which approved of Nestorius and deposed Cyril. Emperor Theodosius rather confusingly accepted the decisions of both synods and arrested Nestorius and Cyril. As the emperor investigated the issues, it became clear that Cyril's views commanded the majority (Cyril also supported his cause with considerable bribery); so in a few months the patriarch of Alexandria was allowed to return to his see in triumph and Nestorius's deposition was upheld. With imperial prompting, Cyril eventually worked out a compromise with the more moderate Syrian theologians led by John of Antioch in 433. This "Formula of Reunion" shows that he was willing to accept some variety in christological vocabulary, provided that this did not compromise the essential issue of the single subjectivity of the God-man. In his last decade of life Cyril continued to write on Christology, attacking Theodore of Mopsuestia and Diodorus of Tarsus, another Antiochene thinker, in a treatise of 438. His final synthesis of his Christology, entitled *On the Unity of Christ*, was composed about 440. During these years the prolific patriarch also wrote a large polemical work *Against the Books of the Impious Julian*, a detailed refutation of the pagan emperor's attack on Christianity composed as early as 363. (Apparently, there were still enough pagans around to make this apologetic effort worthwhile.) Many of Cyril's letters are important dogmatic tracts, and a number of his twenty surviving sermons, especially Homily 11 on the Mother of God, also contain important doctrinal teaching.

Reading Cyril

Cyril's late treatise on Christology is the best summary of his thought; see *St. Cyril of Alexandria: On the Unity of Christ*, trans. John Anthony McGuckin (Crestwood, N.Y.: St. Vladimir's Seminary Press, 1995). Cyril's important letters to Nestorius exist in a full translation by P. E. Pusey, *The Three Epistles of St. Cyril (The Dogmatic Letters to Nestorius)* (Oxford: Oxford University Press, 1872), and there are excerpts in many collections of doctrinal texts. Pusey also did a translation of Cyril's *Commentary on John*, Library of the Fathers of the Church 43 (Oxford: Oxford University Press, 1872).

Bibliography

Walter J. Burghardt. *The Image of God in Man according to Cyril of Alexandria.* Washington, D.C.: Catholic University Press, 1957.

Aloys Grillmeier. *Christ in the Christian Tradition: From the Apostolic Age to Chalcedon.* New York: Sheed and Ward, 1965, 400–12.

John A. McGuckin. *St. Cyril of Alexandria: The Christological Controversy.* Leiden: Brill, 1994. The most recent survey of Cyril's contribution to doctrine.

Patrology III, 116–42.

Robert L. Wilken. *Judaism and the Early Christian Mind: A Study of Cyril of Alexandria's Exegesis and Theology.* New Haven: Yale University Press, 1971. One of the few works to treat Cyril the exegete seriously.

Young, 240–65. A clear summary.

12

PETER CHRYSOLOGUS
(C. 380–450)

FEAST: JULY 30

I N 448 Eutyches, the head of a monastery near Constantinople, wrote a circular letter to the most important bishops of the Roman Empire seeking support for his christological views. Peter, the archbishop of Ravenna, penned a tactful response at Christmas of that year, reminding the monk of the dangers of speculation on divine mysteries and counseling him to depend on the faith of the bishop of Rome. "In all things, honorable brother," he said, "we exhort you to attend in obedience to what the Most Blessed Pope of the city of Rome has written, because Saint Peter lives and presides in his own see and offers the truth of faith to those who seek it" (Letter 25 in the collection of the Letters of Pope Leo I). Fittingly, it was Leo's famous Letter, or *Tome*, setting out the doctrine of the two natures united in the one Person of Christ, that played a major role in Eutyches' condemnation at the Council of Chalcedon in 451.

Little is known of Peter of Ravenna. (The ninth-century life by Andrew Agnellus — the text in which he first received the title "Chrysologus," or "Golden-Word" — is mostly fiction.) Peter was born at Imola in northern Italy, probably closer to 380 than to 400. He became archbishop of Ravenna about 430, the year of Augustine's death. Ravenna at that time was the capital of the Western Empire, the residence of Emperor Valentinian III and his mother, the pious Galla Placidia. Several of Peter's sermons were delivered in the imperial presence.

Like Augustine, Peter was well trained in the Latin rhetorical tradition, showing familiarity with Cicero, Seneca, and Vergil. Peter was essentially a

preacher. Two collections of his sermons come down to us, about 180 homilies in all, though there are still disputes about the authenticity of some.
He also appears to have composed the brief *Explanation of the Creed*. Peter's
preaching was biblical and liturgical, like that of the other fathers and doctors of the fourth and fifth centuries. One does not go to him for original or
powerful doctrinal formulations, but rather in order to appreciate the cate-
chesis of late antique Christianity. Peter's sermons, written in a correct and
occasionally inspired Latin (e.g., Sermon 74 on the Resurrection), give us a
good picture of the Christian liturgical year as seen through his interpretation of the major texts, especially the gospels, for Sundays and Feast Days.
For Peter, as for the other Latin fathers, the spiritual interpretation of the
liturgical readings is what is essential to good preaching: "The historical nar-
rative should always be raised to a higher meaning and the mysteries of the
future should become known through the figures of the present" (Sermon
36). The bishop's fundamental intent is to teach sound doctrine, encourage
moral living, and to bring his audience to single-hearted devotion to Christ.
A passage from Sermon 108, commenting on Paul's exhortation to present
our bodies as sacrifices to God (Rom. 12:1), illustrates the flavor of the best
of his preaching: "Let Christ be the covering of your head. Let the cross remain as the helmet of your forehead. Cover your breast with the mystery of
heavenly knowledge. Keep the incense of prayer ever burning before you as
your perfume. Take up the sword of the spirit. Set up your heart as an altar.
Free from anxiety, move your body forward in this way to make it a victim
for God."

Reading Peter Chrysologus

Some of Peter's sermons are available in English in *St. Peter Chrysologus: Selected
Sermons,* trans. George. E. Ganss, FC 17.

Bibliography

Very little secondary literature exists.

J. H. Baxter. "The Homilies of St. Peter Chrysologus," *Journal of Theological Studies* 22
    (1921): 250–58.
R. H. McGlynn. *The Incarnation in the Sermons of St. Peter Chrysologus.* Mundelein,
    Ill.: St. Mary's of the Lake, 1956.
Patrology IV, 575–77.
Rusch, 163–65.

13

LEO THE
GREAT
(C. 390–461)

FEAST: NOVEMBER 10

I N 451 Attila the Hun, the "Scourge of God," had been checked in his
invasion of Gaul at the battle of Chalons. His forces were still formi-
dable, however, when in the following spring he crossed the Alps and
invaded northern Italy. After a long siege he captured and destroyed Aquileia
and then marched across the Po valley, leaving death and destruction everywhere. In mid-summer of 452, on the banks of the river Mincius, he was met
by an embassy from the city of Rome led by Leo, its bishop. Amazingly, the
embassy convinced the dreaded Hun to give up his plans to march on Rome.
Historians are still unsure of the reasons for this change of mind. Later legend, immortalized by Raphael in a painting in the Vatican Palace, credits a
miraculous appearance of Peter and Paul in the sky over Pope Leo, bran-
dishing swords of divine vengeance. Whatever the reason, the success of the
bishop's legation brought safety to the city and glory to its leader. As the *Book
of the Popes* put it in its brief biography of Leo, "For the sake of the Roman
name, he accepted a legation, and went to the king of the Huns named Attila
and freed all Italy from the peril of its foes."

Leo, one of the two popes to have merited the accolade "the Great," was
bishop of Rome during one of the ancient city's most fateful eras. Little is
known about his life until he ascended the papal throne, but the context
of his time tells us much about Leo's role and significance. When he was
born, probably about 390, "the Roman name" was still all-powerful. But as
he ascended the ranks of the clergy of Rome, the barbarian invasions made

Roman weakness in the West devastatingly obvious. Alaric sacked Rome in 410, and the weak Western emperor Honorius (395–423) retreated to the impregnable fortress of Ravenna. Increasingly, the city of Rome and much of Italy looked to the Roman bishop for leadership. In Leo they found a leader who combined the *gravitas* and *moderatio* of the rulers of ancient Rome with the *humilitas* of a Christian bishop.

It was while he was serving as archdeacon of Rome on a mission to Gaul that Leo heard of his election as pope in 440. The twenty-one years of his pontificate were taken up with a succession of crises, both political and ecclesiastical (the two often intermingled). The successful embassy to Attila in 452 was followed in 455 by a negotiation with the Vandal King Gaiseric, which opened the city to be sacked by him, but spared the lives of the inhabitants. Leo also had numerous dealings with both the Western and Eastern emperors of his day. His attitude toward imperial power was that of a conservative Roman ecclesiastic who looked to the emperors to defend and protect the church, though he was willing to speak out when he felt the emperor had infringed on ecclesiastical prerogatives (see Letter 104 to Marcian on the ecclesiastical status of Constantinople). Writing to the emperor Leo, the pope reminds him, "You should readily recognize that ruling power was conferred on you not only for the rule of the world, but particularly for the protection of the church" (Letter 156).

Pope Leo had an important role in the evolution of the theory of papal primacy. It is not too much to say that in Leo's letters and sermons we find the first clear and systematic expression of the Petrine theology that has ever since been the guiding principle of the papacy. As a "Roman of the Romans," Leo took over Roman juristic terms, such as *principatus* (preeminence) to describe the position of the bishop of Rome. He also was the first to adopt the ancient Roman title *pontifex maximus*, "High Priest." His interpretation of Christ's promise to Peter, "You are Peter [i.e., rock] and upon this rock I will build my church" (Matt. 16:18), was fundamental. Leo held that ecclesiastical jurisdiction, the power to bind and to loose, had been primarily given to Peter and through Peter to the other apostles. As he put it in one place: "The Lord desired that the dispensing of this gift should be shared by all the apostles, but in such a way that he put the principal charge on the most blessed Peter.... He wanted his gifts to flow into the entire body from Peter himself, as it were from the head" (Letter 10; cf. Letter 14, Sermon 4, etc.). While the subjective graces of the great *apostolus* were his alone, Peter's successor, the bishop of Rome, objectively carries on his position in the church as the *vir apostolicus*. In his third sermon for Christmas, Leo proclaimed, "So, if anything is rightly done and rightly decreed by us, it is of his work and merits whose power lives and whose authority prevails in his see" (Sermon 3.3; cf. Letters 102 and 119). As Peter's vicar and successor, the pope has *plenitudo potestatis* (fullness of power) over the church. On this basis Leo resisted Bishop Hilary of Arles's attempt to claim jurisdiction over the churches of Gaul: "He seeks to subject you to his authority while not allowing himself to be under the jurisdiction of the blessed apostle Peter," Leo protested (Letter 10).

Leo's theology is not speculative or original, but essentially traditional, kerygmatic, and christological. As befitting his position as the "rock" of orthodoxy, Leo took a strong stance against heresies and doctrinal errors throughout his pontificate. In the West, he attacked Arians, Manichaeans, Pelagians, and others; but his most important doctrinal struggle was his opposition to christological errors in the East. Christology was the central dogmatic issue of the fifth century, and it is fitting that two contemporaries, Cyril of Alexandria and Leo of Rome, made the most important contributions. Leo's interest in Christology seems to have begun early, because it was at his request that the monk Cassian wrote his *Seven Books on the Lord's Incarnation against Nestorius* (c. 430). Leo's pontificate, however, was to be troubled by the opposite of Nestorius's theology of dividing the human and divine in Christ into "two sons." His major opponents were those who denied that the Incarnate Word possessed a full human nature, the theological position later known as "Monophysitism," or "one-nature" Christology.

Cyril's victory at Ephesus in 431 vindicated the essential unity of Christ the redeemer. But the persistence of dualistic views of the God-Man seems to have prompted some of Cyril's followers to extreme expressions that submerged the human nature of the Redeemer in the Godhead. Cyril had affirmed that Christ was "*out* of two natures," i.e., both human and divine; but because he did not distinguish between *physis* ("nature," for Chalcedon) and *hypostasis* ("person"), his language was not always clear about the continuing full humanity of Christ after the Incarnation. The controversy was brought to a head by Eutyches, the abbot of an important monastery in Constantinople, who taught that after the Incarnation there is only one divine nature in Christ, the human nature being so absorbed into the divine that Christ's flesh was not consubstantial with our own. Eutyches was supported by many of Cyril's followers, especially in Alexandria; but Flavian, the patriarch of Constantinople, summoned him to a synod of bishops in 448 and had him excommunicated. Eutyches, however, had powerful friends, both at the court of the emperor Theodosius II and among the bishops of the East, notably Dioscurus of Alexandria. Theodosius summoned a council to consider the quarrel and named the wily and intemperate Dioscurus as president. Leo was invited to attend, but he argued that this was against custom. Instead, he sent legates, and on June 13, 449, addressed a letter to Flavian, the famous *Tome* (Letter 28) that expressed the faith of the Western church and roundly condemned Eutyches, that "extremely foolish and altogether ignorant man."

Leo's intervention did no good. In August of 449, the "Robber Synod" (*Latrocinium*), as Leo called it, rehabilitated Eutyches and deposed and arrested

Flavian amid a turmoil unusual even for the early church synods. Leo refused to accept the proceedings and protested in vain to the emperor. In July of 450, however, Theodosius died, and Eutyches lost his imperial support. The emperor Marcian summoned a new council, and Pope Leo, somewhat reluctantly at first, again sent legates. When the almost five hundred bishops met at Chalcedon in October of 451, Dioscorus and his followers were condemned and deposed. Then the bishops had the creeds of Nicaea and Constantinople read out, as well as two of Cyril's Letters, and Leo's *Tome* to Flavian. The bishops shouted: "This is the faith of the fathers and the apostles. Peter has spoken through Leo. Cyril taught this too; Leo and Cyril taught the same." The moment signaled a remarkable consonance between Leo's theology of papal primacy and the developing mechanism of ecumenical councils, which had previously paid little attention to the bishop of Rome. The council fathers at first resisted drawing up a new statement of faith, but under imperial pressure eventually a creed was composed which combined Cyrillan emphasis on the unity of person, or subject, in Christ (eight repetitions of "one and the same") with Leo's stress on the continuing integrity of both natures. "One and the same Christ, Son, Lord, Only-Begotten, is to be acknowledged in two natures without confusion, without change, without division, without separation; the distinction of natures being in no way abolished because of the union, but rather the characteristic property of each nature being preserved and concurring in one person or hypostasis."

Leo did not know Greek, so he was not familiar with the debates about the proper Greek terminology to describe the duality of humanity and divinity and unity of the one subject in Jesus Christ, the redeeming God-Man. It was precisely for this reason that the majority of Greek bishops who met at Chalcedon in 451 enthusiastically accepted his firm and clear declaration of the two natures and one Person in Jesus — the "hypostatic union" Christology that has ever after been the touchstone of the orthodox view of East and West. As the *Tome* put it: "It is equally perilous for people to believe that the Lord Jesus Christ is simply God and not a human being, or a mere human being and not God." Both in this famous letter, as well as in Letter 165, his other major christological document, Leo was particularly careful in his teaching on the complicated question of the *communicatio idiomatum*, that is, the way in which, in the case of the single subject who is Christ, human things are said of God and divine things of a human. "Since, therefore, the characteristic properties of both natures and substances are kept intact and come together in one person, lowliness is taken on by majesty, weakness by power, mortality by eternity, and the nature that cannot be harmed is united to the nature that suffers in order that the debt which our condition involves may be discharged" (Letter 28).

Reading Leo

Of Leo's letters 123 remain. Most can be found in *St. Leo the Great: Letters,* trans. Edmund Hunt, FC 34. Leo's ninety-six surviving sermons are available in *St. Leo the Great: Sermons,* trans. Jane Patricia Freeland and Agnes Josephine Conway, FC 93. The pope's Christmas sermons (nos. 21–30) are particularly fine.

Bibliography

Far too little has been written about Leo, at least in English.

W. J. Halliwell. *The Style of Pope St. Leo the Great.* Washington, D.C.: Catholic University of America Press, 1939.
Trevor G. Jalland. *The Life and Times of St. Leo the Great.* London: SPCK, 1941. The most complete account, but rather old.
Patrology IV, 589–612. The best recent survey.
E. P. Pepka. "The Theology of St. Peter's Presence in His Successors according to St. Leo the Great." Ph.D. Dissertation: Catholic University of America, 1986.

II. MEDIEVAL DOCTORS

14

GREGORY
THE GREAT
(540–604)

FEAST: MARCH 12

IN 591, when he sent off the thirty-five books of his masterpiece, the *Morals on Job,* to his friend Bishop Leander of Seville, Pope Gregory I prefaced the work with a brief autobiographical letter. In it he recalled his conversion to the monastic life eighteen years previously: "Even after I was filled with heavenly desire, I preferred to be clothed in secular garb. What I ought to seek in relation to the love of eternity had already been revealed to me, but long-standing habit so bound me that I could not change my outward life.... Finally, I fled all this with anxiety and sought the safe haven of the monastery. Having left behind what belongs to the world (as I mistakenly thought at the time), I escaped naked from the shipwreck of this life." This letter captures the paradoxical relation between contemplation and action, flight and engagement, that is found throughout Gregory's life. In the whirlwind of activity that marked his ecclesiastical career as legate to Constantinople, deacon, and then bishop of Rome (590–604), he always was nostalgic for the contemplative peace of the monastery. Gregory's life mirrors the ambiguous, but necessary, relation between action and contemplation that he explored so often in his writings.

Gregory was born about 540 into an important senatorial family. As a young man he served as prefect of Rome. Most of his adult life was lived in the midst of the Lombard invasions, the last and worst of the barbarian onslaughts that devastated Italy at the end of the Western Empire. At the time of his conversion to the monastic life, Gregory used his family resources to found seven monasteries and entered the house he established in

Rome (St. Andrew on the Coelian hill) as a simple monk. But his talents were too obvious to remain hidden, and Pope Pelagius II convinced him to take on the legatine position about 578. He was to spend the next twenty-six years in public roles that eventually made him one of the most effective of the bishops of Rome (and one of only two ever declared a *doctor ecclesiae*). Though he was of ancient Roman stock and deeply committed to the welfare of the empire, his accomplishments as pope laid the foundations of *christianitas*, medieval Latin Christendom.

Gregory was one of the most widely read and cited authors in the medieval period, perhaps second only to Augustine. His influence on the history of monasticism was of special importance. In the words of Patrick Catry, "Benedict gave Western monks a rule; Gregory gave them a mysticism." (Gregory's "Life of Benedict" in the second book of his *Dialogues* provides our only early source for the saint's career.) Nevertheless, Gregory is not much read today, perhaps because of the bad press he has received from some historians of theology (e.g., Adolph Harnack) and also due to the prolixity of his style, better suited to the contemplative leisure of monastic reading than our own hurried skimming of texts. Not to read Gregory, however, would be to deprive oneself of an encounter with one of the most sensitive and complex of the doctors of the church.

Gregory was not a speculative theologian or even a great dogmatician; he was primarily an exegete and a preacher, a "moralist of conversion" (in Jacques Fontaine's words) whose writings were formative for the biblical culture of the Middle Ages. We read Gregory, then, primarily as a guide for living the Christian life. Gregory's touchstone for how to live is found in the spiritual meaning of the Bible. As he once put it, "Allegory [i.e., spiritual interpretation] creates a kind of machine to lift the soul far separated from God back up to him" (*Commentary on the Song of Songs*, chap. 2). His central works, the *Morals on Job*, the *Homilies on Ezekiel*, the *Forty Gospel Homilies*, and the *Commentary on the Song of Songs*, were all exegetical and homiletic.

Gregory's exegesis is essentially christological. All the events and persons of the Old Testament are prophetic of Christ, that is, the total Christ consisting of both head and members. In the preface to the *Morals on Job* he says: "Because our Savior has shown himself to be one person with the holy church whom he assumed . . . , any person [of the Old Testament] who signifies him designates him at one time with respect to the Head and another with respect to the body." Gregory's exegesis, then, relates to both Christ and the church. In addition to his exegetical works, the pope wrote two very popular texts, *The Pastoral Rule*, a treatise on the proper mode of life for bishops, and the *Dialogues*, a collection of the stories and miracles of the holy men of Italy. As pope, Gregory also left a large correspondence of more than eight hundred letters.

When we read Gregory we are constantly struck by the dialectic that governs his moral and mystical teaching, especially the alternation between the *inner* and the *outer*, which is also expressed in such polarities as light-darkness, silence-sound, above-below, joy-fear, elevation-temptation, satisfaction-hunger, and contemplation-action. While Gregory places ultimate value in the former of each of these polarities, in our present fallen condition he insists that it is the interaction between the opposites which is vital to achieving spiritual equilibrium. This is evident in looking at how the pope presents two key terms in his theological vocabulary: compunction and contemplation.

Compunction literally means "piercing" (see Acts 2:37, where the apostles' audience at Pentecost is "pierced to the heart"). For Gregory compunction describes the central attitude of the Christian life. It begins with the compunction of fear, i.e., terror over coming judgment and sorrow for sin, but it is meant to lead to the higher compunction of love, which is characterized by intense longing for God and even the joy of tasting him in this life. The compunction of love leads to contemplation, one of the most popular terms in Gregory's vocabulary (he might even be called "the doctor of contemplation"). *Contemplatio* is a protean term for Gregory and the Western monastic tradition. Most broadly it refers to any kind of attentive regard, but more technically it signifies the kind of single-minded and total attention that is to be given to God alone, an attention involving all the spiritual senses.

For Gregory, the history of salvation is the history of contemplation. Adam and Eve were created to contemplate God within themselves, but their fall led to a loss of the ability to contemplate and the triumph of mere exteriority. (Gregory's pessimistic, even lugubrious, statements about the world and the flesh always refer not to creation itself, a good product of God's action, but to the fallen world of human sinfulness.) The Word became man in Christ in order to restore to us the possibility of contemplating God, if only imperfectly and fleetingly, as we were created to do. The proper balance of the inner experience of contemplation and the outer fulfillment of love of neighbor leads us on to the full and final contemplation to be found in heaven. In this long and difficult journey, temptation and human frailty continue to play an important role, reminding us of the humility and lower compunction that must always accompany us in this life. What especially characterizes Gregory's descriptions of the life of compunction and contemplation is the intensity of his desire for heaven, where we will finally be free of the polarities of fallenness.

While it is Christ who is both the model and the source of the grace that restores contemplation to us, the Holy Spirit as the "Spirit of Life" (see Ezek. 1:20) conveys this grace to the members of Christ's Body, the church. Gregory's writings contain important teaching on the seven gifts of the Holy Spirit (based on Isa. 11:2–3), which are seen as the crown of the life of grace given us in the sacraments, especially the Eucharist, and through the three theological virtues (faith, hope, and charity). In this teaching, as in much else, Gregory manifests his position as one of the central moral and mystical teachers in the history of the church.

Reading Gregory

Gregory's masterpiece, the *Morals on Job,* was translated into a flowery and archaic English in the mid-nineteenth century. We still lack a good English anthology of key passages from this vast work of almost two thousand pages (e.g., see the preface for his view of scripture, and book 5.28–37 for a mini-treatise on contemplation). However, two of Gregory's major scriptural works are now available: *Gregory the Great: Forty Gospel Homilies,* trans. David Hurst (Kalamazoo, Mich.: Cistercian Publications, 1990); and *The Homilies of Saint Gregory the Great on the Book of the Prophet Ezekiel,* trans. Theodosia Gray (Etna, Calif.: Center for Traditionalist Orthodox Studies, 1990). The interested reader should take them in that order. The *Pastoral Rule,* or *Pastoral Care,* has been translated by Henry Davis, ACW 11, and a version of the *Dialogues* by Odo John Zimmerman is found in FC 39.

Bibliography

John C. Cavadini, ed. *Gregory the Great: A Symposium.* Notre Dame, Ind.: University of Notre Dame Press, 1995. A collection of papers that gives a good sense of current interest in Gregory.

R. A. Marcus. *Gregory the Great and His World.* Cambridge: Cambridge University Press, 1997. A summary by one of the masters of Gregory's life and times.

Bernard McGinn. *The Growth of Mysticism: Gregory the Great through the Twelfth Century.* New York: Crossroad, 1994, chap. 2.

Joan M. Peterson. *The Dialogues of Gregory the Great in Their Late Antique Cultural Background.* Toronto: PIMS, 1984. Helpful for putting the miracle stories of the *Dialogues* in perspective.

Jeffrey Richards. *Consul of God: The Life and Times of Gregory the Great.* London: Routledge & Kegan Paul, 1980. A good introduction to the man and his times.

Carole Straw. *Gregory the Great: Perfection in Imperfection.* Berkeley and Los Angeles: University of California Press, 1988. A sensitive account of Gregory's theology.

15

ISIDORE
OF SEVILLE
(C. 560–636)

FEAST: APRIL 4

I N 625, the Spanish bishop Braulio of Saragossa heard a report that
his friend, Bishop Isidore of Seville, had finished the great work that
Braulio had requested of him. He quickly wrote: "I . . . ask with every
kind of supplication that, mindful of your promise, you bid that the book of
Etymologies, which I have heard is now finished with the Lord's favor, be sent
to your servant, because, as I am aware, you sweated it out for the most part
at my request" (Collection of Isidore's Letters, no. 10). But Isidore was by
no means finished with this large encyclopedia of all knowledge, sacred and
profane. It was not until 632 that he wrote to Braulio saying that he had
finally sent off the manuscript, "though uncorrected because of my ill health"
(Letter 13). Braulio apparently helped correct and edit the work, which can
well be described as *the* basic reference work of the early Middle Ages (over
one thousand manuscripts are known!). Though modern readers may find
this massive early encyclopedia slow going, Braulio and his contemporaries
knew that the immense learning enshrined in the book was both a religious
and a cultural necessity in the primitive world of the barbarian West after the
fall of Rome. All the doctors of the church have been great educators, but
few have had to teach on lower grade levels than Isidore.

Isidore was born of Hispano-Roman nobility about 560. The Visigothic
kings converted from their traditional Arianism to Catholic orthodoxy at the
Third Council of Toledo in 589, about the same year that Isidore entered
the monastic life. His older brother Leander was bishop of Seville before him
and a close confidant of Pope Gregory I. Isidore's education and formation

as a monk prepared him for election to succeed his brother in 600. Unlike Leander, Isidore took little interest in maintaining ties with Rome, nor with Byzantium, toward which he was distinctly hostile because of the brief Byzantine reconquest of parts of Spain under the emperor Justinian. During the long years of his episcopate, Isidore was active as an advisor to the Visigothic kings of Spain and an apologist for the new form of Christian monarchy that was being developed in the West. He was also an eager organizer of synods, such as the Fourth Council of Toledo (633), which was primarily concerned with liturgical issues, but which was also significant for disseminating Augustine's teaching that the Holy Spirit proceeded from both the Father and the Son, the *filioque* teaching that still represents a point of tension between Eastern and Western Christians. Although Isidore was obviously an active episcopal leader, his writings reflect his personality as more of a scholar and polymath.

Isidore's writings fall into five categories. The first and best known are his reference books, practical educational manuals designed to pass on the learning of the ancient world to the newly forming society of Western Christendom. The most noted of these are the twenty books of the *Etymologies* that the bishop compiled from the writings of the fathers and from scholia, florilegia, and other collections representing the accumulated knowledge of classical antiquity. "Etymology," as defined by Isidore, "is the origin of words, when the meaning of the word or name is deduced through interpretation" (bk. 1.29). The bishop knew that many words were given their meaning by human convention, and that others that came from barbarian languages were unknown to the Greeks and Latins, but he insisted that the effort of getting to the root meaning of a term was the best approach to determining its significance: "When you see where a word comes from, you understand its meaning more quickly. A known etymology is the most evident kind of investigation."

The twenty books of the *Etymologies* begin with the seven liberal arts (bks. 1–3), and move on to medicine, law, and time (bks. 4–6), before reaching three theological books dealing with scripture and other sacred writings (bk. 6), God and holy persons (bk. 7), and the church, Jews, and pagans (bk. 8). The later books of the *Etymologies* turn to the investigation of the various aspects of the created world: (1) animate things, that is, humans and animals (bks. 9–12); (2) inanimate things, such as elemental physical realities, the world, buildings, metals and stones, etc. (bks. 13–16); and finally (3) the arts practiced by humans, such as farming, war, ship-building, painting, acting, cooking, and almost everything else (bks. 17–20). The following is just one example of Isidore's hunt for meaning through usually fanciful derivations of words based on verbal similarities. Under the heading "On Drink" (bk. 20, chap. 2), we read: "Drinking [*potio*] comes from the Greek, for they call it *potos*. Water [*aqua*] is generally so named because its surface is even [*aequalis*]; hence we have 'seas' [*aequora*].... Wine [*vinum*] is so called because drinking it quickly fills the veins [*venas*] with blood." Isidore of Seville also wrote a number of other reference works, including *Two Books of Differences*, dealing with grammatical and theological questions, as well as a treatise on physics and cosmography, *The Nature of Things*.

The bishop of Seville's other writings fall into the categories of exegetical works, dogmatic treatises, historical writings, and miscellanea, including a few letters and canonical works. Isidore was not an original mind, so his exegetical and dogmatic works are monuments to tradition, rather than works that are read for any independent contribution they make. He wrote handbooks of the allegories of the Bible and a series of biographical sketches of biblical figures, *The Birth and Death of the Fathers*. His survey *The Numbers Which Are Found in the Holy Scriptures* was the first of its kind, though the content is taken from patristic authors. Some of his historical writings, especially *The History of the Kings of the Goths, Vandals, and Suevi* and his *Major Chronicle*, a world chronicle down to 615, have independent value as sources for his time. Although Isidore's perspective was narrowly Spanish, the rapid diffusion of his modest, but useful, textbooks to Gaul, the British Isles, and Germany made him an important figure in the education of the new Europe.

Reading Isidore

None of Isidore's theological writings exist in English. *Isidore of Seville: Etymologies, Book II*, trans. Peter K. Marshall (Paris: Les Belles Lettres, 1983) is devoted to the definitions of rhetoric and dialectic among the liberal arts. See also *The Letters of Isidore of Seville*, trans. Gordon B. Ford, Jr. (Amsterdam: Hakkert, 1970), and *Isidore of Seville: The History of the Kings of the Goths, Vandals, and Suevi*, trans. Gordon B. Ford, Jr., and Guido Donino (Leiden: Brill, 1970).

Bibliography

The best literature on Isidore is in French and Spanish.

Judith Herrin. *The Formation of Christendom*. Princeton, N.J.: Princeton University Press, 1987, 233–49. A good appreciation of Isidore's contribution.
Patrick Jerome Mullins. *The Spiritual Life according to Isidore of Seville*. Washington, D.C.: Catholic University of America Press, 1940.
Pierre Riché. *Education and Culture in the Barbarian West: From the Sixth through the Eighth Century*. Columbia: University of South Carolina Press, 1978. Provides a survey of the historical context of Isidore's educational role.
Rusch, 198–204.

16

BEDE THE VENERABLE

(C. 673–735)

FEAST: MAY 25

SOMETIME BETWEEN 716 and 731 the Northumbrian monk Bede composed a poem on the Last Judgment at the request of his friend Bishop Acca of Hexham. In a literary topos familiar to a medieval audience (though, of course, the scene may also have been real), Bede pictures himself seated in the garden of his monastery at Jarrow during a pleasant afternoon. Suddenly a violent wind springs up and destroys his peaceful frame of mind, reminding him of the fearful testing that awaits each human at the approach of the Last Day:

> And so I remembered the sins I had committed,
> And the stains of life, and the hateful time of death,
> And the great Day of Judgment with fearful testing,
> And the strict Judge's perpetual anger toward the guilty.

("Judgment Day," lines 6–9)

Bede's version of the last things — judgment, heaven, and hell — in the remainder of the poem, while not exactly original, tell us much about the man and his times. Although the Latin church, following the authority of Augustine and others, had turned against apocalyptic attempts to predict the date of the End, this by no means ruled out a sense of the psychological imminence of Doomsday from exercising a powerful role in the formation of Western Christendom. Bede, like Gregory the Great, presents us with the paradoxical picture of someone who lived in the "shadow of the Second Com-

ing," and for that very reason expended amazing energy to build up a better
Christian society before the Last Day.

Bede was born about 673 in the Wearmouth area in the Anglo-Saxon
kingdom of Northumbria. The collapse of the Roman Empire in the West
had left Britain open to invasion by Germanic tribes from the continent. For
over two centuries before Bede's birth conflict between these invaders and
the native Britons, as well as subsequent struggles among the various Germanic kingdoms pervaded the island. The conversion of the Anglo-Saxons
to Christianity, effected both from the north by Celtic missionaries and from
the south by bishops and monks sent from Rome, had done little to modify
their bellicose nature. But monasticism had also flourished in these troubled
times, both as the engine of missionization and as a haven of culture. The
whole context of Bede's life was a monastic one.

In his *Ecclesiastical History of the English People*, completed in 731, Bede
left us an autobiographical sketch which gives us the following account of
his early years. "When I was seven years of age," he tells us, "by the care
of my kinsmen I was put in the charge of the reverend Abbot Benedict and
then of Coelfrith to be educated." Bede was an oblate, that is, a boy offered
to the monastery as a gift for God. But this did not mean that he did not
love the monastic life. "From then on," he continues, "I have spent all my
life in this monastery, applying myself entirely to the study of scripture. Amid
the observance of the discipline of the Rule and the daily task of singing in
the church, it has always been my delight to learn or to teach or to write"
(*Ecclesiastical History* 5.24). Unlike the wandering Celtic monks, Bede was an
ideal Benedictine in his practice of "stability of place" (see *Rule of Benedict*,
chap. 58).

Bede's life, uneventful in relation to the external world, was filled with the
inner activity of a scholar and teacher. Bede began as a pupil of Benedict Bis-
cop, the Northumbrian nobleman who had founded Wearmouth in 674. In
682 Benedict sent the young boy along with the group under the command
of Coelfrith to start a second foundation at Jarrow. Bede always maintained
great loyalty to the memory of these masters. Ordained a deacon about 692,
he was advanced to the priesthood sometime shortly after 700. "From the
time I became a priest," as he says in the autobiographical fragment, "until
the fifty-ninth year of my life I have made it my business, for my own benefit and that of my brothers, to make brief extracts from the works of the
venerable fathers on the holy scriptures, or to add notes of my own to clarify
their sense and interpretation." Bede, like so many of the other doctors of the
church, saw himself first and foremost as a biblical exegete.

The most pressing intellectual necessity in the disturbed centuries after
the collapse of Rome in the West was the need to preserve the wisdom of the
past, especially the theological sciences required by the church. Among those
who handed on the heritage of the fathers for its later medieval flowering,
Bede's name stands out. If Isidore of Seville at the beginning of the seventh

century had the reputation as the great "encyclopedist" of the early Middle Ages, Bede, in the early eighth century, was almost his equal in breadth of knowledge, as well as being a more original thinker.

Bede's writings fall into three main classes: scientific and educational works; historical works; and biblical works. In addition, we have some miscellaneous writings, including poems, homilies, letters, and hagiography. In order to be able to read the Bible and the fathers, medieval monks cultivated the seven liberal arts and the textbooks necessary for learning them. As the masters of liturgy, monks also needed to be able to know how to calculate time, not least in order to determine the proper date of Easter every year. Bede's writings on grammar (*The Art of Meter, Rhetorical Usages and Tropes,* and *On Orthography*) reflect the former preoccupation, while his treatise *On Times* and the late work *The Calculation of Times,* the most important calendrical handbook of the early Middle Ages, demonstrate his role as a monastic educator. Like Isidore and in partial dependence on him, Bede also wrote a cosmographical encyclopedia, *The Nature of Things* (c. 725).

The Northumbrian monk is best known in the English-speaking world, however, for his historical accomplishments, especially the *Ecclesiastical History of the English People.* History was another of the preoccupations of medieval monks. Earlier monastics had adapted Eusebius of Caesarea's *Chronicle* and *Church History* as models for telling the story of God's providence made manifest in the course of human history. Eusebius's providential history had centered on the conversion of the Roman Empire; later monastics adapted the genre to the Christianized barbarian tribes, inheritors of Roman glory. Bede brought the new genre of providential national histories to its height, and did so with a commitment to research and historical accuracy rare in the Middle Ages and still praiseworthy today. Bede also composed other historical works, such as the *History of the Abbots,* an account of his monastery from its foundation down to 716. As the father of English historical writing — and the only English *doctor ecclesiae* — the genial and devoted monk-scholar has attracted devotion from English-speaking Catholics and non-Catholics alike.

Bede's scientific and historical writings, however, were always intended to serve the central meaning of his life: liturgical prayer and the study of scripture that informed and enriched the *opus Dei,* "God's work," as Benedictines called the monastic liturgy. Many asides in his writings, as well as the moving letter written by his pupil Cuthbert describing the master's death in 735, attest to his devotion to the mass and the singing of the psalms in the monastic office. Bede composed a wealth of commentaries on the books of the Old and the New Testaments, mining the patristic literature he knew so well, but also expressing his own research and attempts to penetrate to the spiritual meaning of the text. Notable among the monk's Old Testament exegesis are his *Commentary on Genesis, On the Tabernacle* (commenting on Exod. 24–30), *On the Temple* (on 3 Kings 5–7), *On the First Book of Samuel, On the Song of*

Songs, and *Thirty Questions on the Book of Kings*. Among the many New Testament books on which he commented, his *On the Gospel of Luke, On the Acts of the Apostles, On the Seven Catholic Epistles*, and *On the Apocalypse* are of special importance. Bede was unusual in his time in exegeting not only books that the fathers had favored, such as Genesis, but also in taking on works like Acts and the Catholic Epistles for which there was little exegetical tradition. Bede's keen mind took a greater interest in the literal meaning of the biblical text than most early medieval exegetes, but his essential concern was always with the nourishing richness of the spiritual senses. "Such is the fecundity of the holy scriptures," he said, "that a verse which is usually written within a brief line could fill many pages, if it were examined by scrutinizing the expressions more diligently for the great sweetness they contain within" (*On the Song of Songs* 4.11).

Reading Bede

Bede's *Ecclesiastical History*, the most famous and most readable of his works, can be found in many translations. Especially recommended is *Bede: The Ecclesiastical History of the English People*, edited with an introduction by Judith McClure and Roger Collins (Oxford: Oxford University Press, 1994). Only recently have some of Bede's exegetical works been translated into English by Cistercian Publications and the University of Liverpool. Among the offerings by Cistercian Publications, see *The Commentary on the Seven Catholic Epistles*, trans. David Hurst (1985); *The Commentary on the Acts of the Apostles*, trans. Lawrence T. Martin (1989); and *The Homilies on the Gospels*, trans. Martin and Hurst (1991). The University of Liverpool Press has made available *Bede on the Tabernacle*, trans. Arthur Holder (1994); *Bede on the Temple*, trans. Sean Connolly (1995); and *Bede: A Biblical Miscellany*, trans. W. Trent Foley and Arthur Holder (1999).

Bibliography

Peter Hunter Blair. *Northumbria in the Days of Bede*. New York: St. Martin's Press, 1976. A fine survey of Bede's context.

Gerald Bonner, ed. *Famulus Christi: Essays in Commemoration of the Thirteenth Centenary of the Birth of the Venerable Bede*. London: SPCK, 1976. Twenty-two useful essays.

George Hardin Brown. *Bede the Venerable*. Boston: Twayne Publishers, 1987. A good introduction.

Charles W. Jones. "Some Introductory Remarks on Bede's Commentary on Genesis," *Sacris Erudiri* 19 (1969–70): 115–98. Studies Bede's exegesis.

Benedicta Ward. *The Venerable Bede*. Kalamazoo, Mich.: Cistercian Publications, 1998. The best guide to Bede.

17

JOHN OF DAMASCUS
(C. 675–749)

FEAST: DECEMBER 4

L ITTLE IS KNOWN of the life of John of Damascus, monk of Mar Saba
(St. Sabbas) in the Judean desert near Jerusalem. The legendary *Life*
that appeared centuries after his death tells an interesting story that
is supposed to have taken place some time after his entry into the monastery (c. 710). John, a noted composer of hymns, had written a hymn for a
fellow monk to commemorate the death of his brother. John's master, an old
monk whose cell he shared, attacked him for compromising his monastic vow
to spend his life weeping and mourning for sin and enjoined a demeaning
penance on him. But the Blessed Virgin appeared to the older monk in a
dream and told him that John should be allowed to write as many books and
compose as many hymns as he could. The story is probably legend, a legend
created to explain John's vast literary production.

John has the distinction of being the last Greek father to have been recognized by the bishops of Rome as a *doctor ecclesiae*. He also is unusual because
his life was set, not in the Christian Eastern Empire of the earlier Greek fathers and doctors, but under the rule of the new religion of Islam that in
one generation had conquered much of the Middle East in the mid-seventh
century. Paradoxically, this fact prevented John from suffering persecution, or
worse, when he attacked the Iconoclastic Byzantine rulers for their heretical
views in the late 720s.

The Ummayad Caliph Yazid conquered the ancient city of Damascus in
Syria in 635. Yanah ibn Mansur ibn Sargun (to give John the Arabic name
he used in his early life) was born in Damascus probably around 675 to a

high Christian official named Sergius in the service of the Ummayad Caliphs. He himself served the caliph Abd-al-Malik, who ruled from to 685 to 705, probably as a tax collector. Al-Malik's successor, however, was less favorable toward Christians, so the pious John decided to abandon public life and enter the monastery of Mar Saba. Here he became the protégé of Bishop John V of Jerusalem, who ordained him to the priesthood c. 720. In 726 the Byzantine emperor Leo III issued a decree forbidding the veneration of sacred images (i.e., icons) and ordering their destruction throughout the empire. The motivation for this unprecedented act is still debated by historians, but the reaction by bishops, monks, and the faithful was predictable outrage. Patriarch Germanus of Constantinople protested and was deposed, and a general persecution of the "image-venerators" (iconodules) was begun. John of Damascus was one of the first to launch a theological defense of icons, composing *Three Apologies against Those Who Attack the Divine Images* during 729 and 730. Although other theological voices were later to write important defenses of icons (especially St. Theodore of Studios in the early ninth century), John's *Apologies* remain the basis for the theology of images in both East and West. The core of John's response rests on two foundations: first, a careful analysis of the relation between image and archetype; and second, insistence on the dramatic change introduced by the Incarnation. As he says in the sixteenth chapter of the *First Apology*: "In former times God, who is without form or body, could never be depicted. But now when God is seen in the flesh conversing with humans, I make an image of the God I see. I do not worship matter; I worship the creator of matter who became matter for my sake."

John of Damascus was a prolific writer, preacher, and hymnodist. Only a few of his sermons survive, most notably his *Homilies on the Dormition of Mary*, one of the clearest early witnesses to the Assumption, declared a dogma of the church by Pius XII in 1950. How many of the surviving hymns ascribed to John are actually his is difficult to know. Many short treatises survive from his pen, but his greatest contribution lay in two massive works of synthesis in which the monk of Mar Saba sought to distil the wisdom of the Eastern fathers for the benefit of his own and succeeding generations. One of these, a work that John called *Sacred Things*, but that is known to history as *The Sacred Parallels*, survives only in fragmentary fashion. This was a *summa* in three books of the moral and ascetical teaching of the Bible and the fathers, both those before and after Nicaea. John's most important work, however, was *The Fountain of Knowledge* (*Pege Gnoseos*), a dogmatic synthesis in three parts that he wrote at the request of his fellow monk, Cosmas, after the latter had become bishop of Maiuma near Gaza in 743. Although *The Fountain of Knowledge* was not the first attempt at a doctrinal *summa* (Theodoret of Cyrrhus had written one in the fifth century), no previous work was as complete and profound as that of John. Its usefulness was especially evident to the great scholastics of the Latin West. Translated in the twelfth century by Burgundio of Pisa under the title *The Orthodox Faith* (*De Fide Orthodoxa*), it was widely used by many medieval theologians and doctors, not least of all Thomas Aquinas.

John of Damascus has sometimes been seen as a mere compiler of the thoughts of others. The modest words he uses in his prefatory Letter to Bishop Cosmas lend credence to this: "I shall add nothing of my own, but shall gather together into one those things which have been worked out by the most eminent teachers and make a compendium of them." This is the voice of all good Orthodox theology, where fidelity to tradition has never ruled out creative thought, though it has often moderated claims to originality. As John put it in his *First Apology*, chap. 2: "First of all, I grasp the teaching of the church through which salvation is planted in us as both foundation and pillar." (Modern theologians often boast of their originality when they are merely putting old ideas in new garb; older theologians of both the Eastern and Western traditions tend to do the reverse.) While much of what John has to say is, indeed, based on identifiable sources, the structure of his synthesis, as well as many of its details, testify to his own theological insight and ability.

The first part of the *Fountain of Knowledge*, called *Dialectica*, is a remarkable summary of the philosophical knowledge necessary for doing theology (one can well see why the scholastics were sympathetic to the doctor from Damascus). John explains his reasons for beginning thus: "First of all, I shall set forth the best contributions of the philosophers of the Greeks, because whatever there is of good has been given to humans from above by God." John's philosophical handbook, furthermore, is not as dependent on the Platonic speculation employed by many earlier fathers as it is on the Aristotelian teaching concerning the philosophical concepts necessary for all clear reasoning and argumentation. For the most part, the sixty-eight chapters of this part follow the commentators on Aristotle's *Categories*, particularly Porphyry and Ammonius. But John, like Leontius of Byzantium and other late antique Greek theologians who had turned to Aristotle to help make doctrinal vocabulary more precise, also introduced discussions of key terms that had been worked out in the course of the ongoing trinitarian and christological controversies — *hypostasis, enhypostaton, anhypostaton, prosopon* (i.e., person), etc. (see chaps. 29, 42–45, 48, 66).

The second part of the work consists of 103 chapters refuting "the absurdities of the heresies hated by God, so that by recognizing the lie we may more closely follow the truth" (Preface). The first eighty are copied from the *Panarion*, a fourth-century anti-heretical book of Epiphanius of Salamis, though John adds important material on the heresy of Messalians (chap. 80). The final chapters, though they may not be by John, contain new material on a number of heresies, especially the Ishmaelites (i.e., Muslims) and the Iconoclasts.

Finally, the hundred chapters of the dogmatic third part of the *Fountain of Knowledge* crown this important compendium. With the exception of Pope

Leo I's *Tome*, all the sources John uses are Eastern, and they are also all post-Nicene, reflecting the orthodox consensus forged in the fourth and fifth centuries, especially by Athanasius, Cyril of Alexandria, and the Cappadocians (Gregory of Nazianzus is John's favorite). John also makes use of many later sources, such as the Dionysian writings, Leontius of Byzantium, and Maximus the Confessor. The division of the chapters into four books was done by the Latin translators and copyists, but it reflects the basic structure of the work. Book 1 deals with God one and three (in chaps. 1–14). Book 2 concerns creation (in chaps. 15–30), while book 3, the richest part of the whole, takes up Christology (in chaps. 45–73). Christology also occupies the first eight chapters of book 4, which goes on to treat faith, the sacraments, Mary, saints and relics, icons, and evil, and ends with a chapter on the resurrection of the body.

Reading John of Damascus

There is a full translation of the *Fountain of Knowledge* by Frederic H. Chase, Jr., in *Saint John of Damascus: Writings*, FC 37. This volume also has a good introduction to John. John's anti-iconoclastic writings are available in *St. John of Damascus: On the Divine Images*, trans. David Anderson (Crestwood, N.Y.: St. Vladimir's Seminary Press, 1980).

Bibliography

Works specifically devoted to John in English are sparse. He does take a place of honor in discussions found in two good studies of Eastern Orthodox theology:

John Meyendorff. *Byzantine Theology: Historical Trends and Doctrinal Themes*. New York: Fordham University Press, 1974.
Jaroslav Pelikan. *The Spirit of Eastern Christendom (600–1700)*. Chicago: University of Chicago Press, 1974.

18

Peter Damian
(1007–1072)

Feast: February 21

IN 1063 the recently retired Peter Damian, cardinal bishop of Ostia, wrote to his friend Pope Alexander II the following complaint: "As far as you are concerned, Venerable Father (who have agreed to my laying down of my episcopal office), I was to have leisure for contemplation and letter-writing. But I am never free of the press of business!...People who need advice for their souls are not lacking; still more difficult are those who want to extract a pontifical decision from me, though I am no longer a bishop" (Letter 96). Peter was not the first or the last to realize that retirement was not what it was cracked up to be.

Peter's complaint reveals much about his life. Though he was an austere hermit who had fled the world to engage in severe ascetical practices, Peter was raised to the highest echelons of the Roman curia at a time when the papacy was in the midst of the movement that changed its relationship to the Western church. Though the popes had claimed primacy over the church since the days of Leo I, this claim became effective in a new way in the eleventh century with the Great Reform movement. This program to cleanse the church and clergy of moral abuses and outside control is often called the Gregorian Reform, since Peter's friend, the monk Hildebrand, who later led the church as Pope Gregory VII (1073–85), was its most strenuous proponent. Still, it is worth noting that it was not Gregory who was eventually named a *doctor ecclesiae*, but Peter, the monk of Fonte Avellana.

Peter was born at Ravenna in 1007 and studied in the schools of northern Italy, which were among the best of their time. Peter played an important

role in two of the new movements of religious life in Western Europe in the
first century of the second millennium: monastic revival and papal reform. In
order to understand the significance of these movements and Peter's role in
them, we need to back up a bit and consider the history of Western Europe
since the time of the death of last Latin doctor, Bede, in 735.

Bede, as we noted, lived in a time of considerable turmoil. The late eighth
century in the West, however, witnessed the formation of what has been
called the "First Europe," that is, the rise of the Carolingian empire solidi-
fied by Charlemagne (emperor 800–814). This was a new effort at organizing
a Christian society, a *renovatio imperii* (renewal of empire), not merely a
pretense of its continuation. The political alliance forged between the Carolingian dynasty and the papacy was another sign of the emergence of a new
religio-cultural entity whose center of gravity had shifted north of the Alps
and westward toward the Atlantic. Charlemagne encouraged a reorganization
of monasticism, as well as a revival of schools and learning. Original minds
from all over Europe flocked to the Carolingian court. Figures like the En-
glishman Alcuin (d. 804), Charlemagne's friend and advisor, and especially
the Irish genius John Scottus Eriugena (d. c. 880) made important contributions to theology. Sadly, the promise of the Carolingian "First Europe" was
cut short by internal weaknesses and the external attacks of a new wave of
barbarians. Europe entered into an "Iron Age" of social, religious, and intellectual decline and near anarchy from about 875 to roughly 1050. All aspects
of society suffered. Monasteries were destroyed or else declined in their fer-
vor and practice of Benedict's *Rule*. Educational opportunities were few; as a
consequence, little theological discussion was possible. Even the papacy de-
teriorated into a sad period when for many decades it was the plaything of
the violent ruling families of the Roman nobility — a kind of "Mafia Era" of
the papacy.

During Peter Damian's lifetime this state of affairs took a dramatic turn for
the better. Given the fact that monasticism was so central to the religious and
theological life of the early Middle Ages, the revival of the monastic life was
a spiritual prerequisite for beginning to work on putting Christendom back
on the right track. Monastic reform had begun in the dismal tenth century
with the foundation of new houses, such as Cluny in Burgundy (910), and
the revivification of monasteries that had declined, such as Gorze near Metz.
The revival of monasticism also hearkened back to the original impetus of
the hermits of the desert. Around the year 1000 a series of deeply ascetic an-
chorites emerged in Western Europe. While devoted to the solitary life, these
men, not unlike the original desert fathers, also became beacons of sanctity to those around them, and sometimes fervent critics of the corruption
of their time.

Peter Damian, or "Peter the Sinner Monk" (*Petrus peccator monachus*) as
he called himself, needs to be understood against this background of monastic reform, severe asceticism, and vigorous (even violent) critique of a sinful

world. About 1036, the well-educated Peter decided to abandon the world and enter the monastery of Fonte Avellana, which practiced a strict eremit-ical version of Benedict's *Rule* that had been introduced by St. Romuald. Though Peter's commitment was to abandoning the world, the needs of the world soon called him forth from his cell, like many other monks, to travel, to teach, and above all to preach against the evils of eleventh-century Italy. Peter was particularly exercised over the corrupt lives of priests. His *Book of Gomorrah* (Letter 31), for example, is a fierce attack on homosexuality among the clergy. Many of his 180 surviving letters (Peter made no distinction be-tween personal letters and treatises in letter form) feature criticisms of the evils of his time.

In 1043 Peter was made prior of Fonte Avellana. It was also during the decade of the 1040s that he became associated with the call to free the pa-pacy from the clutches of the Roman aristocracy and restore the popes to a position where they could take the lead in the moral and ecclesiastical re-form so desperately needed in Christendom. Like others, Peter first looked to the powerful German emperors to help in this task; but by the middle of the eleventh century a party of reform-minded clerics was emerging in the Roman curia. They were convinced that the Roman church needed to free itself from all outside control, even of the German emperors, in order to return to the primatial position that Leo I and others had laid out. Peter Damian, whose fame in Italy as its moral conscience was now widespread, became associated with this group, and friendly with its leader, Hildebrand. It was at Hildebrand's exhortation that Peter Damian was made a cardinal, that is, one of the major clerics of the diocese of Rome and a papal advi-sor, probably in 1057. Over the next fifteen years until his death at Faenza in 1072, Peter, notwithstanding his unsuccessful attempt to retire in 1063, became a major troubleshooter for the reform party of the curia, being sent on numerous diplomatic missions throughout Italy and even into France and Germany. He often complained about these tasks, but his loyalty to the re-form that eventually was to free the papacy from the control of lay leaders, even the quasi-sacral authority of the successors of Charlemagne, meant that he could not refuse the demands placed upon him.

Peter Damian rarely wrote on dogmatic or speculative themes. His tract *On Divine Omnipotence* (Letter 119), written to abbot Desiderius of Monte Cassino about 1065, is one exception; another is the short summary of doc-trine found in Letter 81. Most of Peter's writings are in the form of moral and spiritual advice. It may not be unfair to call the cardinal bishop of Ostia the "Lugubrious Doctor." The times in which he lived were difficult. Wherever he looked he found not only pain and suffering, but also evil and corrup-tion — and he was never slow in denouncing them in the strongest possible terms. (Contrasting the usually pessimistic Peter Damian with the optimism of say, Francis de Sales, tells us much about the diverse personalities that can be found in the list of the *doctores ecclesiae*.) Peter's writings not only contain many jeremiads against evil, but also encourage the severe ascetic practices that his age saw as necessary to restrain and correct vice. His defense of the practice of public flagellation for monks and laity, *The Praise of the Flagellants,* will strike many as strange today. Nonetheless, Peter is far from being always sad, angry, or dourly ascetic. His treatise *The Perfection of Monks* is among the best short presentations of the meaning of the monastic life and the contemplation that is its goal (the influence of Gregory the Great is quite marked, as would be expected). Peter has a message of encouragement for all Christians, directing their attention to the ark of the church that is the only safe haven from the evils of the world. Participation in the sacramental life of Christ's mystical body brings the faithful who endeavor to live according to the moral and spiritual demands of the gospel a true foretaste of heavenly joy. In a number of Peter's writings, such as his book *The Lord Be with You* (Letter 28) and his Letter 23, "Concerning True Happiness and Wisdom," we find many moving passages on the unity of the church, the role of the sacraments, and the life of prayer and contemplation. In the former work the monk and cardinal testified to the role of Spirit as the inner principle of life for all Christians: "Although holy church is divided into the great number of people involved, she is fused into one by the fire of the Holy Spirit.... By the power of the Holy Spirit who dwells in each and at the same time fills all, our solitude is at once plural and our community is singular" (Letter 28.14–15).

Reading Peter Damian

In recent years scholars have come to view all of Peter's writings as letters, eschewing the earlier distinction between epistles and treatises. A full translation of the 180 surviving letter/treatises of Damian is currently underway. See *The Letters of Peter Damian,* trans. Owen J. Blum, FC, Medieval Continuation 1, 2, 3, and 5, comprising Letters 1–120 thus far. Among the older translations, see *St. Peter Damian: Selected Writings on the Spiritual Life,* trans. Patricia McNulty (London: Faber & Faber, 1959).

Bibliography

Owen Blum. *St. Peter Damian: His Teaching on the Spiritual Life.* Washington, D.C.: Catholic University of America Press, 1947. Still the most useful general account in English.
Irven M. Resnick. *Divine Power and Possibility in St. Peter Damian's "De divina omnipotentia."* Leiden: Brill, 1992.
J. Joseph Ryan. *Saint Peter Damian and His Canonical Sources: A Preliminary Study in the Antecedents of the Gregorian Reform.* Toronto: PIMS, 1956.

19

Anselm of Canterbury
(1033–1109)

Feast: April 21

F LASHES OF INSIGHT that lead to momentous discoveries in the history of thought, both real and legendary, are famous. Think of the story of Archimedes in his bath discovering the principle of the displacement of water, or Sir Isaac Newton and the apple. The history of theology displays at least one similar incident. It took place in the monastery at Bec in Normandy sometime in the year 1077. The Italian-born monk, Anselm, had completed a treatise on the existence and nature of God in 1076, but was dissatisfied with the long chain of arguments in the work. "I began," he tells us, "to ask myself if it might be possible to find one argument which would need depend on nothing else but itself and that alone would suffice to prove that God really exists and that he is the Highest Good requiring nothing else." The task, however, proved more difficult than Anselm imagined, and he finally gave up in despair and tried to put the problem out of his mind. But he was not successful; it had become an obsession. "Then, one day," his account goes on, "when I was exhausted by vigorously resisting its relentlessness, the solution that I had despaired of finding suddenly appeared in the turmoil of my thoughts so that I eagerly embraced the idea which in my distraction I had been rejecting." This was the discovery of Anselm's noted "ontological," or better, analytical, argument for the existence of God as laid out in the treatise he called the *Proslogion*. (According to this argument, still debated in our own century, God's existence is necessarily implied in conceiving of him as "that than which nothing greater can be thought.") This moment of insight after months of effort typifies Anselm's theological mind. The great modern

103

theologian Bernard Lonergan once described Anselm as a "theologian's theologian" because he was interested in only the most difficult problems and also because he never relented in his attempts to find the best arguments.

Anselm was born in Aosta in northern Italy probably in 1033. After some years of wandering, in 1060 he entered the reformed monastery of Bec, which had become famous as an intellectual center under another Italian, Lanfranc, the master of its school. Anselm succeeded Lanfranc in this position. His spiritual writings, the influential *Prayers* and *Meditations,* were composed between 1070 and 1080, as were also his earliest theological works. (Anselm's prayers were important in disseminating a new form of personal, Christ-centered devotion.) He became abbot of Bec in 1078 and continued his writing, producing a number of treatises on the philosophical foundations of theological reasoning (*On Grammar, On Truth,* and *On Free Choice*), as well as the first of his treatises concerning the fall and redemption of humanity.

Although Anselm would have preferred to remain in the monastery, his position as abbot brought him into contact with many of the famous rulers of the day, who took note of his talents. Hence, it was not surprising that William II, the Norman king of England, chose him to succeed Lanfranc as archbishop of Canterbury. Anselm's tenure as primate of England was not a happy one. He was not a good administrator, and his adherence to the reforming policies of Pope Gregory VII and his successors brought him into conflict with the imperious King William, difficulties that continued under his successor Henry I. Anselm was twice forced into lengthy periods of exile, returning permanently to England only in 1107, two years before his death. Despite the turmoil of these years and the frequent traveling forced upon the aging archbishop, Anselm continued his investigation of redemption and other complex philosophico-theological issues. His masterpiece, *Why the God-Man?,* was written between 1094 and 1098. His treatises *The Virgin Conception and Original Sin* (1100), *The Procession of the Holy Spirit* (1102), *Letters on the Sacraments* (1107), and *The Harmony of Foreknowledge, Predestination, and the Grace of God with Free Choice* (1108) testify to his unflagging pursuit of knotty theological issues.

Anselm gives the lie to the simplified distinctions that are often used to characterize medieval theology, such as that between monastic and scholastic theology, or between doctrinal and speculative theology, or even between philosophy and theology. His writings contain all these forms of thought, demonstrating that he never felt any tension between reason and faith, or doctrine and speculation. Although a monk, Anselm's search for "necessary reasons" (*rationes necessariae*), that is, arguments that would reveal the necessity and inner intelligibility of the truths of faith, was a key aspect of the development of scholasticism. Making his own the Augustinian view of the task of the theologian as that of "faith seeking understanding" (*fides quaerens intellectum*), Anselm insisted that the concrete experience of belief forms the foundation for good theology. As he once put it, "He who will not believe will not understand, for he who will not believe will not gain experience, and he who has not had experience will not know" (*Letter on the Incarnation of the Word*, chap. 1). Nevertheless, the necessary reasons which Anselm sought were not only designed to give joy to the believer; they also had an apologetic function, namely, "to answer, on behalf of our faith, those who while unwilling to believe what they do not understand, deride others who do believe" (ibid., chap. 6).

Anselm's major contributions to theology concentrate on two essential doctrines: the existence and attributes of God, and redemption. The long debate over the validity of his analytic argument for the existence of God found in the first chapters of the *Proslogion* has distracted attention from the fullness of the teaching of Anselm's two treatises on God. Although he became dissatisfied with the chain of arguments found in his first work, the *Monologion*, which he called "a meditation on the being of God," the tract is a good example of a treatment of the nature and properties of God, one and three, in a standard Western Christian form going back to Augustine. More original was the famous *Proslogion*, not only for its development of the analytical proof (chaps. 2–4), but also for its rich and more concise teaching on the divine attributes. From this same period comes his *Reply to Guanilon*. (Guanilon was a monk who had questioned the adequacy of the *Proslogion* proof.)

Although all scholastic theologians insisted that there could be no contradiction between reason and faith, they differed on how far the truths of faith could be proven on the basis of necessary reasons. In this regard Anselm went beyond many later scholastics, such as Thomas Aquinas, in finding necessary reasons for the Incarnation of the Word of God in his treatise *Why the God-Man?* Modern research, however, has cleared up one misunderstanding regarding the kind of proofs Anselm intended. The unbelievers (*pagani*) he was addressing in the book were not ancient pagans or some generic form of unbeliever, but rather contemporary opponents, that is, Jews and Muslims, who shared at least some of the axioms on which the archbishop based his arguments (e.g., that humanity was created for blessedness by a good God, and that humans have sinned and cannot attain blessedness without forgiveness). *Why the God-Man?* is really a series of four essays organized into two books. The first essay (bk. 1, chaps. 1–10) is negative, a brilliant destruction of the traditional explanation for redemption — the necessity for Christ's deceiving the devil because the fiend had acquired "rights" over humanity in the fall. The second essay (1.11–25) is an extended analysis of the necessity for salvation based on the notion of satisfaction, that is, that God's justice demands that sinners repay "something greater than that for the sake of which you were obliged not to commit the sin" (1.21). The third essay (2.1–6), the heart of the work, demonstrates that the God-Man alone both "can" as God and "ought" as man make such satisfaction. Finally, the last essay (2.7–22) shows that the God-Man, in conformity with the Christology of the Council of Chalcedon, must be perfect God and perfect man united in the one Person of the Word. Though few theologians believe that Anselm's "necessary rea-son" for the Incarnation is more than what is called a "fitting reason" (*ratio conveniens*), his treatise was a crucial one in the development of a Western theology of redemption.

Reading Anselm

There are good translations of Anselm's two most important works, the *Proslogion* and the *Why the God-Man?*, in *A Scholastic Miscellany: Anselm to Ockham,* ed. and trans. Eugene R. Fairweather (Philadelphia: Westminster, 1957). *The Prayers and Meditations of Saint Anselm* by Sister Benedicta Ward (New York: Penguin, 1973) is a sensitive rendering of his spiritual writings. Translations also exist of most of Anselm's other philosophical and theological works.

Bibliography

Karl Barth. *Anselm: Fides Quaerens Intellectum: Anselm's Proof for the Existence of God in the Context of His Theological Scheme.* Richmond: John Knox, 1960. Though Barth's interpretation of Anselm's proof is controversial, it is always instructive to see one theological giant engage another.

G. R. Evans. *Anselm and Talking about God.* Oxford: Oxford University Press, 1978.

Jasper Hopkins. *A Companion to the Study of St. Anselm.* Minneapolis: University of Minnesota Press, 1982. A fine vade-mecum for reading Anselm.

R. W. Southern. *St. Anselm and His Biographer: A Study of Monastic Life and Thought 1059–c. 1130.* Cambridge: Cambridge University Press, 1963. A study of Anselm and his biographer Eadmer within the context of Anglo-Norman monastic life and thought.

————. *Saint Anselm: A Portrait in a Landscape.* Cambridge: Cambridge University Press, 1990. The finished fruit of Southern's lifelong study of Anselm. A superb biography.

20

BERNARD OF CLAIRVAUX

(1090–1153)

FEAST: AUGUST 20

O N EASTER SUNDAY in the year 1112 there was a great commotion at the door of a poor monastery in Burgundy. A crowd of noblemen had arrived and were waiting outside, not to loot the monastery or to make complaints about land disputes, as was so often the case. Rather, they all wanted to sign up. How had so many been drawn to make this dramatic choice at the same time? The answer is Bernard of Clairvaux.

Many stories are told about Bernard, "the difficult saint," who bestrides the twelfth century as no other figure. Among the most revealing is how, after he had made his decision to enter the monastery of Citeaux in the early months of 1112, he was not content that his election of what he was convinced was the best form of monastic life should be a solitary one. Rather, he traveled back and forth in feudal Burgundy, cajoling his friends and relatives to heed God's call and accompany him to the "New Monastery," as it was called. The hagiographers say that "mothers hid their sons when Bernard came near, and wives clung to their husbands to prevent them from going to hear him" (*First Life*, chap. 6). However exaggerated these stories, when Bernard arrived at Citeaux's gate that Easter with thirty companions the Cistercian order was on the way to becoming the great success story of twelfth-century monasticism. There were to be no less than 343 Cistercian houses by the time of Bernard's death.

Bernard of Clairvaux was persuasive, daunting, sometimes even overbearing. His vocation was that of a contemplative monk hidden from the world; the reality was that of a figure whose force of personality and conviction of his purpose made him indispensable to the running of the church for roughly a quarter-century (c. 1128–53). Bernard was acutely aware of the contradiction between his calling and his life. In one place he says: "I am a kind of chimaera of my age, neither cleric nor layman" (Letter 250). The many church-political issues he took part in, and especially his relentless pursuit of some distinguished figures whose theology he took exception to (e.g., Peter Abelard and Gilbert of Poitiers), may make him seem like a cold and arbitrary inquisitor. Nothing could be further from the truth. Bernard's emotional warmth and deep sensitivity made him immensely charming — "the great seducer," as his premier modern student, Jean Leclercq, referred to him. Unlike other seducers, however, Bernard's real aim was to help fallen humans be "seduced by" their true lover, Jesus, the Divine Bridegroom.

Bernard was born in 1090, a middle child in the large family of a pious knight and his wife. He must have received a fine primary education, given the magnificence of his Latin style. (Along with Augustine, Bernard is the supreme master of Christian Latin.) The young nobleman's decision to enter the struggling monastery of Citeaux, which had been founded in 1098, was unusual. Citeaux's commitment to a more rigorous and contemplative style of monastic life than that of the established Benedictine houses, like the great abbey of Cluny (also in Burgundy), had not led to much success before Bernard's arrival. Historians still argue about how much the order's sudden growth was due to Bernard and how much to the inherent advantages of the new model of monasticism.

By 1115 Bernard was made abbot of Clairvaux, one of the four new foundations of Citeaux ("The Four Daughters," as they are called). For about a decade, the young abbot was relatively silent. It must have been during this time that he absorbed the profound knowledge of the Bible and the fathers that was the foundation of his subsequent writing. (Bernard himself was later called "The Last of the Fathers.") By the mid-1120s Bernard was already engaged in extensive writing of letters, treatises, and biblical commentaries. Although the power of his personality helps explain why he was such an important political figure in his time, it is the extraordinary depth of his mystical writings that have guaranteed him an important role in the history of theology. In perhaps no other *doctor ecclesiae* is the style so much a part of the message — a fact to keep in mind when one reads him in translation.

Bernard's first major ecclesiastical engagement was with the papal schism of 1130–37, in which his active support and many travels in favor of Innocent II helped Innocent eventually to triumph over the antipope Anacletus. The next decade saw countless other involvements in both local and international church politics. In 1145, one of Bernard's former monks ascended the papal throne as Eugene III. The former Cistercian called on Bernard to preach the Second Crusade. After some reluctance, the abbot plunged into this work with enthusiasm, but the failure of the expedition in 1148 led him to a period of depression and doubt in which he wrote his important treatise *On Consideration* (c. 1148–53), criticizing the politicization of the papacy. The great abbot died in 1153, just as a new cast of major figures in both church and state were coming on the scene.

Bernard's extensive writings fall into three main categories: sermons, which are to be thought of as biblical-liturgical commentaries; treatises; and letters. Although most of his hundreds of sermons that survive are "written rhetoric," that is, carefully edited compositions with only a distant relation to actual preaching, there is no reason to doubt that Bernard in the flesh was one of the most effective preachers in the history of Christianity. Bernard's masterpiece is the eighty-six sermons he composed on the Song of Songs between 1135 and his death. Although these comment on only a third of the Song, their circular and compact mode of presentation, in which the part reveals the whole, make them the most complete summary of the abbot's teaching about the loving union between Jesus, the Divine Bridegroom, and the bride who is both the church and each of her members. Bernard's *Sermons on the Liturgical Year* are an extended meditation of 125 sermons on the mystery of redemption lived through the church's annual participation in the saving events of Christ's life. Bernard also left a large number of sermons gathered together as *Sermons on Different Topics*. The abbot's eight treatises vary widely in length and topic. Some, like *On Grace and Free Choice* are primarily doctrinal, dealing with the anthropological and soteriological foundations of the mystical life. Some are directed to monastics, such as *On the Steps of Humility and Pride* and *On Precept and Dispensation;* others are more general, especially *On Loving God,* a summary of the mystical path of love. Finally, Bernard left 548 letters, some of them treatises in letter form. Bernard and his secretaries carefully edited and organized these letters into a *speculum ecclesiae* (mirror of the church), that is, a handbook to illustrate the obligations and opportunities proper to each mode of life within Christ's mystical body.

Bernard has always been recognized as a supreme mystical teacher, but it is important to remember that his teaching about the soul's union with Christ is rooted in a profound dogmatic theology centered on the notion of humanity as made in "the image and likeness" of God (Gen. 1:26). Through Adam's sin the free choice that is the core of our divine likeness is deeply damaged and humans are self-condemned to wander in "the region of unlikeness," where they continue to sin because they no longer have contact with God, who is pure spirit. Humans are trapped in fallen flesh, and it is only the divine initiative in taking on flesh that opens up the path back to God. As Bernard put it in typically symbolic language in *Sermon on the Song of Songs* 6: "Thus human beings lost and changed their glory for the likeness of a grass-eating beast. God had mercy on their errors and deigned to come forth from the shady dark mountain [i.e., of his divinity] and place his tabernacle in the sun [i.e., in the Incarnate Word]. He offered his flesh to those who knew only flesh so that through it they might come to know spirit too." What Bernard called "the carnal love" of Christ was thus the necessary first stage in the ascent to God which restores the image and likeness.

In various places in his writings Bernard provided different models for the transition from carnal to spiritual love, which is also the ascent to loving "union of spirit" (*unitas spiritus*) with the Word made flesh. What today we would call mystical experience or, perhaps better, mystical consciousness of the direct presence of the Word (see *Sermon on the Song of Songs* 74), is a brief foretaste of the freedom from the misery of fallen existence which is the heavenly goal of the restoration process. Though Bernard held that these tastes of the Word's presence could be enjoyed by all Christians, he obviously thought that training in the monastery, "the school of charity," was the best form of preparation for such experience.

Bernard's analysis of the modalities and progress of the love affair between God and the soul as seen in the spiritual interpretation of the Song of Songs is one of the supreme achievements of Christian mysticism. Bernard insisted that his readers should use the Song to guide their own experience and analyze their experience as a key to grasping the inner depth of the Song's spiritual meaning. Through this mutual interaction they could begin to regain the true "order of charity" (*ordo caritatis*) that the bride speaks of in Song 2:4: "He has ordered charity in me" (*Ordinavit in me caritatem*).

Reading Bernard

Cistercian Publications has made available most of Bernard's writings in new translations. One might begin with the treatise *On Loving God*, which provides a handy summary of the abbot's teaching, but there can be no substitute for immersion in the *Sermons on the Song of Songs*. I would recommend the following as especially important: Sermons 1–8 (a good introduction to the whole); 23 (the stages of the mystical life); 31 (seeing God); 50–51 (the order of charity); 74 (Bernard's personal account of the Word's visit); and 80–85 (love and the recovery of the divine likeness). *On Loving God* and most of these sermons can also be found in *Bernard of Clairvaux: Selected Works*, trans. G. R. Evans, CWS 55.

Bibliography

Michael Casey. *Athirst for God: Spiritual Desire in Bernard of Clairvaux's Sermons on the Song of Songs*. Kalamazoo, Mich.: Cistercian Publications, 1987. A revealing study of Bernard's masterpiece.

Etienne Gilson. *The Mystical Theology of Saint Bernard of Clairvaux*. New York: Sheed and Ward, 1940. One of the first works to reveal the depth of Bernard's theology.

Jean Leclercq. *Bernard of Clairvaux and the Cistercian Spirit*. Kalamazoo, Mich.: Cistercian Publications, 1976. One of Leclercq's more general works on Bernard and the Cistercians.

Bernard McGinn. *The Growth of Mysticism: Gregory the Great through the Twelfth Century.* New York: Crossroad, 1994. Chap. 5, summarizes Bernard's doctrinal and mystical thought.

Thomas Merton on St. Bernard. Kalamazoo, Mich.: Cistercian Publications, 1980. Gathers Merton's valuable essays on Bernard into a single volume.

John R. Sommerfeldt, ed. *Bernardus Magister: Papers Presented at the Nonacentenary Celebration of the Birth of Saint Bernard.* Kalamazoo, Mich.: Cistercian Publications, 1992. Thirty-one essays provide an overview of recent scholarship on the abbot.

21

Anthony
of Padua
(1191–1231)

Feast: June 13

I N LATE 1222 the two new orders of mendicants, the Franciscans and
the Dominicans, held an unusual event — a joint ordination of some
of their members in the town of Forli in northern Italy. According to
hagiographical tradition, the Franciscan superior asked that one of the assembled brethren preach a sermon for the occasion, but both the Dominican
and Franciscan friars present begged off saying that they had not had sufficient time to prepare. Whereupon the superior ordered a short and stout
Portuguese friar, who had joined the order just a year before, to give the
homily. His eloquence and knowledge of scripture so astonished those present
that he was soon appointed public preacher and lector in theology for the
other Friars Minor. This position, the first properly theological office in the
new Franciscan order, was confirmed by Francis himself in 1224 when he sent
the following letter to the still new friar: "Brother Francis sends greetings to
Brother Anthony, my bishop. I'm pleased that you are reading sacred theology to the brethren, as long as you do not extinguish the spirit of prayer and
devotion with study of this kind, just as it says in the Rule."

Though little is known about Anthony's life (his reputation as a miracle-
worker is totally posthumous, for example), his position as the first Franciscan
theologian and his fame as a preacher make him a significant figure in the
evolution of the movement begun by the humble man of Assisi who addressed Anthony as "my bishop." Anthony is scarcely a typical doctor of the
church. He left no ponderous theological treatises, only a group of sermons
on the liturgical year that have been little read outside Franciscan circles.

These homilies, however, reveal why the Portuguese friar acquired such fame in his brief life. They also have much to say about the relation of the Franciscan movement to key currents in medieval theology and to the renewal of church life in the thirteenth century.

Anthony (whose given name was Ferdinand) was the son of a Portuguese knight. As a teenager, he entered a house of canons regular (priests living according to the *Rule of St. Augustine*) not far from Lisbon. His studies for the priesthood in this environment were conducted under teachers who were familiar with the thought of the theologians of the famous School of St. Victor at Paris. The young Ferdinand's theological education initiated a contact with Victorine thought that was later evident in many Franciscans, not least Bonaventure.

Ferdinand was probably ordained in 1220, the same year as the martyrdom of five Franciscans who had gone off to preach to the Muslims of Morocco. Inspired by their example, he received permission to enter the mendicant order, adopted a new name, and set off for North Africa. Brother Anthony, however, was not fated to become a martyr. His ship was blown off course to Sicily, and he then journeyed north to attend the General Chapter of Franciscans held at Assisi on Pentecost, 1221. At the chapter Anthony was accepted into the Romagna province of the order and began his teaching career. Over the next decade he preached and taught in both northern Italy and southern France. His reputation for sanctity of life and the fervent support of the friars and townspeople of Padua (who had to fight with other claimants over his body) led to his canonization less than a year after his death — quicker even than the canonization of St. Francis!

Anthony's writings consist of two sermon collections, the *Sunday Sermons* first written down about 1223–27 and redacted about 1230, and the *Festal Sermons,* put down in 1230–31 at the request of Cardinal Rainaldo di Jenne, the future Pope Alexander IV. The late twelfth century and the beginning of the thirteenth had witnessed a renewed emphasis on the importance of preaching, evident both in the creation of handbooks for preachers and in ecclesiastical teaching. In 1215 the Fourth Lateran Council had proclaimed: "Among the things which pertain to the salvation of the Christian people the food of the word of God is known to be especially necessary.... Therefore, we command that fitting men be ordained...whom the bishops may have as assistants and cooperators, not only in the office of preaching, but also in hearing confessions, assigning penances, and the other things that pertain to the salvation of souls" (Constitution 10). Anthony's sermons were a response to this challenge. By providing exemplary material for preaching to the friars who had been put under his tutelage, Brother Anthony was not only fulfilling the mandate given by Fourth Lateran, but also furthering Francis's wish that his little brothers inspire others to follow the gospel both by word and by example.

Anthony's sermons were not exercises in speculative theology, but were eminently practical teaching that can be characterized under three headings: liturgical, scriptural, and moral. The sermons are always geared to the liturgy of the Sunday or feast day being treated. In the "Prologue" he wrote to his *Sunday Sermons* Anthony says that his main endeavor is to build a "chariot" for raising the soul to heaven out of the spiritual understanding of scripture, using quotations from the Old and the New Testaments as found in four sets of liturgical readings: the Sunday gospels, the Old Testament passages found in the Divine Office for the day, and the introits and epistles for the mass. Each sermon follows an original five-part structure that seeks to illustrate the "concordance," or inner agreement, of the four scriptural texts of the feast.

Anthony was a master of the spiritual interpretation of scripture, employing a rich web of allegorical meanings in order to direct his listeners to amend their lives and cultivate deeper love for God and neighbor. Modern audiences may find his constant allegorizing somewhat tedious, but the friar's medieval listeners doubtless delighted in the allegorical explanations of biblical events and names and in the interpretation of various animals that he adopted from ancient sources. Anthony's message is intensely practical, emphasizing the necessity for penance and giving constant moral instruction. When he does preach doctrine, it is always presented in a simple and traditional manner. Like Francis, he found in the poverty and suffering of Jesus the center of the gospel message. As he put it in the sermon for the Fifth Sunday after Easter: "The only wealth the Lord had was his suffering on the cross, which he left as an inheritance to his children. Hence he says, 'Do this in memory of me' (Luke 22:19), namely, in memory of my suffering.... The spirit of poverty and the inheritance of Christ's suffering are sweeter than honey and the honeycomb in the hearts of truly loving souls."

Reading Anthony

Little of Anthony is available in English, but the reader can get a good sense of the character of his sermons from *Anthony of Padua: Sermons for the Easter Cycle,* ed. George Marcil (St. Bonaventure, N.Y.: Franciscan Institute, 1994).

Bibliography

Most of the better studies are in Italian. One useful English book is:

Sophronius Clasen. *St. Anthony: Doctor of the Church.* Chicago: Franciscan Herald Press, 1973.

22

Albert the Great
(C. 1200–1280)

Feast: November 15

LBERT, provincial of the Dominicans in Germany (1254–57) was at it again. On one of his many travels, he had chanced upon a captive ostrich, a rare but not unknown bird in medieval Europe. Inherited wisdom had it that the ostrich possessed such a powerful digestive system that it would greedily devour anything offered it, including iron. The bishop was trying to feed the ostrich the metal without success. Albert was not crazy. He was doing something quite rare in the Middle Ages — he was experimenting! In his work *On Animals* he says: "It is said of this animal that it eats and digests iron, but I have not experienced this, because when I frequently offered iron to many ostriches they did not consume it" (*On Animals* 23.24.139).

Albert's *On Animals,* as well as his other writings as a naturalist, are filled with remarks like "I saw," "I observed," "I witnessed," "I have consulted." He had little sympathy with Pliny, whose *History of Animals* was a standard authority; "Pliny in fact has said a great deal that is false," he declared. Though we should scarcely expect a thirteenth-century thinker to have the same attitude toward the natural world as a twentieth-century scientist, there was eminent justification in the 1941 decree by Pius XII naming Albert the Patron Saint of Physical and Natural Scientists. Albert's view of the created universe as a subject for study is well expressed in a famous phrase: "The whole world is theology for us, because the heavens proclaim the glory of God" (*Commentary on Matthew* 13.35). The title "Universal Doctor" (*doctor universalis*) given to the German Dominican in later centuries aptly expresses the breadth of his passionate concern for all knowledge — natural, philosophical, and theological.

Albert was born of a well-to-do family in Lauingen in the diocese of Augsburg probably around 1200. While he was a student at Padua in the 1220s he joined the Dominican order, inspired by the preaching of Jordan of Saxony, Dominic's successor as master general. The new friar was sent back to Germany about 1230, first to Cologne to study theology and then to Hildesheim and Freiburg, where he served as lector. During this time he published the first of his many writings, the treatise *On the Nature of the Good*. About 1240 Albert went on to Paris, where he was promoted to master of theology in 1245. During this period he completed the required *Commentary on the Sentences of Peter Lombard*, as well as a number of other lengthy works, such as the *Summa on Creatures*. Albert also began to teach and comment on the writings of Aristotle and the *corpus Dionysiacum*, the body of treatises ascribed to Dionysius the Areopagite, the supposed pupil of St. Paul. Though neither the pagan philosopher nor the Christian Neoplatonist were strangers to the academic world of the thirteenth century, Albert's role as an interpreter of their thought was as important as any of his other contributions to the history of philosophy and theology.

In 1248 Albert returned to Cologne to head the new Dominican *studium generale*, or general house of theology. Recent study has seen this foundation and Albert's innovative teaching as the beginning of an important tradition in German philosophy, theology, and mysticism. A young Italian friar, Thomas Aquinas, who had begun his studies with Albert in Paris, followed his master to Cologne, absorbing his knowledge of Aristotle, Dionysius, and much else. Albert continued his extensive commentarial writing, even after 1253 when he was elected provincial of the vast German province of the order. His numerous duties and travels in this office did not prevent him from writing his treatise *On the Soul* and from disputing the Averroistic reading of Aristotle before the papal court (*On the Unity of the Intellect against the Averroists*). His pupil, Thomas, now his successor as master at Paris, was to take up these same issues more than a decade later.

In 1258 Albert was back in Cologne teaching at the *studium generale*. In 1259 he was a member of the important commission which reorganized the studies of the Dominicans to make sure that rigorous training was mandated, both in philosophy and theology. Then, in 1260, the pope unexpectedly named him bishop of Regensburg. Although both he and the order resisted, Albert eventually had no choice but to acquiesce. As bishop, Albert tried to provide an example of poverty and spirituality, but the politics involved in the episcopal office proved most unwelcome, and his resignation was accepted in 1262. For the next few years the ex-bishop lived a wandering life in Italy and Germany, performing various functions for the papacy and the order. Finally, in 1269 he returned to Cologne, where he took up the teaching that had always been closest to his heart. Here he completed his own

Summa of Theology probably about 1277. Albert also attended the Second Council of Lyons in 1274, and the story that he went to Paris in 1277 to defend the reputation of his deceased student, Thomas Aquinas, during the attacks against him is probably true. At some stage before his death, the aged Albert began to suffer from memory loss and stopped teaching. But it is also possible that after such a busy life in which he had been at the beck and call of many, Albert just wanted some peace and quiet — time to devote to increased prayer. This is what is suggested by a story told by the Dominican chronicler Henry of Herford about his last years. "He used to retire often to a solitary place to pray and chant, considering himself as already dead. When he was visited by the archbishop of Cologne, the recluse refused to open the door of his cell, but responded quite simply: 'Albert is not here; he's gone'" (*Book of Memorable Matters*, 202). Albert died in Cologne and is buried in the crypt of the Dominican church there.

Albert wrote an astonishing amount — forty huge volumes. Like Thomas Aquinas, and in contrast to many other thirteenth-century doctors, his writings extend over both philosophy and theology. He went beyond Thomas in his numerous works on natural science. Albert and Thomas shared a common perspective about the necessary relation between philosophy and theology (a view recently seconded by John Paul II in his encyclical *Fides et Ratio*). While Albert's view of the relation of the two sciences lacks the clarity of presentation found in Thomas, he was a pioneer in investigating this crucial aspect of Christian thought. According to Etienne Gilson, the twentieth-century historian of Christian philosophy, Albert was the first scholastic master to recognize the great difference between patristic thought and the new philosophical science made available by translations from Greek and Arabic and thus to insist that theology was a science distinct from philosophy. This meant that the fathers did not enjoy the same kind of authority in medicine, science, and philosophy that they did in theology. In his *Commentary on Peter Lombard's Sentences* he rather daringly said: "In things pertaining to faith and morals Augustine is more to be believed than the philosophers, if they disagree; but if we're discussing medicine, I would rather believe Galen, or Hippocrates; and if we're talking about the natures of things, I would rather believe Aristotle or someone else expert in natural science" (*In II Sent.* d.13, a.2). But Albert was no fideist when it came to the sciences. He said that while Aristotle was the greatest philosopher, he too was only human and could therefore err. Albert, in fact, had a keen nose for error, and little sympathy for its more obvious examples. While Thomas Aquinas was almost always an example of equanimity in argument, Albert's writings are dotted with testy remarks about those he criticized.

Albert was the first *systematic* Aristotelian commentator of the Latin West. At the beginning of his interpretation of Aristotle's *Physics*, he says, "Since there are three essential parts of real philosophy, ... which parts are natural science, or physics, and metaphysics, and mathematics, our intention is to make all these parts intelligible to the Latins." Significant as this endeavor was for the role of Aristotle in medieval thought, we must not let it obscure Albert's importance as a biblical commentator and especially as a key figure in the history of Dionysianism. In comparison with the work of his younger contemporaries, Thomas Aquinas and Bonaventure, Albert's theology has rightly been judged less systematic, more occasional, and at times eclectic. His genius lay in the diversity of his interests and the incredible energy with which he pursued so many forms of knowledge. If there is a core to the German Dominican's thoughts about the deepest issues of theology, it can be argued that it rests in his attempt to bring together the Dionysian vision of the world as an emanation, or theophany, from God, with the metaphysics of Aristotle and the many other philosophers that he studied so assiduously.

Reading Albert

A number of Albert's scientific writings have been translated, at least in part. Among these are *The Book of Minerals,* and books 22–26 of *On Animals* (under the title *Man and Beasts*). Unfortunately little of his theological writing is available in English. One exception is the Dominican's *Commentary on Dionysius's Mystical Theology* in *Albert and Thomas: Selected Writings,* translated and introduced by Simon Tugwell, CWS 60. The introduction to this volume contains a good treatment of Albert.

Bibliography

Albert the Great, Theologian: Essays in Honor of Albertus Magnus (1280–1980) in *Theological Studies* 44, no. 4 (October 1980). Eight essays on aspects of Albert's theology. The best thing in English.

Francis J. Kovach and Robert W. Shahan, *Albert the Great: Commemorative Essays.* Norman: University of Oklahoma Press, 1980. Contains only philosophical essays.

James A. Weisheipl. *Albertus Magnus and the Sciences.* Toronto: PIMS, 1980. Again, mostly nontheological pieces.

Hieronymous Wilms. *Albert the Great: Saint and Doctor of the Church.* London: Burns, Oates & Washbourne, 1933. Old, but still useful.

23

Bonaventure of Bagnorea

(1217–74)

Feast: July 15

O NE DAY in about 1223 or 1224, Francis of Assisi was passing through the town of Bagnorea on the border between Latium and Umbria. A wealthy middle-class couple brought him their sickly young son, John, to have him touched by the *poverello*, who had acquired a reputation as a wonder-worker. The boy was cured, and, when he grew up, became the most famous thirteenth-century Franciscan after Francis himself, Brother Bonaventure, the first and foremost Franciscan doctor.

John received his early instruction at the Franciscan house in Bagnorea before going on to the faculty of arts at Paris, where he studied between 1236 and 1242. In the following year, he entered the order, taking the name Bonaventure. He remained in Paris between 1243 and 1248, studying theology under several of the early Franciscan masters. Bonaventure then ascended the academic ladder between 1248 and 1257, until he was recognized as a master by the Paris theology faculty. It was during these nine years that he composed most of his technical theological works: his vast *Commentary on the Sentences of Peter Lombard* (1250–52), several biblical commentaries, a series of important disputations — *Disputed Questions on the Mystery of the Trinity* (1254) and *Disputed Questions on the Knowledge of Christ* (1254–55) — and his brief introduction to theology, the *Breviloquium* (1257). His little summary of human knowledge called *The Reduction of the Arts to Theology* also seems to come from this period.

In 1257 at the age of forty Bonaventure was elected minister general of the Franciscan order with the mandate to defend the order against its numerous detractors. He also sought to bring harmony to the order, which had experienced conflict between the "spirituals," who resisted all modifications of Francis's ideals and used the thought of the twelfth-century apocalyptic thinker Joachim of Fiore to enhance the world-historical importance of the Franciscans in the last days, and the more moderate "conventual" party, which was willing to adjust the ideal of poverty and thought that apocalyptic expectations were dangerous delusions. Bonaventure's efforts were largely successful during his own lifetime, but the interior and exterior problems of the order were to surface after his death and to provide much drama for the next fifty years.

During his busy generalate (1257–74), Bonaventure still found time to write and preach, though most of his works were pastoral, spiritual, and mystical in content. As general, he also wrote much about the order and its ideals and practices. The best known of the works from this period are *The Mind's Journey into God* (1259), Bonaventure's summary of the mystical ascent following the model laid down by Francis, and the *Life of St. Francis (Legenda major)*, the official biography of the saint that Bonaventure wrote in 1261. Other important spiritual writings from this period include *The Tree of Life*, a meditation on Christ's life, and *The Triple Way*, a systematic outline of the spiritual life. In the last years of his life, Bonaventure was engaged in polemics, defending the Franciscans against their attackers in his *Defense of the Poor* (1269) and combatting the radical Aristotelians of the university of Paris in three series of sermon lectures — *The Ten Commandments, The Seven Gifts of the Holy Spirit*, and his final theological synthesis, *The Collations on the Hexaemeron*. Bonaventure was made a cardinal by Gregory X in 1273, a year before his death at the Second Council of Lyons.

Although Bonaventure does not speak about his own experience of God, his spiritual treatises give him a central place in the history of Christian mysticism — "the prince of mystical theology," as Pope Leo XIII called him. The Franciscan doctor anchored his mystical teaching in a profound christocentric theological synthesis, one of the most impressive in the entire history of theology. In his *Collations on the Hexaemeron* he provides the following brief formula of his vision of truth, both theological and philosophical: "The Word expresses the Father and the things made through him, and he is foremost in leading us to the unity of the Father who brings all things together.... [He] is the metaphysical center that leads back [*reducens*] and this is the sum total of our metaphysics: emanation, exemplarity, and consummation" (*Coll. on Hex.* 1.17).

"Emanation" is the term Bonaventure uses to describe God's activity, or "fontality," as the First Principle of all things. We must distinguish, however, between two forms of fontality in God. All three Persons of the Trinity have fontality in relation to the creation of the universe, but this fontality is rooted in the mystery of the Father, "in whom is the fountain-fullness (*fontalis plenitudo*) for the production of the Son and the Holy Spirit" (*Questions on the*

Trinity 8.2). Bonaventure's dynamic view of the Trinity, in which the three Persons are distinguished in terms of the processions within the Godhead, is close to that of many of the Greek fathers. He integrates the dynamic activity of all three Persons into every aspect of his theology: the Father is the ultimate mystery of origin and return; the Son is the "expressive Word" in which the Father says himself and all things; and the Holy Spirit is the divine agent who actualizes the goal offered us in the Word made flesh. Thus, emanation, exemplarity, and consummation reveal the mystery of the Trinity, as he says in a text from his treatise the *Soliloquy:* "At the beginning of every good work not without reason should we invoke him from whom every good comes forth as from its origin, through whom every good is produced as its exemplar, and to whom every good is brought back as its end. This is the ineffable Trinity: Father, Son, and Holy Spirit" (*Sol.* prol.).

Exemplarity helps us to gain some understanding of the Word in the three states of his being: the Uncreated Word, the Incarnate Word, and the Inspired Word. Emanation demands exemplarity, that is, expression of the unknowable inner mystery of divine life. For Bonaventure every word is "an expressed and expressive likeness." Therefore, the Word is the Father's "expressed likeness," that is, a divine Person who expresses, absolutely, fully, and uniquely, the reality of the Father. But the Word is also the Father's "expressive likeness," a denomination that helps us understand why Bonaventure loves the formula of *Verbum increatum–Verbum incarnatum–Verbum inspiratum.* As the Uncreated Word, the Second Person is expressive of the Father as speaker and is the exemplary cause of the created universe. "In the very same Word in which the Father speaks himself, he speaks whatever he speaks" (*Questions on the Trinity* 4.2). The Word as expressive likeness also reveals the fact that the Second Person takes on flesh as the *Verbum incarnatum* in order to express the message of salvation to fallen humanity. Finally, the Word is also expressive to us as the *Verbum inspiratum* of the Bible in which God addresses us. The only way back to the source of all, the divine "fountain-fullness," is through the center, or *medium,* who has become the *mediator* by taking on flesh — Jesus Christ.

The process of consummation, return, or "reduction" (*reductio*) as Bonaventure loved to call it, forms the third moment in his theological synthesis. Reduction is most evident as a mental activity, that is, the way in which the mind "brings back" any form of truth to the eternal reasons upon which it is founded (this is why all sciences can be "reduced" to theology). Although Bonaventure, like other scholastic theologians, made use of Aristotelian logic in the details of his technical theological writings, the essence of his way of doing theology is founded upon the reductive arguments that are designed to reveal the universal trinitarian analogies found in all created reality (hence the constant ternary distinctions found throughout his writings). Reduction as a way of revealing the truth, however, is founded upon reduction as the basic metaphysical law of the universe according to which all things are ultimately drawn back into the divine source. This takes place in and through the Word, but also through the love that is the Holy Spirit as the bond between the Father and the Son.

Bonaventure's theology of creation and return has a deep affinity with the cosmic vision found in St. Francis's "Canticle of Brother Son." His understanding of Christ, the *Verbum incarnatum*, is also based upon Francis as the perfect "expressed likeness" of Christ in his life of poverty and his reception of the stigmata, the marks of the crucified Savior. Summing up the meaning of the *poverello* in the *Life of St. Francis*, he put it this way: "The most Christian of men, who strove by perfect imitation to be like the living Christ while alive, like the dying Christ in dying, and like the dead Christ after death — and therefore merited to be adorned with his expressed likeness [i.e., the stigmata]" (*Life* 14.4). In both *The Mind's Journey into God* and the *Life*, Bonaventure shows how Francis provides a model for our incorporation into Christ both *vertically*, that is, by contemplative ascent, and *horizontally*, by his function in salvation history as the Angel of the Sixth Seal predicted in Apocalypse 7:2, a harbinger of the coming contemplative state of the church on earth (in this Bonaventure utilized a modified form of the corporate apocalyptic mysticism of Joachim of Fiore). Francis leads the believer to Christ, who is the only way to God.

Bonaventure's christocentricism is found throughout his works, both those of academic theology and the more popular spiritual sermons and treatises. The "Seraphic Doctor" (as he came to be called) was one of the most influential voices in furthering the meditative and contemplative appropriation of the mysteries of Christ's life that formed so large a part of late medieval piety. Meditation was to be directed primarily to the Nativity in which God gave himself totally to humanity and the Passion in which he gave himself totally back to God on humanity's behalf. The centrality of the Passion is beautifully illustrated in *The Mind's Journey into God*. Here Bonaventure lays out six stages in the contemplative ascent toward God (a movement both upward and inward into the soul's depths), culminating in the level of suprarational *intelligentia*, which, through grace, gazes upon God first as one pure and necessary existence (*esse*), and then as three equal Persons in the mystery of overflowing goodness (*bonum*). The mind cannot understand this coincidence of opposites, but it can enter into its very life in a final seventh stage by contemplation of "the totally wondrous union of God and man in the unity of the Person of Christ" (*Mind's Journey* 6.4). This transcendent passing beyond (*transitus*) is essentially an affective state in which, impelled by love, we imitate Christ by dying to the world and giving ourselves wholly to God in the darkness of sacrificial love.

Reading Bonaventure

Most of Bonaventure's theological and spiritual treatises and disputed questions are available in English, but only some of his sermons and fragments of his biblical commentaries and *Commentary on the Sentences*. The best place to begin is with *The Mind's Journey into God* and *The Life of St. Francis*, which can be found in *Bonaventure: The Soul's Journey into God*, trans. Ewert Cousins, CWS 5. For the saint's overall view of theology, first turn to *The Reduction of the Arts to Theology*, and then to the *Breviloquium*. More meaty fare can be found in the translations of the *Disputed Questions on the Mystery of the Trinity* and the *Disputed Questions on the Knowledge of Christ*. These writings are available in the series *Works of St. Bonaventure* (St. Bonaventure, N.Y.: Franciscan Institute, 1979–).

Bibliography

J. Guy Bougerol. *Introduction to the Works of St. Bonaventure*. Paterson, N.J.: St. Anthony Guild Press, 1963. A good, detailed introduction to Bonaventure's life, context, and thought by a great modern Bonaventure scholar.

Ewert H. Cousins. *Bonaventure and the Coincidence of Opposites*. Chicago: Franciscan Herald Press, 1978.

Etienne Gilson. *The Philosophy of St. Bonaventure*. Paterson, N.J.: St. Anthony Guild Press, 1965. Though primarily known as a student of St. Thomas, Gilson shows his deep affinity with Bonaventure in this classic book.

Zachary Hayes. *The Hidden Center: Spirituality and Speculative Christology in St. Bonaventure*. New York: Paulist Press, 1981. Perhaps the best introduction to Bonaventure's theology.

Bernard McGinn. *The Flowering of Mysticism: Men and Women in the New Mysticism (1200–1350)*. New York: Crossroad, 1998, 87–112. Surveys Bonaventure's contribution to mysticism.

Joseph Ratzinger. *The Theology of History in St. Bonaventure*. Chicago: Franciscan Herald Press, 1971.

24

Thomas Aquinas

(1224–74)

Feast Day: January 28

I N THE YEAR 1269 King Louis IX of France was hosting a dinner party. Among the guests was the chief Dominican theologian at the University of Paris, Thomas Aquinas, who had been given a seat of honor next to the king. As the meal proceeded, Thomas, known to be a man of few words outside class (his seminary classmates had dubbed him "the dumb-ox"), grew more and more quiet. At one point, to the amazement of all, this "very fat" (*pinguissimus*) friar's great fist pounded the table, and he exclaimed, "That settles the Manichees!" Thomas's prior, who was also at the meal, touched his hand, and said: "Master, master, you are at dinner with the king of France, not in your cell!" Coming to his senses, Thomas apologized for this breach of etiquette, saying, "Excuse me, your Majesty, I thought I was at my desk . . . and I have begun a work against the Manichees." As befits the courtesy of one saint seated next to another, the king was not offended, ordering his secretary to take down Thomas's argument against the dualist heretics at once (Bernard Gui, *Life of St. Thomas*, chap. 25).

The single-mindedness of Thomas's dedication to truth will be evident to anyone who has ever read any of his works and marveled at their clarity, power, and perspicacity. If Augustine had the greatest influence on the evolution of the concept of *doctor ecclesiae* in the late patristic period, Thomas Aquinas has enjoyed an equally important reputation among the postpatristic doctors of Western Christianity. It is important, however, to reflect on the nature of Thomas's authority, given the importance of his teaching on the role of doctors already pointed out in Part I. As Thomas rightly insisted, "because the teaching of the catholic doctors has its authority from the church, we must abide by the custom of the church more than the authority of... any doctor" (*Quodlibetal Questions* 4.2).

The conviction that Thomas Aquinas was *the* official voice of all Roman Catholic theology had a relatively short shelf-life, given the more than seven hundred years since his death. (Its regnant period was between the encyclical *Aeterni Patris* of 1879 and the Second Vatican Council of 1962–65.) But to see the great Dominican as one among a host of witnesses to the truth is not to diminish his contribution; rather, it helps us to put him in the perspective that he himself adopted. Thomas would have welcomed the contemporary view that places him *in* the list of doctors, rather than over it. He always insisted that theology proceeds more by argumentation than by the invocation of authority in areas that are still open to discussion.

Thomas was born in 1224 at Aquino south of Rome from a noble family of mixed German and Italian origin. His parents had earmarked him for a distinguished ecclesiastical career, but he upset their plans by entering the new order of poor preachers, the Dominicans, in 1244. After early training in Naples, he was sent on to Paris and then Cologne, where he studied under Albert the Great from 1245 to 1252. His relatively brief academic career of only two decades, extraordinary for its productivity, falls into three parts. Thomas taught at Paris from 1252 to 1259, being promoted to master of theology in 1256. Then, as was customary with the mendicant orders that had to service their houses of theology all over Europe, he was called back to teach in Italian Dominican theologates and for the papal court (1259–68). In the midst of the crisis over the use of Aristotle in theology that developed in Paris in the late 1260s, Thomas was given the unusual privilege of being recalled to the theological center of the West, where he taught from early 1269 to mid-1272. Finally, he was again sent back to Italy to head up a new theological center at Naples. Here, something happened to the prodigy. On December 6, 1273, Thomas suddenly stopped writing. His hagiographers spoke of a divine vision that convinced him that all that he had written seemed "like straw." Modern scholars have speculated on a stroke, or some kind of mental and physical breakdown. Some months later, Thomas died in the spring of 1274, while on his way to the Second Council of Lyons.

At the beginning of his *Summa of Theology*, Thomas discusses the nature of what he calls "sacred teaching" (*sacra doctrina*) — a term he preferred to "theology" because it emphasized the actions of teaching and being taught over the static sense of a set of abstract principles enshrined in books (which is perhaps what "theology" suggests even more today than in the thirteenth century). Thomas says that sacred teaching enshrines two kinds of truths: those that can be attained by human reason on its own, such as God's existence and attributes; and those that surpass any created understanding, because they reveal the inner divine realities, such as the Trinity and the mystery of God becoming man in Jesus Christ. For the Dominican, the former kind of truth is the realm of philosophy, though due to the darkening of the human intellect in Adam's fall, these truths are also taught in the Bible. The second form of strictly supernatural truth — the truths that are necessary for salvation — can be made known only by God's revelation. This fundamental distinction between the natural and the supernatural realms, epistemological as well as soteriological, governs the whole of Thomas's teaching, providing it with a clarity and system second to none among all the *doctores ecclesiae*.

The distinction between natural and supernatural truth also helps explain Thomas's dual career as both philosopher and theologian. Although the majority of the Dominican's writings are theological, his recognition of an independent, if subordinated, role for philosophy has given Thomas an important place in the history of philosophical thought, even among those who do not share his religious commitment. Nevertheless, Thomas was primarily a theologian; his two great *Summae* are both theological works, not exercises in philosophy, however much he respected and utilized that discipline. Trying to see how Thomas related natural and supernatural truth in his many writings provides one way into understanding his contribution to the history of Christian doctrine.

Thomas's efforts as teacher and writer fall into three broad categories. Like all scholastics, what he wrote is based upon, often even a transcript of, what he taught day-in and day-out to seminarians. Medieval university professors were first and foremost commentators who explained the meaning of authoritative texts, especially the Bible. It is only in recent decades that the investigators have begun to understand Thomas's role in the history of exegesis (he wrote eleven biblical commentaries, some of considerable length). Although he did not reject the spiritual sense, the friar was especially concerned with the literal meaning of the Bible, "since all the [other] meanings are founded upon one, that is, the literal, from which alone argument can be drawn" (*Summa of Theology* Ia.1.10). Of course, Thomas's understanding of the literal meaning of the Bible was far from modern historical-critical attempts to recover the original situation of the text, but it does represent a more "common-sense" approach to the essential doctrinal message of scripture than that of many of his contemporaries. (For example, Thomas read the book of Job as a message about providence rather than an occasion to reflect on the patriarch as a type of Christ.)

Thomas's commentarial role is also evident in his early *Commentary on Peter Lombard's Sentences* (1254–56), an effort required of all scholastics. Though this large work will always be a mine for scholars tracing the development of his mind, its greatest significance rests in the fact that while writing it Thomas came to rethink how to teach *sacra doctrina*. His own *Summa* implicitly criticizes the Lombard's organization, finding that it does not adhere to "sound educational method" (*ordo disciplinae*). Along with his biblical and *Sentence* commentaries, Thomas composed two other sets of interpretations of texts for more advanced students. The first dealt with important

Neoplatonic theological works, such as Pseudo-Dionysius, Boethius, and the *Book of Causes* (which Aquinas recognized was based on a pagan philosophical work). The second was his set of commentaries on Aristotle (twelve texts of varying length).

The relationship between Thomas Aquinas and Aristotle is essential for understanding the nature of his theology and the controversies it provoked. (Some of Thomas's more Aristotelian positions were actually condemned by the bishop of Paris in 1277 as dangerous and heretical!) Much of the philosophical language used in Christian theology between c. 300 and 1200 had been based on the reception and transformation of aspects of the Platonic philosophical tradition. Aristotle's logical works always had some currency, but it was not until late in the twelfth century that an influx of new translations of the "philosopher's" books on cosmology, psychology, and metaphysics became well known. The systematic cogency of the Aristotelian philosophical corpus made it immediately attractive to medieval scholastics and their drive to create a new "scientific" model of theology — this despite Aristotle's contradictions of Christian belief on such issues as the creation of the universe in time, the existence of providence, and personal immortality. Aristotle had been attacked early in the thirteenth century, but the usefulness of his philosophy led to its reentry into the teaching curriculum by the 1240s when the young Thomas was well trained in Aristotle by Albert the Great. Thomas's own commentaries on the Greek philosopher were an attempt "to stand Aristotle on his head," that is, to show how Aristotelian philosophy, properly interpreted, provided a sound basis for what natural reason could know about truth and thus was a useful "handmaid" for Christian theology. Thomas was never an Aristotelian fundamentalist, one who believed everything the "philosopher" had written was reason's "gospel truth." But, in contrast to his contemporary Bonaventure, he always gave Aristotle the benefit of the doubt — utilizing him whenever possible, correcting him when necessary, and insisting that an "independent" philosophy could not contradict revealed truth. The sharp disagreement between Bonaventure's view of Aristotle and that of Thomas is rooted in their differing conceptions of the relations between philosophy and theology.

These biblical, philosophical, and theological commentaries serve as the broad foundation upon which Thomas erected the vast palace of his theology. The structure can be seen as consisting of two main parts: specialized theological investigations, which work out problems and respond to contemporary issues; and the great systematic syntheses, which organize all sacred doctrine in a manner appropriate for effective learning. A master of theology (*magister theologiae*) like Thomas was not only a commentator, but also a "disputator," someone who was obliged several times a year to engage in public disputations on theological topics. Like other scholastics, Thomas took advantage of this practice to compose series of questions on some of the most perplexing areas in theology — sixty-three disputations arranged under seven titles on such topics as "Truth," "Evil," "God's Power," "The Soul," "The Virtues," etc. The at times numbing detail with which Thomas explored the problems raised by these philosophico-theological issues show how these "questions" provided him with insights that were crucial for the positions he took in the two major systematic works he produced in the last fifteen years of his life. Equally important for his *summae* were the numerous short treatises (*opuscula*) that Thomas worked on during his teaching career (about sixteen works in all). These were often responses to contemporary issues, such as the debates over the status of the mendicant orders, or concerning the use of Aristotle. Thomas also composed letter-treatises, and even left some sermons and liturgical pieces (e.g., the Office for the Feast of Corpus Christi) among his more than a hundred recognized writings.

Thomas's readers have most often — and rightly — directed their attention to his two attempts to survey the whole of Christian teaching: the *Summa against the Gentiles* (1259–64) and the *Summa of Theology* (1266–73). More than any other doctor, Thomas sought to provide a total overview of the understanding of faith. He did this in conformity with the twofold distinction of truths noted above. The *Summa of Theology* is a work of dogmatic theology, that is, a reflection on how the believer tries to understand the biblical message about salvation and its teaching on both natural and supernatural truths. The *Summa against the Gentiles,* on the other hand, is a work of apologetic, or missionary, theology, designed to help Dominican friars convert Muslims and Jews in the Spanish mission. Here Thomas primarily investigates how to demonstrate the truths of natural knowledge about God (bks. 1–3), but does not neglect arguments showing the "fittingness" of those truths that surpass reason (bk. 4).

The structure of Thomas's *Summa of Theology* is as revelatory of his synthetic perspective as is every detail of its execution. Though Thomas's love for Aristotle has always been obvious, recent scholarship has shown that his integration of philosophy into the task of faith seeking understanding was also much indebted to Platonism. The Dominican even structured his *Summa of Theology* according to the Platonic paradigm of *exitus-reditus*, that is, how all things come forth from and finally return to God. The "First Part" of the *Summa* (Ia) deals with God both in Godself and as the First Cause of the production of all things, with the treatment of God as one occupying questions (qq.) 2–26, and the Trinity being investigated in qq. 27–43. Then Aquinas turns to a consideration of the created universe, first in itself (qq. 44–49), and next according to its various kinds of creatures: angels and the creatures of the first five days of the Genesis account (qq. 50–74); and then an extended discussion of humanity as the creature embracing both the spiritual and material realms (qq. 75–102). The Ia concludes with a treatment of providence (qq. 103–19).

As Thomas moved into the Second (IIa) and Third (IIIa) Parts of the *Summa,* where he investigates the return of all things to God as their Final

Cause, it is obvious that what had been initially intended as an introduction to theology for beginners was becoming a vast (and ultimately unfinished) work. The Second Part is divided into two sections. A full description cannot be given here, but a glance at the outline of the questions shows the incredible detail of Thomas's treatment of the natural and supernatural acts by which God draws us to beatitude, the enjoyment of ultimate felicity in the divine vision. The Dominican's status as a supreme moral theologian is evident in this section of the *Summa* (longer than Ia and IIIa combined). Finally, the Third Part of the *Summa* treats the *way* by which God restores all things to the goal, that is, Christ, the God-Man, and the sacraments which bring Christ's saving power to the believer. Here too, Thomas's commitment to distinguishing natural and supernatural truth is evident. In contrast to Anselm, he holds that there can be no "necessary reason," or philosophically demonstrative argument, for the Incarnation, because this would impinge on divine freedom. Revelation alone teaches us this mystery, though reason guided by faith can find many "fitting arguments" (*rationes convenientes*) for the Incarnation and the other truths of salvation history.

Reading Thomas Aquinas

There are complete translations of both of Thomas's great *Summae*, and these are where even the neophyte should start to read the "Angelic Doctor." For the *Summa of Theology*, the English Dominicans at Blackfriars twice translated the text: in three large volumes in 1920, and a second version in sixty volumes in the 1960s. The *Summa against the Gentiles* has also been fully translated: *Saint Thomas Aquinas: Summa contra Gentiles*, trans. Anton C. Pegis, 4 vols. (Notre Dame, Ind.: University of Notre Dame Press, 1975). I begin my students with the first thirteen questions of Part I of the *Summa of Theology*, even though these are as profound as anything Thomas ever wrote. The Dominican's technical vocabulary and the density of his mode of presentation should *not* put readers off; no great thinker has ever been more interested in clarity than Thomas Aquinas. Most of Thomas's *opuscula* and many of his disputed questions also exist in translation — a full list cannot be given here. In recent years some of Aquinas's commentaries, biblical and nonbiblical, have begun to be translated, though not the long *Commentary on the Sentences of Peter Lombard*.

Bibliography

There is a multitude of books about Aquinas; only a few of the most helpful and important can be listed here:

Brian Davies. *The Thought of Thomas Aquinas*. Oxford: Clarendon Press, 1993. A recent clear and comprehensive introduction.

Etienne Gilson. *The Christian Philosophy of St. Thomas Aquinas*. New York: Random House, 1956. The classic work of the greatest student of Thomas of the first half of the twentieth century.

Norman Kretzmann and Eleonore Stump, eds. *The Cambridge Companion to Aquinas.* Cambridge: Cambridge University Press, 1993. Concentrates on philosophical issues.

Bernard J. F. Lonergan. *Verbum: Word and Idea in Aquinas.* Notre Dame, Ind.: University of Notre Dame Press, 1976. Lonergan's breakthrough in understanding Thomistic epistemology. Also important is the same author's *Grace and Freedom: Operative Grace in the Thought of St. Thomas Aquinas.* New York: Herder and Herder, 1971.

Thomas F. O'Meara. *Thomas Aquinas Theologian.* Notre Dame, Ind.: University of Notre Dame Press, 1997. A brief summary of Thomas and the history of Thomism.

Jean-Pierre Torrell. *Saint Thomas Aquinas.* Vol. 1: *The Person and his Work.* Washington, D.C.: Catholic University of America Press, 1996. The most up-to-date and detailed treatment of Thomas's life and the creation of his writings.

James A. Weisheipl. *Friar Thomas d'Aquino: His Life, Thought, and Work.* Garden City, N.Y.: Doubleday, 1974. Older, but still useful on the background to Thomas's life as a university man.

25

CATHERINE OF SIENA

(1347–80)

FEAST: APRIL 29

I N JUNE OF 1375 a public execution took place in Siena. A young man named Niccolò di Toldo had been convicted of plotting against the city and was sentenced to be beheaded. Although he had not been a fervent Christian during his life, as Niccolò approached death he underwent a conversion through the ministrations of Catherine Benincasa, a pious Dominican tertiary, or lay sister, of the city. Shortly after his death, Catherine described the event in a letter she sent to her confessor, Raymond of Capua. The letter (no. 31 of her collection) is both a description of the execution, a meditation on redemption, and an invitation to Raymond and others to plunge into the redeeming blood of Christ.

Catherine tells Raymond: "I went to visit the one you know and he was so comforted and consoled that he confessed his sins and prepared himself very well. He made me promise that for the love of God that when the time came for the execution I would be with him." On the morning of the execution Catherine let the condemned man rest his head on her breast. She says, "I sensed an intense joy, a fragrance of his blood — and it wasn't separate from the fragrance of my own, which I am waiting to shed for my gentle Spouse Jesus." At the place of execution, Catherine blessed Niccolò and encouraged him with the words, "Down for the wedding, my dear brother, for soon you will be in everlasting life." Her account goes on: "I placed his neck on the block and bent down and reminded him of the blood of the Lamb. His mouth said nothing but 'Jesus!' and 'Catherine!; and as he said this I received his head into my hands, saying 'I will!' with my eyes fixed on divine Goodness.

Then was seen the God-Man as one sees the brilliance of the sun. His side was open and received blood into his own blood — received a flame of holy desire, which grace had given and hidden in this soul, into the flame of his own divine charity." Catherine says in closing that the fragrance of the blood gave her so much peace that she could not bear to wash it from her hands and clothes.

This mystical experience, powerful and perhaps strange to contemporary taste, provides a revealing insight into Catherine of Siena's teaching on redemption and union with God. While redemption "in the precious blood of the Lamb" (1 Pet. 1:19) was a pervasive theme in the history of Christianity from its New Testament roots down through the fathers and later teachers, no doctor of the church gave it as central a role as Catherine. Blood for the Sienese Dominican is not a concept or a theological abstraction; it is the living experience of God's overpowering, "mad" love. As she says to Raymond at the outset of this letter: "I long to see you engulfed and drowned in the sweet blood of God's Son, which is permeated with the fire of his blazing charity."

Catherine was born in 1347, the twenty-fourth of the twenty-five children of a middle-class family. According to the *Life* written by Raymond, she vowed herself to a life of virginity after receiving a vision of Christ at the age of seven. In 1365, over the objections of her family, she received the habit of the "Sisters of Penance," pious women, usually widows, who were associated with the Dominican order. She then retired to her room for three years and lived a life similar to that of the enclosed women (*inclusae*), or anchoresses, popular throughout the Middle Ages. During this time, she learned to read and engaged in an intensive prayer life that resulted in a famous vision in which, like her namesake the legendary Catherine of Alexandria, she was espoused to Christ (*Life* 1.11). Catherine interpreted this experience as a call to an evangelical lifestyle, so at age twenty-one she began to succor the poor and sick in her native city. She also gradually gathered a group of followers around her to hear her reflections on Christian faith and life. Catherine thus became a model for the union of both contemplation and action in the service of church reform.

Catherine's functioning as an *apostola*, while unusual for a woman, was not totally unprecedented. The legendary accounts about Mary Magdalene had given her an apostolic status that had been called on before by women teachers. In fourteenth-century Italy we can see a number of other examples of apostolic women teachers, such as Angela of Foligno (d. 1309) and Birgitta of Sweden (d. 1373). Each of these, like Catherine, appealed to their direct visionary contact with God to authorize their teachings. Like them, Catherine had to struggle to gain acceptance by convincing her Dominican confessors and other ecclesiastical figures that her revelations were conformable to church teaching and helpful for the salvation of souls. Catherine had her detractors, early and late. Raymond notes, "She was scarcely able to do a single act of devotion in public without suffering from calumnies, impediments, and persecutions, especially from those who ought to have been most favorable to her" (*Life* 3.7). But Catherine persisted, confident in her message from God. The dozen years of her public life saw her gain ever greater fame as a teacher, guide, and conduit for God's message to the world.

Part of the reason for the international reputation of Birgitta and Catherine (unprecedented for women, at least since the time of Hildegard of Bingen) was the perilous state of the church during the Avignon captivity of the papacy. The Swedish seer and the Italian mystic came to be recognized as representatives of God's call for the return of the papacy to Italy, the end of the quarrels of the fractious Italian city-states, and the general reform of the church in head and members.

In the period from 1368 to 1374, Catherine's activities were mostly confined to Siena. During this time she continued to enjoy a variety of mystical gifts, including an experience of "mystical death" (*mors mystica*) in 1370. She also increased the intense fasting that was eventually to lead to her death. In 1374 the learned Dominican Raymond of Capua became her confessor; in the same year Catherine began to exercise a wider ministry, making the first of her journeys outside Siena. In 1375 she traveled to Pisa to intercede with that city not to join the anti-papal league; she also began an extensive correspondence (382 letters) that spread her message more widely. In 1376 Catherine undertook a longer journey, traveling to Avignon to mediate between Pope Gregory XI and the city of Florence, which he had put under interdict. While at Avignon, Catherine urged the pope to return to Rome, an action he finally agreed to, arriving in his rightful see in January of 1377. Catherine spent much of 1377 on another peacemaking venture at Rocca d'Orcia. It was here that she had the mystical experiences that led her to the composition of the *Dialogue*, her most important work. Catherine dictated the book from October 1377 through most of the following year, often correcting the copy in her own hand.

In 1378 Catherine was once again in Florence, this time at the pope's behest, trying to arrange for a cessation of hostilities between the pontiff and the city. On March 27 Gregory died. The election of his successor, Urban VI, soon led to a split in the ranks of the cardinals. The French faction, dissatisfied with the turmoil of Italy and Urban's actions, left Rome for Anagni where they elected the French cardinal Robert of Geneva as Pope Clement VII. He soon returned to Avignon to begin the Great Western Schism, which divided Western Christendom from 1378 to 1417. From the beginning of the schism, Catherine was a strong supporter of the Roman claimant. In November of 1378, the pope called her to Rome. Here, despite her declining health, she continued to write letters on his behalf. Most of Catherine's twenty-six prayers date from this time. By early 1380, Catherine, who no longer took any food at all, was close to death. She miraculously clung to life for a few months, dying on April 29 in her thirty-third year.

Catherine's life was remarkable; her teaching even more so. Although she was by no means the first of the great female theologians of the Middle Ages, her teaching is representative of the new role that women began to take in the twelfth century, with figures like Hildegard, and especially from the thirteenth century on. Within the patriarchal conditions of both the church and society, it was quite difficult for women to take on a teaching role, but the witness of Paul (despite statements that also relegated women to a secondary status) was hard to gainsay. According to the apostle to the Gentiles, "In Jesus Christ there is neither male nor female" (Gal. 3:28); and his text that "God has chosen the weak things of the world to put to shame the strong" (1 Cor. 1:27) was often used by women to defend their right to speak out when male authorities were either silent or confused.

The later Middle Ages witnessed an extraordinary growth of "vernacular theology," i.e., faith seeking understanding in the new vernacular languages of Western Europe and in popular, rather than academic, forms of discourse. Women took a major role in this movement, and hence it is only fitting that one of them (at very least) has achieved the rank of *doctor ecclesiae*. Catherine of Siena's central work, the *Dialogue,* exemplifies the new theology pioneered by women. The *Dialogue* is the record of a conversation between God and Catherine conducted over 167 chapters. Its repetitious and "layered" arrangement is far from the careful articulation of scholastic theology, as seen in Thomas Aquinas, Bonaventure, and others. However, this does not mean that Catherine's message is naive, superficial, or unoriginal. The *Dialogue* is a powerful re-presentation of the theology of redemption first worked out by Anselm and Thomas Aquinas, one designed to make the technical language of the schoolmen a lived and felt reality. Some decades after Catherine died, Jean Gerson was to define mystical theology as an "experiential knowledge of God" (*cognitio experimentalis de Deo*), a form of knowing that would not contradict dogmatic theology, but serve to deepen it. This is what Catherine's *Dialogue* does for the theology of that other great Dominican, Thomas Aquinas.

The ten sections of the *Dialogue* do have their own form of organization — a pattern consisting of Catherine's petition to God, his response, and her return of thanksgiving. We learn to appreciate Catherine's message, not by organizing it according to the categories of scholastic theology, but by "overhearing" it, i.e., by allowing ourselves to enter into the dialogue between herself and God and participate along with her in experiencing the power of divine love (see, e.g., her hymn to God the "mad Lover" in chap. 153). The long allegory "The Bridge" (chaps. 26–87) provides a good insight into the depth of Catherine's teaching. The Bridge is Christ, according to Catherine's deeply symbolic and pictorial mode of presentation. In order to escape the river of sin and mount from earth to heaven we must climb up this bridge's three stairs — Christ's feet representing the soul's affection; Christ's open side figuring the mind's eye, which responds in love to the divine love shown in the crucifixion; and finally Christ's mouth, which is the peace of union with the Divine Lover (see chaps. 26 and 54). Elsewhere Catherine develops a picture of spiritual progress in terms of the transition from mercenary, to servant, and eventually to child and friend (e.g., chaps. 56, 63, and 72). As the Dominican expounds her long Bridge allegory, however, it is the dense evocation of the meaning of key symbols that makes her theology of mystical redemption so rich. The most central of these, not surprisingly, is blood. Christ's blood is our food and inebriating drink (chap. 66), it is our bath and baptism (chap. 75), it is also our bond with him and our ransom (chap. 27). Though Catherine uses a variety of symbols to present her message of the path to loving union with God — water, bread, tree, tears, light, anvil, etc. — again and again she returns to the experience of immersion in blood to express her message, or rather, the message God sends through her. In chapter 66, as in other places, she ties this immersion to the reception of Christ's Body and Blood in the Eucharist. God speaks: "When one communicates sacramentally in loving charity one finds and tastes in the blood because one sees that it was shed through love. And so the soul is inebriated and set on fire and sated with holy longing, finding herself filled completely with love of me and of her neighbors."

Reading Catherine

The *Dialogue* is Catherine's most important work and, despite its length, should be the first read. A good translation is *Catherine of Siena: The Dialogue,* trans. Suzanne Noffke, CWS 17. Suzanne Noffke has also translated *The Letters of Catherine of Siena,* vol. 1 (Binghamton: Medieval and Renaissance Texts and Studies, 1988), containing Letters 1–88; and *The Prayers of Catherine of Siena* (New York: Paulist Press, 1980). Catherine's life by Raymond of Capua has been translated by Conleth Kearns, *The Life of St. Catherine of Siena* (Wilmington, Del.: Michael Glazier, 1980).

Bibliography

Caroline Walker Bynum. *Holy Feast and Holy Fast: The Religious Significance of Food to Medieval Women.* Berkeley: University of California Press, 1987. Has interesting reflections on Catherine's use of food imagery.

Mary Ann Fatula. *Catherine of Siena's Way.* London: Darton, Longman and Todd, 1987.

Igino Giordani. *Saint Catherine of Siena: Doctor of the Church.* Boston: St. Paul Editions, 1975.

Richard Kieckhefer. *Unquiet Souls: Fourteenth-Century Saints and Their Religious Milieu.* Chicago: University of Chicago Press, 1984. Sets Catherine within the wider context of fourteenth-century conceptions of sanctity.

III. MODERN DOCTORS

26

TERESA
OF AVILA
(1515–82)

FEAST: OCTOBER 15

I N ABOUT 1524 a young Spanish girl and her older brother secretly left
their home in Avila in order to travel, "begging bread for the love of
God," to Muslim lands in North Africa to offer themselves for martyrdom. At the bridge leading out of the city they were apprehended by an
uncle who marched them home to a less adventurous life in the midst of a
large family of a pious couple.

This is the event with which Teresa of Avila begins her spiritual autobiography (*The Life*), the earliest and most popular of her works, written
between 1562 and 1565. Her choice of this incident is revealing, because
while *The Life* artfully portrays its subject "Augustine-like" as a sinful soul,
and even a tepid nun for the first two decades of her convent life, the book
cannot really hide the single-minded dedication to the love of God she displayed from her earliest years. Teresa, whose family came from a *converso*,
that is, a Jewish convert background, was many things — religious reformer,
activist founder of convents, ecstatic contemplative, prolific author. What
gives her complex and fascinating life its essential harmony, however, is clear:
the force of her overwhelming desire for God. The seventeenth-century English poet Richard Crashaw captured this center of her personality when he
addressed her as "O thou undaunted daughter of desires!"

Teresa depicts herself as a frivolous young girl who entered the Carmelite
convent of the Encarnación in 1536 more out of "servile fear" than love.
During her first decade in the convent she suffered from many illnesses.

Whatever the state of her spiritual life during these years, in about 1556 she began to experience deeper forms of mystical consciousness that were to grow in intensity down to 1572, when she received the culminating grace of the "spiritual marriage" to God discussed in her final work, *The Interior Castle*, written in 1577. The most noted of these early mystical experiences occurred in 1559 when an angel appeared to Teresa and pierced her heart with a fiery golden spear that left her "totally on fire with great love of God" (*Life*, chap. 29). This "transverberation," the most famous of the physical images of mystical union with God after the stigmata of St. Francis, was widely illustrated, especially in the powerfully erotic sculpture of Gian Lorenzo Bernini in the church of Santa Maria della Vittoria in Rome.

As we have seen in the case of Catherine of Siena, it was a difficult, though not impossible, task for a woman to compose theological literature. Teresa's authorial career was occasioned by the 1559 decree of Fernando de Valdés, grand inquisitor of Spain, who forbade the reading of the vernacular spiritual works that had nourished the piety of Teresa and her nuns. At this juncture, Christ appeared to her and told her he would give her a living book — the book she later externalized in her writings (*Life*, chap. 26). Along with *The Life* and *The Interior Castle* the most important of her writings are *The Way of Perfection* (1565–66) and the *Book of the Foundations* (1573–76), an account of her work in spreading the austere "Discalced" reform of the Carmelite order, which she had begun with the foundation of the convent of St. Joseph at Avila in 1562. During her life and after her death there was an ongoing examination of the orthodoxy of her writings by the Inquisition. Eventually permission was given for their publication in 1588 (they were edited by the great Augustinian mystic, Luis de Léon). Teresa was canonized in 1622.

Teresa of Avila's teaching, along with that of her friend, confessor, and fellow reformer John of the Cross, represents one of the high points in the history of Christian mysticism. Although there was much in their lives and teaching that drew Teresa and John together, the nun's mystical doctrine is her own and differs from that of John in its mode of expression, as well as in some aspects of its content. We should remember that Teresa's works were written primarily as practical guides for her nuns — "how-to" books dealing with both the ascetical and the mystical dimensions of the cloistered life. Nevertheless, Teresa was not exclusivistic. In *The Interior Castle* she explicitly says that souls living in the world cannot be denied entrance into even the final "dwelling place" of spiritual marriage, especially if they strongly desire it (*Castle* 3.1.5). It is perhaps for this reason that Teresa's writings, more than those of many of the scholastic doctors, have continued to attract such a wide range of readers over the past four centuries.

Teresa and John bring to completion the tendency begun among twelfth-century mystical authors (see Bernard of Clairvaux) to probe the inner dimensions of the "book of experience" by exploring the dynamic transformation of the mystical self. In contrast to John, Teresa speaks in her own voice, using the first person story of her soul in *The Life* and thinly disguised third-person accounts found in *The Interior Castle*. The subtlety, delicacy, and vehemence with which she presents her inner states, however, must not be exaggerated, as if her writings are nothing more than some sort of experientialism. Teresa was not seeking to hold up her own experiences as the norm, but rather to show how her mystical consciousness conformed to the teaching of the Bible and the church, and thus could be used as a model for others who desired to find transformation in Christ. The ongoing conversation with her many learned confessors (and some unlearned and unskilled ones) described in the course of both *The Life* and *The Interior Castle* is just one of the techniques she uses to demonstrate this.

Teresa's fundamental concern with the *process* of transformation into God is mirrored in the way that her written works reflect the progress she made over two decades in her higher prayer life (c. 1557–77). Important differences exist between *The Life* and *The Interior Castle*, some that she notes in the latter book and some that are not explicitly cited. (Also some terms, like the "prayer of quiet," are used ambiguously over the course of her writings.) But the spirit of Teresa's mystical message is more important than the details — and that spirit is easily grasped by reading any of her three major mystical texts. Although *The Life* is the most engaging of her works because of its concrete character and revelation of her personality, and although *The Way of Perfection* tells us more about the total spiritual program she wished to see realized in the life of the cloistered community, *The Interior Castle* is the most mature and most succinct of her writings and is therefore the best place for a contemporary reader to gain an appreciation of the Spanish doctor's teaching.

The Interior Castle is one of the most sustained and profound accounts of mystical transformation in the history of Christian theology. Adopting the image of a castle with its walls (=body) and inner rooms or dwelling places (=aspects of the soul) as her main teaching device, Teresa lays out the journey within to the divine light dwelling at the center of the soul. As in many mystical itineraries, the journey is sketched according to seven stages, or "dwelling places," though she insists that there are many other such locations in the interior castle of the soul. If the journey is primarily a movement to the God within, however, it always involves a reciprocity with outward practice, especially in the final seventh stage.

In presenting the seven stages, Teresa, like John of the Cross and other contemporaries, is concerned with analyzing the respective roles of divine grace and human cooperation in the path toward mystical union. The first three dwelling places represent the more active stages, in which we are called to make efforts to cooperate with God's invitation to move toward the light within. The first dwelling place comprises knowledge of our sinfulness, invocation of the need for humility, as well as the moral efforts that mark the beginning stages of prayer. In the second dwelling place mortal sin is left behind as the soul progresses in the life of prayer. The third stage is the life of perseverance in prayer found in those who guard against venial sin — a state in which many devout souls find themselves over a long period of time. In all these active states Teresa insists on the necessity for humility, because the distractions of exterior things and diabolic temptation can easily lead to backsliding in those who are happy with their progress.

The fourth dwelling place begins the stages where God's gratuitous activity of infusing grace takes over and where the soul becomes increasingly passive to divine action. During these stages the soul becomes more and more conformed to Christ — the goal of Teresa's mystical path can be described as both christological and trinitarian. The fourth place mingles the activity reflected in the "consolations" which we acquire by our own meditations and petitions to God with the passivity of the "spiritual delight" given only by God. "However diligent our efforts we cannot acquire it," she says (*Interior Castle* 4.2.6). The last three dwelling places deal with three progressively deeper forms of mystical union. Teresa pictures these stages according to an analogy with human marriage. The fifth dwelling place, also called the "prayer of union," is the "first meeting" of the prospective bride with the Divine Bridegroom and is marked by what Teresa calls the "sleep of the senses," short periods of abstraction from ordinary consciousness. The longest part of *The Interior Castle* deals with the sixth dwelling place, the stage of betrothal and the union of rapture. Here Teresa treats a range of topics, such as the nature of ecstasy, divine locutions, the wound of love, or transverberation, and the forms of visions that accompany these unusual mystical graces. These extraordinary graces marked the acme of the mystical journey in *The Life*. But here the mature Teresa teaches that the goal is higher: the seventh dwelling place, the state of mystical marriage. In this stage the mystic attains a deep union in the Trinity achieved through Christ, one in which "the soul always remains with its God in that center [i.e, of the soul]" (7.2.4). In this permanent union, where direct vision of divine truth is always present (if not always directly adverted to), raptures are left behind, and Mary, the symbol of contemplation, and Martha, the symbol of the active life of service to others, become one.

Reading Teresa

As suggested, the reader would best start with *The Interior Castle,* and then move backward to *The Life* and *The Way of Perfection.* Teresa also wrote *Meditations on the Song of Songs,* which unfortunately survive only in part, and other minor prose works and poems, as well as almost five hundred letters. A good translation of *The Interior Castle* by Kieran Kavanaugh and Otilio Rodriguez can be found in CWS 14. Teresa's other writings can be found in *The Collected Works of St. Teresa of Avila,* trans. Kieran Kavanaugh and Otilio Rodriguez, 2 vols. (Washington, D.C.: Institute of Carmelite Studies, 1980).

Bibliography

Gillian T. W. Ahlgren. *Teresa and the Politics of Sanctity.* Ithaca, N.Y.: Cornell University Press, 1996. A study of how Teresa struggled to get a hearing in Counter-Reformation Spain.

Jodi Bilinkoff. *The Avila of St. Teresa: Religious Reform in a Sixteenth-Century City.* Ithaca, N.Y.: Cornell University Press, 1989. Important for Teresa's historical context.

Michel de Certeau. *The Mystic Fable.* Vol. 1: *The Sixteenth and Seventeenth Centuries.* Chicago: University of Chicago Press, 1992. Chap. 6, contains important reflections on Teresa.

E. W. Trueman Dicken. *The Crucible of Love: A Study of the Mysticism of St. Teresa and St. John of the Cross.* New York: Sheed and Ward, 1963. Although it tries to force a concordance between Teresa and John at times, this detailed study still repays reading.

Mary Frohlich. *The Intersubjectivity of the Mystic: A Study of Teresa of Avila's "Interior Castle."* Atlanta: Scholars Press, 1993. A difficult but rewarding analysis of Teresa's notion of mystical transformation in the light of Bernard Lonergan's cognitional theory.

Alison Weber. *Teresa of Avila and the Rhetoric of Femininity.* Princeton, N.J.: Princeton University Press, 1990. A useful study of Teresa's rhetorical strategy.

Rowan Williams. *Teresa of Avila.* London: Geoffrey Chapman, 1991. A good brief introduction to Teresa's theology.

27

PETER CANISIUS

(1521–97)

FEAST: DECEMBER 21

ON MAY 8, 1521, the Edict of Worms placed the Augustinian monk Martin Luther under the imperial ban, confirming that the papal condemnation of his teaching and his formal excommunication issued on January 3 of that year now had secular authorization. Of the many dates for the beginning of the Reformation (October 1518 is the most popular), this official event ranks high with the other contenders. Whenever the Reformation may have been said to have begun, it is ironic to note that it was on this same May 8 of 1521, in the Dutch city of Nijmegen, that Peter Kanis, future *doctor ecclesiae* and "hammer of heretics," the foremost opponent of Lutheranism in sixteenth-century Germany, was born. What is more, in the same month a Basque soldier named Ignatius of Loyola was gravely wounded in the wars between France and Spain. The ex-soldier Ignatius was to experience a conversion during his convalescence and go on to found the Jesuit order, the bulwark of the Roman Catholic counterattack against the Reformation. Peter Kanis, known to history as Peter "Canisius," was Ignatius's personal choice to lead the Catholic resistance in Germany. This confluence of events highlights controversies we now find painful, yet they are an unavoidable part of the history of Christianity and its doctors.

The story of the doctors of the church has always been connected with the history of the divisions in Christianity. In the fourth and fifth centuries, the first major group of doctors worked to combat Arians, Nestorians, Monophysites, and other heretics. No Arian churches survive (though there have always been individual Arians, such as the English poet John Milton). Nestorian and Monophysite Christian communities exist to this day. Many of the later medieval doctors (e.g., Anselm, Bonaventure, Aquinas) were involved in the polemics between Eastern and Western Christendom, divisions that are still sadly evident. The sixteenth century, however, witnessed an even more divisive era of the history of Christianity. Western Christendom, for all its variety, had maintained a basic, if messy, unity during the Middle Ages. This was fractured in the sixteenth century when Protestant Christianity broke away from the medieval consensus and when modern Roman Catholicism reformulated the medieval church in new directions.

All of the post-1500 *doctores ecclesiae* (the sixteenth century saw the birth of more doctors than any other century since the fourth) had impeccable anti-Protestant credentials. Of the sixteenth-century doctors, two (Teresa of Avila and John of the Cross), were personally removed from the areas where the struggle between Protestants and Catholics was most intense, though they were resolutely anti-Protestant. The lives of the other four doctors (the Jesuits Peter Canisius and Robert Bellarmine, the Capuchin Lawrence of Brindisi, and Francis de Sales) were deeply interwoven with the tensions, controversies, and polemics over the soul of Christendom.

Peter Kanis lost his mother at an early age, but his father and stepmother raised him in an atmosphere of great devotion. Nijmegen at that time was part of the archdiocese of Cologne, so Peter went there to study. His father wished him to marry and pursue a worldly career, but Peter took a vow of celibacy and pursued courses in theology. In 1542 he heard a series of sermons delivered by Peter Faber, the first disciple of Ignatius of Loyola. (The Jesuit order had gained official papal approbation in 1540.) Peter made the "Spiritual Exercises" that Ignatius had created to help believers make a fundamental election, or choice of life. As a result of this experience, he decided to enter the new order, becoming the first German Jesuit. On May 8, 1543, his twenty-second birthday, he wrote: "I, Peter Canisius of Nijmegen, today make a simple vow to God and the Virgin Mary, before St. Michael the Archangel and all the saints, that I will place myself under the obedience of the Company called that of Jesus Christ" [i.e., the Jesuits]. Peter was ordained in 1546 and began his career as writer and editor with an edition of the sermons of the German mystic John Tauler, as well as the works of two doctors of the church, Cyril of Alexandria and Leo the Great. He then served as a theological consultant at the first sessions of the Council of Trent (1545–63), the meeting of Catholic bishops summoned by Paul III to combat Protestantism and to reform the corrupt practices that had led to the split in Western Christendom.

At this point, it is important to distinguish between two aspects of the Roman Catholicism of the sixteenth century — Catholic Reform and Counter-Reformation. Throughout the late medieval period, voices had been raised against the many abuses in Latin Christendom. In the sixteenth century, even before Luther's reaction, reform movements were underway in many areas — doctrinal, organizational, devotional, and moral — that blossomed as the century progressed. This is what historians refer to when they speak of "Catholic Reform." Nevertheless, the tremendous challenge presented by Luther and the other early Protestant leaders provoked a polemical reaction, a "Counter-Reformation," which sought to refute Protestantism as heretical and to combat it by every means possible. The Council of Trent was the foundation of the Counter-Reformation, though many of the council documents also dealt with issues of Catholic Reform. Peter Canisius and the other non-Spanish doctors of the sixteenth century were both "Counter-Reformationists" in their opposition to Protestant theology, as well as "Catholic Reformers" in their commitment to improving Roman Catholicism.

Peter was soon summoned to Rome by Ignatius himself, who quickly recognized the talents of the young man from Nijmegen. After several years of service in Italy, in 1549 he was sent back to Germany at the request of Duke William IV of Bavaria, who was anxious to find teachers and preachers to combat the inroads of Protestantism in his domains. Peter was to labor in this contested vineyard for the rest of his life.

Although Luther had died in 1546, Protestantism continued to spread in Germany. The major ground of contention between the Roman Catholic and the Reformed versions of Christianity now centered on the south German lands. The retention of these areas for Roman Catholicism was in large part due to the activities of the new apostolic orders, such as the Jesuits and Capuchin Franciscans, who were not fettered with the abuses of the older religious congregations and whose energy and total obedience to the Counter-Reformation program created by the Council of Trent became legendary. Without this defense, Roman Catholicism might have become a largely "Mediterranean" form of Christianity. Its European-wide dimensions, as well as the wider global presence begun by the spread of Catholicism to the New World in the sixteenth century, were closely tied to the new religious orders.

Peter Canisius's older contemporary among the early Jesuits, St. Francis Xavier (1506–52), was the paragon of early Jesuit success in the "foreign" missions of India and China. Peter's strenuous efforts in Germany were an equally impressive story in the realm of the "internal" mission to revitalize moribund Catholicism and to combat Protestantism. Over a period of almost fifty years (1549–97), Peter was active in a variety of German-speaking cities: Ingolstadt, Vienna, Prague, Augsburg, Dillingen, Innsbruck, and Freiburg in Switzerland. He took part in the 1557 Colloquy of Worms, one of the last attempts to reach a compromise with Protestantism, but he found the discussions useless. In 1561 he was again present at the sessions of the Council of Trent, addressing the assembly on the Eucharist and Index of Prohibited Books. The most important initiative of Peter and the Jesuits against Protestantism, however, was educational. Wherever he went, Peter founded schools, colleges, seminaries, and even what became the university of Freiburg. A better educated clergy and laity, Peter rightly thought, was the key to resisting Protestantism.

Peter Canisius was not only a founder, an organizer, and an active provincial leader of the Jesuits, he was a powerful preacher (five volumes of sermons survive), as well as an effective writer. Though he treated many subjects, it was not as an original theologian that Peter made his mark, but as a catechist. Luther's large and small catechisms, published in 1529, had done much for the spread of the Reformation. Though other Catholics had tried to counter Luther's popular appeal, none of the previous Catholic entries into the arena of popular catechisms had been very successful. Peter's ability to give a clear and correct communication of standard Catholic teaching provided the answer that German Catholics had needed. His catechisms became instant best-sellers and remained in use down to the nineteenth century.

Peter composed three catechisms, each adapted for a particular audience. In these works, the Jesuit eschewed direct attacks on Protestantism, but refused to compromise on any of the issues under dispute between Protestants and Catholics. The *Great Catechism* (*Summa doctrinae christianae*), first published in Vienna in 1555, was designed for the clergy and educators. Employing a question-and-answer format, the work consisted of 213 questions in sixty-nine folio pages. Peter divided the book into two sections. The first was devoted to "Wisdom," treating the Creed, the Lord's Prayer, the Hail Mary, the ten commandments, the precepts of the church, and the seven sacraments (emphasizing those denied by Protestants). The second part was devoted to "Justice" and aimed at producing a solid Catholic piety. It treated such topics as the four kinds of sin, the cardinal virtues, the gifts of the Holy Spirit, and the evangelical counsels. To convey the church's teaching to wider audiences, Peter adapted his catechism for children, publishing the *Baby Catechism* (*Catechismus minimus*) in 1556. Even more popular was the version he made for adolescents in 1559, the *Small Catechism of Catholics* (*Parvus Catechismus catholicorum*). These works, often reprinted, translated, and illustrated, avoided scholastic terminology, basing the presentation of the faith on scripture and the fathers. It is ironic that of all the doctors of the church, Peter Canisius, who could well be called the "Catechism Doctor," is not mentioned in the recent *Catechism of the Catholic Church* (see Appendix III).

Reading Peter Canisius

Versions of Canisius's *Catechisms* were made in English for the service of the Counter-Reformation activities of the Jesuits. One of these has been reprinted: *St. Peter Canisius: A Summe of Christian Doctrine [1592–96]*, English Recusant Literature 35 (Menston, England: Scolar Press, 1971).

Bibliography

James Brodrick. *Saint Peter Canisius, S.J. 1521–97.* Baltimore: Carroll Press, 1960. This large biography (over eight hundred pages) contains everything anyone would ever want to know about Canisius, though it is also quite readable.

28

JOHП OF
THE CROSS
(1542–91)

THE SUMMER HEAT in the Spanish city of Toledo can be almost murderous, especially if one is imprisoned in a cell six feet by ten with only a high slit in one wall for light and ventilation. This was the case in June 1578, for the prisoner, known to history as St. John of the Cross, who had been captured six months before by members of his own Carmelite order as a renegade and troublemaker. Such was the Christian charity of John's religious brethren that he had been subjected to many terrible punishments, including daily scourging and near starvation. These trials had brought him close to death. One stifling summer evening, however, John overheard a love song being sung in the street outside his prison — a young man was serenading his girl friend with the words: "I am dying of love, dear. What shall I do? Die!" Suddenly, the friar was carried off into an ecstatic experience of the overwhelming power of divine love. When he returned to the more quotidian realm of poetic inspiration, he began to compose a lyric he later called the "Cántico espiritual" ("Spiritual Canticle") to try to express what he had experienced. This poem and another written down shortly after his escape, "En una noche oscura" ("On a Dark Night"), formed the basis for the mystical *summa* that John was to write after his almost miraculous escape from prison on August 16, 1578.

John of the Cross was born in 1542 as Juan de Yepes y Alvarez into a poor family in Castile. At the age of twenty-one he joined the Carmelite order, a religious group that had begun in the twelfth century as hermits in the Holy Land, but that in the later Middle Ages had evolved as a mendicant order spread over Western Europe. The ongoing tension in the history of the Carmelite order between eremitical retreat and active involvement in pastoral ministry influenced the career of John and the woman who was his penitent, his inspiration, and his mystical confidant, Teresa of Avila.

Between 1564 and 1568 John studied at Salamanca, receiving a solid theological training in one of the centers of Counter-Reformation theology. In September of 1567 he met Teresa of Avila, who had just begun her reform of the Carmelite nuns, seeking to return those members of the order who were willing to the ascetical and contemplative traditions that had been neglected in recent centuries. In November of 1568, John accepted the reformed habit sewn for him by Teresa herself, changed his name to Brother John of the Cross, and became the spearhead in expanding Teresa's reform among the male Carmelites. Reaction against the reform movement, however, was strong. The conflict within the Carmelite order between the adherents of the status quo and the reformers (the groups later came to be termed "Calced" and "Discalced," over the issue of whether footwear was allowed) was what led to John's nearly fatal prison experience.

For five years (1572–77), John was the confessor at the convent of the Encarnación in Avila, where Teresa herself was prioress for part of the time. Though their time together was brief, these two giants of the Carmelite reform and premier mystics of the sixteenth century obviously had a close personal bond and influenced each other to a remarkable degree. Still, there were differences between their temperaments and teachings that later homogenizing tendencies in twentieth-century neoscholastic theories of mysticism glossed over all too easily. In 1575 the political struggle within the Carmelite order shifted in favor of the anti-reform movement. This allowed John's enemies within the order to kidnap and imprison him (Teresa complained to everyone within hearing distance, including the king of Spain). After his escape, Friar John, empowered by his near-death experience, began his writing career. First, he recorded the two poems that reflected his experience of God while in prison, and then, between 1582 and 1587, he wrote a remarkable series of prose works commenting on these two prison poems, as well as a third lyric, "Llama de amor viva" ("The Living Flame of Love") that he had composed in a state of ecstasy in 1585.

Most of the doctors of the church expressed their teaching in prose, although often the rhetorical prose of sermonic eloquence. Ephrem, the "Harp of the Holy Spirit," is the only other doctor whose inspiration as a poet compares to John of the Cross. John, however, is unique in the way in which he interwove the poetic and prose expressions of his doctrine of mystical purgation and transformation. On the basis of three relatively brief poems (forty stanzas of the "Spiritual Canticle," eight for the "Dark Night," and only four for the "Living Flame"), John constructed an impressive edifice of four commentaries of over a thousand pages to "explain" (insofar as there can be any explanation) the mystery of the love affair between God and humans. From

the perspective of literary criticism, John's poems, in the words of Gerald Brenan, mark him as "one of the supreme lyric poets of any age or country." The
theologian Hans Urs von Balthasar went so far as to say that it is as a poet
rather than a prose writer that John is a doctor of the church, but it is not
really necessary to choose between the poet and the expositor.

John continued to work for the Carmelite reform in various capacities after
his escape from prison. His service in ecclesiastical offices, however, was less
important than his continuing penetration into the "dark night of the soul"
that leads to union with God, as well as his guidance of those who turned
to him for advice in making this perilous and difficult journey. In 1587 the
Discalced Carmelite reform finally won approval by Pope Sixtus V, but this
was not the end of John's trials. In 1590 John told his brother Francisco that
Jesus had spoken to him one evening when he was praying before a crucifix
and told the friar that he could ask for any favor he wished. In conformity
with his commitment to inner suffering and negation, John responded, "Lord,
make me to suffer and be despised for your sake." John got his wish. Because he had incurred the wrath of the new vicar general of the Discalced
Carmelites, he was dismissed from his offices in 1591 and suffered greatly
from persecution and illness before his death on December 14, 1591. John
died as the midnight bell for Matins was being rung with the words "Tonight
I shall sing matins in heaven" on his lips.

In the Carmelite's four great mystical treatises he daringly comments on
his poems as if they were the equivalent of the biblical love-lyric, the Song of
Songs, that had provided the base text for so much of the history of Christian
mysticism. This is not because John had any exalted view of himself or of
his poetic gifts — utter negation of self was the core of his teaching — but
because he was convinced that these poems were not his but God's: a true
"re-creation" of the Bible's Song of Love. In response to the request of Sister
Ana de Jesús, John wrote a commentary on the "Spiritual Canticle" between
1582 and 1584, expounding it as an allegory of the soul's journey to God
through the traditional stages of the purgative, illuminative, and unitive ways.
This was later revised on the basis of an expanded text of the poem (1585–
86). John's shorter prison poem, "In a Dark Night," became the subject of
a longer work in two parts, the book he called *The Dark Night of the Ascent
of Mount Carmel* (1582–85), traditionally divided into *The Ascent of Mount
Carmel* and the shorter *Dark Night of the Soul*. John dealt with only the first
three stanzas of this brief poem in these books, but in such length that this
text on the purgative aspect of his mystical teaching has often been given
more attention than his reflections on the higher mystical stages found in
the other works. Finally, John wrote two commentaries on the third of his
mystical poems, "The Living Flame." The first version was composed about
1585, and the revised text was completed in the last months of his life.

The complex evolution of John's four mystical commentaries is worth reviewing, if only because it underlines how difficult it is to get a full sense of

his teaching without reviewing all his works. Taken as a whole, they constitute an exposition of mystical transformation unrivaled in its scope and depth
of analysis. Like Teresa, John is much concerned with careful analysis of the
relation between human and divine activity in the path to union. Where he
goes beyond Teresa (without necessarily disagreeing with her) is in the ample
attention he gives to the role of the faculties of the soul in the production of
the mystical "self," that is, the person who has attained what John calls "sub-
stantial union" with God in the "center of the soul" (see especially *Spiritual
Canticle,* stanza 39).

The necessity for purging the human subject of all its selfish attachments
had always been emphasized by mystics. The infinite distance between God
and human can be overcome only by a radical negation of all our customary
ways of thinking and acting. Other contemporary mystics, like Catherine of
Genoa (d. 1510), had given purgation a central role in their teaching, but no
one before John of the Cross had emphasized the "dark night" of purgation so
emphatically and analyzed it with such subtlety. As for another contemporary
(with whom he would not have liked to be compared), that is, Martin Luther,
for John of the Cross it is the dark and painful way of reliance on faith alone
that leads to God. "For a soul to attain to the state of perfection," John says
(*Ascent* 1.1.1), "it ordinarily has to pass through two principal kinds of night,
which spiritual persons call purgations or purifications of the soul. Here we
call them nights, for in both of them the soul journeys, as it were, by night,
in darkness." John says that the term "night" is appropriate for three reasons:
first, because purgation involves stripping away "desire for all worldly things";
second, because the road the soul must travel is that of faith, "which is as
dark as night to the understanding"; and third, because "God is equally dark
night to the soul in this life" (*Ascent* 1.2.1). The first night is the "night
of the senses," the second is the "night of the spirit." John divides each of
these nights into two parts, an active night where we cooperate with grace
in the process of stripping away what divides us from God, and the passive
night "wherein the soul does nothing and God works in it" (*Ascent* 1.13.1).
The highest stage (though John insists that all the nights go on at the same
time) is the passive night of the spirit, which is "an inflowing of God into the
soul that purges it from all its ignorances and imperfections, habitual, natural,
and spiritual, and which is called by contemplatives infused contemplation,
or mystical theology.... This divine wisdom is not only night and darkness
for the soul, but it is likewise affliction and torment" (*Dark Night* 2.5.1–2). In
the mysticism of John of the Cross "nothing" (*nada*) is everything. The soul
must be reduced to nothing in order to find the Nothing that is God.

The highest stage of purgation, terrible as it is, overlaps with the traditional levels of illumination and union that John treats in detail in his two
other works, *The Spiritual Canticle* and *The Living Flame of Love.* Here again,
John shows himself to be not only a master of the previous mystical teaching of Latin Christendom, but also a doctor of great originality. In these

works the love-language of the poetic base text comes to the fore. In *The Spiritual Canticle* pure disinterested love leads the soul through the various stages of purgation (stanzas 1–12) to the spiritual betrothal, or stage of illumination and rapture (stanzas 13–21), which prepares it for the ultimate experience possible in this life, the full union of spiritual marriage (stanzas 22–35), which is a foretaste of the union of glory in heaven (stanzas 36–40). As the last stanzas of *The Spiritual Canticle* and the whole of *The Living Flame of Love* insist, mystical union is essentially trinitarian — a form of knowing by unknowing, that is, an indescribable intuitive and intersubjective sharing in the life of the three Persons of the Trinity. "There would not be a true and total transformation of the soul," John says, "if the soul were not transformed in the three Persons of the Most Holy Trinity in an open and manifest degree.... For the soul, united and transformed in God, breathes in God into God the very same divine breath that God, when she is transformed in him, breathes into her in himself" (*Spiritual Canticle*, Stanza 39.3).

Reading John of the Cross

There are many versions of John's poems. My favorite is Roy Campbell, *Poems of St. John of the Cross* (New York: Pantheon, 1951). For a selection of the prose works, see *John of the Cross: Selected Writings*, CWS 53. The complete four commentaries exist in two good versions, the first by the noted scholar of Spanish mysticism E. Allison Peers, and the more recent version of Kieran Kavanaugh and Otilio Rodriguez, *The Collected Works of John of the Cross* (Washington, D.C.: ICS, 1991).

Bibliography

Gerald Brenan. *St. John of the Cross: His Life and Poetry.* Cambridge: Cambridge University Press, 1973. A sensitive appreciation of John's life and poetry.

Crisógono de Jesús Sacramentado. *The Life of St. John of the Cross.* London: Longmans, Green, 1958. The standard biography, though there are later editions in Spanish.

God Speaks in the Night: The Life, Times, and Teaching of St. John of the Cross. Trans. Kieran Kavanaugh. Washington, D.C.: ICS, 1991. A good collection of essays.

Jacques Maritain. *Distinguish to Unite, or The Degrees of Knowledge.* New York: Scribner, 1959. Chaps. 8–9 contain an important analysis of John's view of contemplative knowing and union.

Steven Payne. *John of the Cross and the Cognitive Value of Mysticism.* Dordrecht: Kluwer Academic Publishers, 1990. An important analysis of mystical knowing in John.

Edith Stein. *The Science of the Cross.* Chicago: Henry Regnery, 1960. Recently canonized Carmelite nun's study of John.

Karol Wojtyla. *Faith according to St. John of the Cross.* San Francisco: Ignatius Press, 1981. A translation of the present pope's doctoral dissertation.

29

ROBERT BELLARMINE
(1542–1621)

FEAST: SEPTEMBER 17

N MARCH 3, 1599, Pope Clement VIII advanced the Jesuit scholar and theologian Robert Bellarmine to the position of cardinal of the Roman Catholic Church. During his pontificate, which lasted from 1592 to 1605, Clement had already established a track record for promoting distinguished figures to the purple, as witnessed in his making the noted church historian Cesare Baronio a cardinal in 1596. In elevating Robert Bellarmine, however, the pope went out of his way to praise the recipient with these words: "We elect this man because the Church of God has not his equal in learning." The Jesuit order and Robert himself protested against the promotion in vain. When Robert attempted to urge objections during the ceremony, the imperious pope commanded him to keep silent under pain of excommunication. Robert's advancement was not only a good witness to Clement's discernment of character, but also a not-so-covert criticism of his predecessor, Pope Sixtus V (1585–90), whose death had prevented him from putting Cardinal Bellarmine's greatest work, the *Disputations about the Controversies of the Christian Faith against the Heretics of the Age*, on the "Index of Forbidden Books." (In this work Robert had argued that the papacy had only indirect power in temporal affairs — a position which angered Pope Sixtus.)

Robert Bellarmine was born in Montepulciano in Tuscany of an impoverished noble family. His uncle, Marcello Cervini, reigned briefly as the reforming Pope Marcellus II in 1555, but the young Roberto made his way up the church hierarchy not by traditional nepotism, but by his power of in-

tellect and tenacity of will hidden in a slight and sickly body. In 1560 he
entered the Jesuit order and studied subsequently at Rome, Padua, and Louvain. Ordained in 1570, he taught at Louvain until 1576, combatting the
errors of the Protestants and Michael Baius (1513–89), a Louvain professor of theology who adhered to a strict late Augustinian position on grace
and free will and whose views were condemned by Pius V in 1567. In 1576
Bellarmine was recalled to Rome to take up the new chair of "Controversial
Theology" at the Jesuit Collegium Romanum, which had been founded by
Ignatius Loyola in 1551, but was officially recognized in 1582 by Pope Gregory XIII (from whom it receives its name, the "Gregorian University"). Here
Bellarmine began to give lectures to prepare Jesuits and other clerics to answer the challenge posed by Protestant theology. These eventually grew into
the most important sixteenth-century Roman Catholic theological response
to Protestantism, the three volumes of the *Disputations* (1586–93). The publication of these volumes, the first systematic refutation of the Protestant
position, marked a new era in the theological encounter between Catholicism and Reformation Christianity. Bellarmine was not a polemical ranter,
but an immensely learned and methodical opponent that Protestant theologians could not ignore. Although he was well trained in the philosophical
argumentation of the great age of "Second Scholasticism," as Catholic theology of the sixteenth and seventeenth centuries has been called, Bellarmine
utilized a good deal of the historical research that he and Cardinal Baronio
had compiled against the Protestant position. The *Disputations* may not have
made many converts, but they initiated thousands of pages of response and
counterargument from Protestant controversialists.

In 1592 Bellarmine was made rector of the Roman College. The same
year also saw the publication of the "Sixto-Clementine" version of the Vulgate on which the Jesuit had expended much labor to clean up the errors that
Pope Sixtus had introduced with his own arbitrary editing of the first version.
Like his Jesuit confrere Peter Canisius, Bellarmine entered the catechetical
arena, publishing a very popular *Brief Christian Doctrine* in 1597 (it was translated into sixty-two languages), and a more expanded catechism, *The Longer
Declaration of Christian Doctrine,* in 1598. After 1599, Bellarmine's life combined his skills as a controversialist with the day-to-day toil of a busy curial
official. In 1602 Pope Clement surprisingly named him bishop of the poor diocese of Capua, and Robert exercised the pastoral office there with distinction
until 1605, when he was called back to Rome for the papal conclave which
eventually elected Paul V (1605–21).

Pope Paul insisted that Bellarmine remain in Rome, where he could utilize
his talents. The Jesuit defended the pope's action in placing Venice under
interdict in 1606. In 1609 he wrote an anonymous pamphlet attacking the
loyalty oath that James I of England had demanded from his subjects, since
it involved a rejection of the papacy and Catholic doctrine. The king himself
responded and Bellarmine wrote a rejoinder under his own name. In 1610 the

Jesuit returned to the issue of papal power in an attack on royal absolutism entitled *The Power of the Pope in Temporal Affairs against William Barclay*. Bellarmine's ongoing insistence on the right of the popes to depose monarchs in this work was deeply controversial, even to many Catholics. Another doctor of the church, Francis de Sales, though he respected Bellarmine, wrote to a friend in 1611: "I have not found to my taste certain writings of a saintly and most excellent prelate in which he touches on the indirect power of the pope over princes. Whether his theory is right or wrong is not for me to judge, but only that at the present time, when we have so many external enemies, I think it behooves us not to cause any stirs within the body of the church."

Robert Bellarmine was a theologian and historian, but no scientist. As a firm Aristotelian and adherent to the literal sense of the Bible, as well as in his official capacity as the head of the Holy Office, the curial congregation in charge of protecting the faith, Bellarmine played an unfortunate role in the early stages of the case against Galileo. In 1616 he personally delivered the command to Galileo to cease teaching that the earth revolved around the sun — another example of the fallibility of all the *doctores ecclesiae*.

The last decade of Bellarmine's life, however, was more devoted to the writing of spiritual works than to controversy. In 1611 he published his large *Commentary on the Psalms* and later a number of devotional treatises. Two of these can be considered classic works: *The Mind's Ascent to God by the Ladder of Created Things* (1615) and *The Art of Dying Well* (1620). Unlike Bonaventure's work of the same title (which he knew and admired), Bellarmine's book on the ascent to God is not a mystical text, but rather a rhetorical panegyric in the Renaissance mode designed to lift the soul up to admiration and love of God through praise of the created universe. In this sense *The Mind's Ascent* is a kind of commentary on "The Contemplation for Obtaining Love," which ends Ignatius's "Spiritual Exercises." It also reflects the anti-mystical tenor that had developed in the Jesuit order at the end of the sixteenth century. So too *The Art of Dying Well*, though it taps into the long medieval tradition of handbooks for the dying, is a new kind of book — a sober, ascetic, and deeply moralistic meditation on death of an almost Stoic character.

Reading Robert Bellarmine

The Mind's Ascent to God and *The Art of Dying Well* are now available in *Robert Bellarmine: Spiritual Writings*, trans. and ed. John Patrick Donnelly and Roland J. Teske, CWS 61. The only part of the cardinal's *Disputations* to be translated is the important section on political authority, *De laicis sive saecularibus*. See *De Laicis or the Treatise on Civil Government by Robert Bellarmine*, trans. Kathleen E. Murphy (New York: Fordham University Press, 1928). Also available in English is *The Power of the Pope in Temporal Affairs against William Barclay* trans. George Albert Moore (Chevy Chase, Md.: Country Dollar Press, 1950).

Bibliography

Richard J. Blackwell. *Galileo, Bellarmine, and the Bible.* Notre Dame, Ind.: University of Notre Dame Press, 1991. A study of Bellarmine's involvement in the beginnings of the Galileo case.

James Brodrick. *Robert Bellarmine: Saint and Scholar.* Westminster, Md.: Newman Press, 1961. An excellent biography; to be preferred to Brodrick's original two-volume work published in 1928.

John Courtney Murray. "St. Robert Bellarmine on the Indirect Power," *Theological Studies* 9 (1948): 491–535. Classic study of Bellarmine's view of papal power by a great modern theologian.

30

LAWRENCE
OF BRINDISI

(1559–1619)

FEAST: JULY 22

O CTOBER 9, 1601. The army of Holy Roman Emperor Rudolph II under the command of archduke Matthias confronted a much larger Turkish force outside Alba Regalis (today Szekesfehervar) in the middle of the Hungarian plain. In the Archduke's train was a chaplain, the Capuchin friar Lawrence of Brindisi, who had been sent by Pope Clement VIII to spread the Capuchin reform and missionize against heresy in Austria and Bohemia. Friar Lawrence addressed the troops, encouraging them to fight boldly and promising them victory: "Forward! Victory is ours," he shouted. Then, astride a horse and waving his crucifix, he led them against the Turks. In the thick of the battle, exposed to every danger, he miraculously emerged unscathed. The Christian army triumphed and Friar Lawrence was hailed as a hero; his wonder-working crucifix was later treated as a relic. Lawrence of Brindisi is the only doctor of the church to have led an army in battle.

The future doctor was born at Brindisi in 1559 as Giulio Cesare de Rossi. Educated by the conventual Franciscans both in Brindisi and Venice, he entered the Capuchin branch of the Franciscan order at the age of sixteen, taking the name Lawrence (Lorenzo). The Capuchin reform, begun in 1526, was an attempt to return the order to the more ascetic and fervent days of St. Francis. Their austerity and devotion made them one of the most important religious groups in the Catholic reaction to the rise of Protestantism that we call the Counter-Reformation. Friar Lawrence's life and writings bear ample witness both to this Catholic counterattack and to the impetus of the internal Catholic reform movement of his era.

Friar Lawrence was sent to the university at Padua to pursue philosophical and theological studies. Here his prodigious memory allowed him to master many languages, both ancient and modern, including Hebrew and Syriac. Ordained a priest in 1582, he spent seven years as lecturer in theology and novice master before becoming first the provincial of Tuscany and then one of the members of the Superior Council of the Capuchin order. It was during this period (1596–1602) that Lawrence was called upon to travel beyond the Alps to set up new houses, convert Protestants, and eventually to serve as a military chaplain. The reputation he acquired in ably fulfilling these tasks led him to be elected minister general of the Capuchins in 1602. Lawrence's talents as linguist, preacher, administrator, and diplomat were recognized by a succession of pontiffs and by many of the rulers of Europe. He traveled over much of Europe, walking barefoot in rain and snow. After he refused to serve for a second term as minister general in 1605, Pope Paul V sent him once again to the court at Vienna with a mandate to work for converting heretics. Here he engaged in controversy with the Lutheran theologian Polycarp Leyser and wrote the most important of his polemical works, the *Representation of Lutheranism* (*Hypotyposis Lutheranismi*) in 1607–8. This work had three parts: a personal attack on Luther; a doctrinal refutation of Lutheran errors; and a rebuttal of the pamphlet Leyser had written against him. Unfortunately, Lawrence was so busy with his ambassadorial tasks that he never published the book.

Both Jesuits and Capuchins became deeply embroiled in the political maneuverings of this age of conflict between Protestants and Catholics, conflicts that also involved political and dynastic ambitions. In France, the "Grey Eminence," the Capuchin Joseph of Paris, was soon to become Cardinal Richelieu's right-hand man in his anti-Hapsburg policies between 1624 and 1638. Between 1609 and 1618 Lawrence exercised a rather similar, if less partisan, role as diplomat for the papacy, the Hapsburgs, and especially his close friend, Duke Maximilian of Bavaria. Perhaps the most notable of his diplomatic successes was in gaining the support of Philip III of Spain for the Catholic League that Maximilian had organized to oppose the Evangelical Union of Protestant princes (1609–10).

Worn out by his many activities and travels, Lawrence eventually retired to Naples in 1618, only to have to take on one more delicate diplomatic task. The nobility of Naples, chafing under the oppression of the Spanish viceroy Don Pedro Osuna, asked Lawrence to appeal to the king of Spain to have him removed. In secrecy Lawrence traveled to Madrid and then on to Lisbon to meet the king. Difficult negotiations ensued. Osuna was eventually recalled, but not before Lawrence, exhausted by his travels and diplomatic activities, had died on July 22, 1619.

Lawrence of Brindisi wrote an incredible amount for a person who was kept so busy. The fifteen volumes of his *Opera Omnia,* edited by the Italian Capuchins, contain 8,451 pages. Most of what survives is in the form of sermons — 804 altogether, often grouped according to the liturgical year. Lawrence, like his contemporary Francis de Sales, had received a broad humanistic education. His optimism and emphasis on the love of God above all things is reminiscent of the bishop of Geneva, but there is no evidence of direct contact between the two. In keeping with his Franciscanism, what is most evident about the Capuchin is his devotion to the universal primacy of Christ and the concomitant stress on Mary the Mother of God. Lawrence's most famous work is what he called the *Mariale,* the most important Mariological treatise of its time. The *Mariale* consists of eighty-four sermons grouped around twelve topics. Particularly important for providing a sense of Lawrence's contribution to Christian teaching are the sixteen sermons commenting on the gospel for the Feast of the Annunciation, which constitute an impressive treatise on the Incarnation.

Reading Lawrence of Brindisi

To the best of my knowledge, nothing from Lawrence's extensive writings has been translated into English. The critical edition is *Opera Omnia,* 15 vols. (Padua, 1928–56). For those who read Latin, the Sermons on the Annunciation mentioned above can be found in vol. 1, 75–159. There is an Italian translation of the whole *Mariale.*

Bibliography

P. Arturo da Carmignano. *St. Lawrence of Brindisi.* Westminster, Md.: Newman Press, 1963. The only recent English life; unfortunately of an older style of hagiography.

D. Unger. "The Absolute Primacy of Christ Jesus and His Virgin Mother according to St. Lawrence," *Collectanea Franciscana* 22 (1952): 113–49. A consideration of one of the essential themes of Lawrence's theology.

31

Francis
de Sales

(1567–1622)

Feast: January 24

I N THE WINTER of 1586–87 a young student in Paris experienced six
weeks of living hell. Nineteen-year-old Francis of Sales (a castle in
Savoy) had been reading theology and had become obsessed with the
issue of predestination. In the contentious debates of the sixteenth century, both between Protestants and Catholics, and within diverse theological
camps in Tridentine Catholicism, predestination had emerged as an issue
both personal and theoretical. Francis had become convinced that he was
one of those whom God, for his own mysterious reasons, had eternally pre-
destined to hell. So powerful was this feeling of damnation that Francis could
scarcely sleep or eat; his health began to deteriorate. Recalling his despair in
a later note (the *Protestation*), he tells us that he tried to express his continuing love for God in the midst of this temptation with the words: "Whatever
happens, Lord, may I at least love you in this life if I cannot love you in
eternity, since no one can praise you in hell." Finally, one evening, as he
was returning from classes, he went into the neighborhood church of Saint
Etienne-des-Grès to pray. Kneeling before the statue of the Virgin Mary, he
began to read the prayer known as the *Memorare* — "Remember, O most
compassionate Virgin Mary, that never was it known that anyone who fled
to your protection, implored your help, or sought your intercession, was left
unaided." Suddenly, even miraculously, his despair was lifted. As his great
spiritual friend, St. Jane de Chantal, to whom he later spoke of the event,
tells us: "He said the prayer through, then rising, it came to him all at once
that his disease had fallen from him like leprous scales, and he felt himself

perfectly and completely whole." According to Francis's own *Protestation*, he heard a voice within him testifying that the temptation had been to "the glorification of my name, which is not He-who-damns [*damnificator*], but Jesus." Francis was ever after a strong spokesman for the importance of human freedom and the universal salvific will of God, agreeing with the Jesuits Luis de Molina (d. 1600) and Leonard Lessius (d. 1623) that God predestines souls to glory according to the merits he foresees. (Augustine held a different view.)

Francis de Sales's rescue from the pit of despair tells us much both about the man and his times. Religious certainty, both in the doctrinal sense and as a personal conviction of salvation, was an issue of crucial concern for Protestants and Catholics. Further, the conviction of the correctness of one's religious profession had cast Europe into the turmoil of the religious conflicts that were to cover Europe with blood down to 1648. A year after Francis's birth in 1567, Catholics had been driven out of neighboring Geneva by the triumph of Calvin's Reformed party, and France's eight Wars of Religion raged from 1562 to 1598 while he was growing up.

Francis was the eldest son of a proud aristocratic family. With his obvious gifts, his father destined him for a career as a soldier, or failing that, a lawyer. After extensive study in Paris (1581–88) and Padua (1588–92), Francis became bold enough to tell his father that he desired to become a priest. He was ordained for the diocese of Geneva in 1593 (the Catholic bishop lived in exile at Annecy) and began his pastoral career as preacher and guide of souls. His biographers and many correspondents testify that few pastors have been more accessible to their congregation; Francis was a model of Paul's desire to be "all things to everyone" (1 Cor. 9:22).

The character of Francis de Sales is justly recognized as among the most humane and winning of all the saints and doctors of the church. In a letter to Jane de Chantal he once said, "I am as human as anyone can possibly be" (*Works* 13:330). It was not a boast, but his way of expressing the solidarity he tried to find with everyone he encountered. In another place he asked, "Haven't I got a human heart and a nature that feels?" (*Works* 14:264). In his education, his literary style, and his broad humaneness, Francis was a perfect example of the Renaissance devotion to humanism; but for him humanism was legitimate only insofar as it aids humans to direct the fullness of their lives and gifts to God. It is not for nothing that his teaching has been described as the acme of "Devout Humanism."

The early years of Francis's priesthood saw him preaching in the Chablais area east and south of Geneva to win back these Reformed territories to Roman Catholicism. Though Francis was a strong opponent of Protestantism, he was unusual for his age in stressing the priority of invitation over coercion. As he put it, "I have said that whoever preaches with love preaches sufficiently against heretics, even though he may never say a controversial word" (*Works* 14:96–97). In 1599 he became coadjutor bishop to Geneva and succeeded to the see he never physically occupied in 1602. In the same year,

Francis spent seven months in Paris, where he made contact with groups of ecclesiastics and pious lay mystics, such as Pierre de Bérulle and Madame Barbe Acarie, who were laying the ground for the great florescence of mysticism in seventeenth-century France. It was during this time that the young bishop emerged in full confidence of his role as a guide of souls and author of the spiritual writings that were to transform post-Tridentine Catholicism.

In 1604 Francis first met a thirty-year-old aristocrat, Jane Frances de Freymont, Baroness de Chantal. After the death of her beloved husband in a hunting accident, she had been eagerly pursuing a more devout life, but one that would be compatible with her familial obligations. The forms of spiritual friendship (*amicitia spiritualis*) that have been important throughout the history of Christian mysticism have never been more evident and productive than in the case of the interchange between Francis and Jane for the nineteen remaining years of the bishop's life. (For some other examples of such bonds in the history of the doctors of the church, see Basil and Macrina, Jerome and Eustochium, Catherine of Siena and Raymond, and especially Teresa and John of the Cross.) Francis became Jane's spiritual guide and confidant, but it is clear that her own pursuit of the higher states of mystical consciousness was also important for his life and writing.

In 1610 the two collaborated to found a new form of religious life for women, the convent of the Visitation of Holy Mary at Annecy. This was the first form of religious life in the modern period created just for women. It was also a new "middle-of-the-road" society, rejecting the often lax late medieval convent life, while not holding the members to the intense asceticism of the newer religious orders, such as Teresa's Discalced Carmelites, which were often physically impossible for older or infirm women. The Visitandines, as they came to be called (there were eighty houses by Jane's death in 1641), were devoted to both interior contemplative prayer and the active apostolate of work with the poor and destitute. The many letters that Francis sent to Jane testify to the depth and importance of their mutual friendship in Christ. (Although about two thousand of her letters survive, Jane mysteriously destroyed almost all the letters she sent to Francis.) Their relationship was by no means static, especially because each partner was convinced that the human affection they felt for each other had to be rooted in something deeper. Francis once wrote to Jane: "Our Lord loves you, my mother; he will have you all his own. Take no other arm than his to support you.... Don't think any longer on the friendship or bond that God made between us — nor of your children, nor of your heart, nor of your own soul" (*Works* 3:115–18).

Francis wrote primarily for those he counseled. Over two thousand of his letters survive (vols. 11–21 of the twenty-six volumes in his collected works), along with many sermons and the *Spiritual Conferences* he gave to the Visitandine community. The bishop's fame, however, rests on two major works that also reflect his guidance of souls. The *Introduction to the Devout Life*, written between 1602 and 1608, began as a series of letters of spiritual direction to Madame de Charmoisy, the semifictional "dearest Philothea" of the text. The five parts of this popular introduction to Christian living fall into two large sections: the first dealing with the fervent soul's conversion to Christ; the second, her advance in the life of devotion. The term "devotion" is crucial to all Francis's writings. At the beginning of the *Introduction to the Devout Life* he defines it as follows: "Devotion is nothing other than that spiritual agility and vivacity by which charity works in us, or we work with her aid, with alacrity and affection." Devotion is the generosity and magnanimity of love. While the term later often came to be associated with a cloying and subservient piety, Francis viewed devotion as something spiritually strong and calm: "I do not desire a fantastic, fussy, melancholy, peevish, and lamenting devotion, but a piety gentle, gracious, calm, peaceable — in a word — that piety that finds favor first with God and then with humans" (*Works* 13:59). Moderation, discretion, insight into self and others, humility, simplicity, and above all "sweetness" (*douceur/suavitas*) are the characteristics of the truly devout life. Sweetness is not to be understood as weakness or mawkishness. It is a manner of life that allows the Christian to be always gentle and gracious toward others without attenuating essential values of the faith.

Henri Bremond, the great student of French spirituality, rightly said that the publication of Francis's *Introduction to the Devout Life* was "a landmark in the history of Christian life and thought." This is not because the *Introduction* represented a new message — most of what Francis said in this and his other books was deeply traditional — but because of the spirit and the way in which Francis was able to present how to live the Christian life to a new age. His optimism, his patience, his compassion, his confidence in the overwhelming power of God's love to overcome sin, and his message that all Christians in all walks of life were called to true devotion make the book one of the treasures of Christian spirituality.

The bishop's other great work was devoted to the higher, mystical dimensions of the Christian life. *The Treatise on the Love of God*, composed between 1608 and 1616, owes much to Francis's interaction with Jane. His reflections on her prayer life and his ability to synthesize the teaching of the great mystics of tradition (not least Teresa of Avila) give this work a unity and clarity rare among the classics of mysticism. The theme of the work is what was always central to Francis's teaching and preaching — pure love, or, in more detail, "the birth, the progress, and the decay of the operations, characteristics, benefits, and excellence of divine love" (Preface). The interior reform of the heart through what Francis called the love of complacence and the love of benevolence (see bk. 5) eventually lead the soul to the love of conformity and love of submission which unite the heart perfectly to God (bks. 7–9). Due to its size (twelve books that run to over five hundred pages), the *Treatise* has been less read than the *Introduction*, but it is an equally important contribution to the history of spirituality.

Reading Francis de Sales

There are many translations of Francis's two main works. Especially recommended are *St. Francis de Sales: Introduction to the Devout Life*, trans. John K. Ryan (Garden City, N.Y.: Doubleday, 1955); and *St. Francis de Sales: Treatise on the Love of God*, trans. Henry Benedict Mackey (Westminster, Md.: Newman Press, 1953). The preface to the latter work is a fine summary of Francis's thought. There are also a number of translations of Francis's letters; see especially *Francis de Sales, Jane de Chantal: Letters of Spiritual Direction*, trans. Péronne Marie Thibert, CWS 59.

Bibliography

Michael de la Bedoyere. *François de Sales*. New York: Harper, 1960. A readable biography.

Henri Bremond. A *Literary History of Religious Thought in France*. 3 vols. London: SPCK, 1928–36. Vol. 1, chap. 3, and vol. 2, chap. 7, contain a classic account of Francis and Jane.

Michael J. Buckley. "Seventeenth-Century French Spirituality: Three Figures." *Christian Spirituality: Post-Reformation and Modern*. Ed. Louis Dupré and Don E. Saliers. New York: Crossroad, 1989, 28–68. Contains a fine brief presentation of Francis.

Ruth Kleinman. *Saint François de Sales and the Protestants*. Geneva: Droz, 1962.

Wendy M. Wright. *Bond of Perfection: Jeanne de Chantal and François de Sales*. New York: Paulist Press, 1985. A study of spiritual friendship.

32

Alphonsus de Liguori

(1696–1787)

Feast: August 1

I N JULY OF 1723 an important civil suit was being heard before the High Court in the Kingdom of Naples. A Neapolitan nobleman, Filippo Orsini, was suing Cosimo III, the Grand Duke of Tuscany, over the rights to the rich fief. The young lawyer who argued Orsini's case was a rising star on the Neapolitan legal scene named Alphonsus de Liguori. Although he had prepared his case meticulously and was sure of victory, Alphonsus had overlooked a technicality and was fighting against powerful political forces. His argument was peremptorily dismissed. Speechless for a few minutes, he finally exclaimed, "O world, I recognize you now. Goodbye to courtrooms!" and stormed out of the chambers. On October 23, over the strenuous objections of his father, he received tonsure and began his studies for the priesthood. Although modern research has shown that Alphonsus's conversion was not instantaneous — the pious youth had long been pondering a religious vocation — the incident in the Neapolitan court was the dramatic push he needed to begin a long career of tireless pastoral service and distinguished writing on moral and spiritual topics.

Alphonsus was born into a family of minor Neapolitan nobility and took his doctorate in law at the age of sixteen. For years before his decision to give up law and enter the priesthood he had practiced a life of devotion and of service to the sick and poor of Naples. After his conversion he was ordained in 1726, and he continued to serve society's outcasts, as well as to try to raise the spiritual level of the Neapolitan clergy. (The social and financial benefits of the clerical status in the Kingdom of Naples had led to a unfortunate glut of ill-educated and often dissolute priests.) In 1732 with his friend Thomas Falcoia, who had been named bishop of Castellamare on the Amalfi coast below Naples, Alphonsus founded a new missionary society (the Missionaries of the Most Holy Savior) to work among the rural poor. In 1749 the group received papal approval under the title the "Congregation of the Most Holy Redeemer," or the Redemptorists as they are popularly known. (The women's branch of the order was approved in the following year.)

Alphonsus did not begin his real literary career until he was almost fifty with the publication of his *Visits to the Blessed Sacrament* in 1745 (a few minor devotional writings had appeared earlier). It is astonishing, then, that he was able to produce so much in the three decades until 1776, when declining health put an end to his writing. He wrote 110 works in the diverse areas of apologetics, dogmatic theology, ascetical and spiritual theology, and especially in moral theology, for which he became most famous. In 1760, Alphonsus reluctantly accepted the see of Sant' Agata dei'Goti in the province of Benevento, where he put into practice the *Reflections Useful for Bishops*, which he had written in 1745. Despite his bad health, he provided a model of episcopal leadership at a time when the Italian church was often so tied to political privilege as to be pastorally ineffective. In 1775, almost totally bedridden, he resigned his diocese. The last dozen years of his life were plagued with severe illness, squabbles within the Redemptorist order, and inner spiritual trials.

Alphonsus wrote a number of apologetic works against the errors of his time, especially Jansenism (the rigoristic and pessimistic theological errors condemned by Innocent X in 1653). The bishop also opposed the Enlightenment views of the French Encyclopedists, then spreading into Italy, especially in his two-volume work *The Truth of the Faith* (1776). But Alphonsus is primarily remembered as a spiritual and moral author, one whose great popularity (he was translated early and often into many languages) did much to form Roman Catholic piety and practice in the nineteenth and early twentieth centuries. The fading of this style of Catholic life in the second half of our century has led to some neglect of the famous moralist, but many aspects of his message still merit reading and study.

Alphonsus was not a mystic, though in such works as *The Direction of Souls Who Wish to Lead a Deeply Spiritual Life* he included advice on mystical matters for confessors, much of it culled from his reading of Francis de Sales and Teresa of Avila, two of his favorite authors. (Most of Alphonsus's writings are liberally sprinkled with quotations from the fathers and doctors of the church, thus forming convenient summaries of tradition.) Alphonsus's interests lay mostly in the areas of asceticism and devotion, as is evident in popular treatises like the *Visits to the Blessed Sacrament* noted above (one of the most influential works in the history of devotion); the *Glories of Mary* (1750), an exposition of the popular Marian hymn the "Salve Regina"; and the *Novena of the Sacred Heart of Jesus* (1758). But where the founder of the

Redemptorists made his greatest impact on the church was in his work as a moral theologian.

Casuistry, that is, the application of general moral principles to particular cases (*casus*) had been implicit in Christian moral theory from an early period. The handbooks written for confessors in the late medieval period contained many case studies, but casuistry as an explicit discipline of moral theology was a creation of the sixteenth-century debates within Tridentine Roman Catholicism concerning the best "systems" to bring to bear on practical moral decision-making. Today, these debates are often difficult to understand — something that may have as much to do with the privatization of decision-making as it does with changes in cultural and theological perspectives. By the mid-seventeenth century, lines had been drawn between the "probabilist" camp, which held that in disputed moral decisions any *probable* opinion could be followed, and the "probabiliorists," who insisted that only the *more* probable opinions would allow the pious believer to remain free of sin. Fine lines often divided the two camps, but this did not prevent probabilists of being accused of "laxism" (favoring almost any view in morally dubious questions) and probabiliorists being seen as "rigorists," that is, adherents of the rigid views of Christianity that were found among the Jansenists. Alphonsus was trained as a probabiliorist and remained a paragon of piety and ascetic practice throughout his life. But his wide experience as a guide of Christians in every walk of life gradually moved him toward the milder probabilist view. In 1746 he issued the first version of his major work of moral theology, disguised as a commentary on a popular treatise by a Jesuit moralist of the previous century. He subsequently developed this as his own *Moral Theology*, published in two volumes (1753–55) and many times expanded and reprinted. Alphonsus also defended his position in a treatise on *The Moderate Use of the Probable Opinion* (1755, and many later editions). Alphonsus's middle-of-the-road view was later known as "Equi-probabilism" — that is, the system that argued that legitimate probable views needed to be in the same range of argument as those contrary to the possible course of action. This was controversial in his own day and for a century thereafter (see above p. 16 for how Jesuit probabiliorists in the 1850s and '60s tried to block Alphonsus's proclamation as a *doctor ecclesiae*). These ancient debates were effectively put to rest in 1950 when Pius XII named Alphonsus as the Patron Saint of Confessors and Moral Theologians.

Alphonsus de Liguori would not have wanted his readers, then or now, to have made a sharp distinction between his spiritual and his moral writings. What is perhaps his central text (he called it "the most devotional and the most useful of my writings") shows the unity of these two sides of his career. *The Practice of the Love of Jesus Christ* was first published in 1768 and went through many subsequent editions. The great twentieth-century Redemptorist moral theologian, Bernard Häring, described it as "a kind of moral theology for lay people as well as priests," because Alphonsus insisted that all persons can find holiness in the life which providence has given them, "the religious as religious, the person in the world as a person in the world, priest as priest, married person as married person, soldier as soldier" (chap. 8.10). The essential theme of the work is God's gracious love toward sinners — an ecstatic and importunate love that invites, almost compels, our loving response. It is in this loving response to God that the healthy conscience, one which makes generous and correct moral decisions, is formed. Alphonsus's message is one of hope, not fear: "Although we have good cause to dread eternal death on account of how we have offended God, we have still greater motives for hoping for eternal life through Jesus Christ, whose merits are of infinitely greater value for our salvation than are our own merits for bringing us to perdition" (chap. 3.2).

Reading Alphonsus

Much of Alphonsus was translated into English in the nineteenth and early twentieth centuries, but most of these works are out of print. The best way to sample the range of the doctor's teaching is in the collection *Alphonsus de Liguori: Selected Writings,* ed. Frederick M. Jones, CWS 94. See also *Alphonsus Liguori: The Redeeming Love of Christ: A Collection of Spiritual Writings,* ed. Joseph Oppitz (Brooklyn, N.Y.: New City Press, 1992).

Bibliography

Frederick M. Jones. *Alphonsus de Liguori: The Saint of Bourbon Naples.* Dublin: Marianella Publications, 1992. The best English study.

Théodule Rey-Mermet. *Alphonsus Liguori: Tireless Worker for the Most Abandoned.* Brooklyn, N.Y.: New City Press, 1989.

33

THÉRÈSE
OF LISIEUX
(1873–97)

D URING HER EIGHTEEN MONTHS of final illness (April 1896 to her death in October 1897), as she slowly died from tuberculosis, the young Carmelite nun Thérèse of the convent of Lisieux tried to keep in touch with the circle of correspondents she had attracted over her few years in the most rigorous of religious orders for women. Often unable to hold a pen due to her sufferings, she was still able to continue work on her autobiographical reflections and to write some of her most moving letters. One of the latter may give some indication of why this young woman, despite her lack of formal theological training, on the centenary of her death was recognized as a doctor of the church by Pope John Paul II. In writing to her spiritual "brother," the missionary priest Adolphe Roulland, on March 19 of 1897 (Letter 191), she repeated a phrase used by another Carmelite doctor, John of the Cross: "The smallest amount of *pure love* [her italics] is more useful to the church than all the works that have been ever achieved....I want to save souls and forget self for them. I want to save them even after my death, so I should be happy if...you would say: 'My God, permit my sister to go on making you loved.'" Thérèse of Lisieux is the doctor of pure love.

The paradoxes of holiness have rarely been better illustrated than in the case of the shy but totally confident young nun who dedicated herself to God. Her purity of intention seems to prove that the modern era, with all its fractions and distractions, is not inferior to ancient or medieval Christianity in being able to provide models of a self-effacement that is as total as it is inspirational. Thérèse the enclosed contemplative became Thérèse the patroness of missions. Thérèse the "Little Flower," whose writings were altered by her own sister, Mother Agnes, to conform to the standards of nineteenth-century bourgeois piety, is revealed in her unexpurgated texts as a far deeper and stronger figure, one whose dark night of the soul was not unlike that of John of the Cross and other great mystics. And now, Thérèse the simple young girl who had never had formal theological training becomes Thérèse the doctor of the church. Even though we now know that the growth of Teresa's cult and her rapid path to canonization in 1925 was engineered by her community on the basis of texts that significantly altered what she was trying to say, this really has made little difference to the impact that she has had and continues to have on twentieth-century Catholicism. When John Paul II recognized her as *doctor ecclesiae* a new chapter began in the long history of the *doctores ecclesiae.*

Marie-Françoise-Thérèse Martin was born on January 2, 1873, in the town of Alençon, the ninth and last child of Louis Martin and Zelie Guerin, who had both contemplated joining religious communities before they married. All their children who survived infancy were to become religious. In the *Story of a Soul,* the spiritual autobiography that Thérèse wrote toward the end of her life, she provides a picture of the stages of her religious growth in this pious family. She was formed in a surrounding in which the lives of the saints were a basic model of education and source of entertainment, and there is no reason to doubt her claim that she dedicated herself to a religious life from as early as she could remember: "From the age of three, I began to refuse nothing of what God asked of me," she later recounted. The first stage in her life ended when her mother died when she was four and she chose her elder sister Pauline as her "second mother." (It was Pauline, who eventually became the superior of her community at Lisieux, who was to manufacture the "cleaned-up" view of Thérèse to speed her canonization.) This second stage was a period of pain and difficulty for the sensitive little girl, the "winter trial of the little flower." On Christmas, 1886, Thérèse experienced a conversion that initiated the third period of her life. "I received the grace of leaving my childhood," she wrote, "in a word the grace of complete conversion. . . . On that night of light began the third period of my life, the most beautiful and most filled with graces from heaven" (*Story of a Soul,* chap. 5). From that time on, Thérèse's great desire was to be allowed to follow her older sisters into the religious life. In November of 1887, Thérèse, her sister Céline, and her father went on pilgrimage to Italy, where they were received in audience by Pope Leo XIII. Thérèse kissed the pope's foot and cast him into consternation by requesting his permission to enter the Carmelite order at the noncanonical age of fifteen. The pope tried to demur with the expressions that all would turn out for the best if she only waited, but Thérèse was insistent and had to be carried off by papal guards without receiving a clear answer.

Finally, on April 9, 1888, Thérèse Martin was accepted into the Lisieux

Carmel as a postulant. She was to spend the less than a decade that remained of her life within its walls. In January of 1889 she became a novice, and finally on September 8, 1890, she was fully professed as a member of the community, taking the name Sister Thérèse of the Infant Jesus and the Holy Face. In 1894, her beloved father died after a trying illness and her biological sister Pauline, now Mother Agnes, ordered her to write down her memories of her childhood, the beginning of the manuscript that was to grow into the *Story of a Soul.* The work consists of three separate manuscripts. The eight chapters of Manuscript A were written between December 1894 and January 1896, at the command of Mother Agnes. Manuscript B (chap. 9) on the vocation of love was written in September of 1896 and addressed to Jesus. Finally, Manuscript C (chaps. 10–11), addressed to Mother Marie de Gonzague, was written in June of 1897 and describes her final days and the "Dark Night" experience that had begun on April 5 of the previous year and was to continue until her death. In this trial Thérèse's sense of God's presence vanished and she lived in the midst of a darkness in which all the joy of belief deserted her. These final chapters of the *Story of a Soul* constitute the core of Thérèse's message.

Thérèse of Lisieux, even more than the two female doctors declared in 1970, represents a new model of the ancient and still-developing office of *doctor ecclesiae*. It is not so much that Thérèse is a woman, but rather that her form of teaching explodes the traditional categories of "doctoral" status even more than Teresa of Avila and Catherine of Siena. The Little Flower's "Little Way," even when shorn of the accretions foisted on it by her managers in life and in death, deliberately eschews traditional theological categories and the usual forms of theological analysis. Nevertheless, the deep wisdom found in the Carmelite's writings has been a major resource for Catholicism over the past century, and not just for what is too easily dismissed as "popular" piety. The great Swiss theologian Hans Urs von Balthasar put it well when he said, "She penetrates straight through all triviality and counterfeit to the simple, naked truth of the gospel." All the *doctores ecclesiae*, of course, sought for nothing more — nor less — than the presentation of the simple, naked truth of the gospel, though they did so in the forms and modes demanded by their age and context. Thérèse's particular expression of the gospel, though couched in the language and images of a piety that often sounds dated today, in its essence is faithful to the foundational meaning of Christianity at the same time that it is startlingly contemporary in its directness and simplicity.

The essence of Thérèse's teaching is total surrender to the love of God, an abandonment which in turn forms the basis for a life dedicated to spreading the message of God's love to others by active love and missionary zeal, either through physical preaching of the gospel, or by prayerful and personal support of missionaries. Thérèse spoke of her teaching as a "Little Way" fit for children. As she put it in chapter 10: "God cannot inspire unrealizable desires. I can, then, in spite of my littleness, aspire to holiness. It is impossible for me to grow up, and so I must bear with myself such as I am with all my imperfections. But I want to seek out a means of going to heaven by a little way, a way that is very straight, very short, and totally new."

The images of "littleness" that she uses of herself throughout her writings — the little flower, the little bird, and the like — may seem sentimental and insipid to some, but they are to be understood in light of the gospel adage, "Unless you change and become like little children you will never enter the kingdom of heaven" (Matt. 18:3). Thérèse's Little Way is not characterized by the smallness of fear, but by the largeness of love: "To satisfy divine Justice," she wrote, "perfect victims were needed, but the law of Love has succeeded to the law of fear, and Love has chosen me as a holocaust, me, a weak and imperfect creature" (chap. 9). Because Thérèse abandoned herself to her sacrificial role so totally — especially in the midst of the physical sufferings and interior desolation of her last months, she knew that God would use her story to spread his message over the world. In the *Story of a Soul* she exclaimed, "Ah! in spite of my littleness, I would like to enlighten souls as did the *Prophets* and *Doctors*. I have the *vocation of the apostle*" (ibid.). Because she had discovered that "MY VOCATION IS LOVE!" [her capitalization], all vocations were in a sense to be hers. During her final months her desire to be a missionary, even a doctor, became a conviction as she surrendered herself ever more fully to God. Among the conversations of her last months, the following is recorded for July 17, 1897: "I feel that my mission is about to begin, my mission of making others love God as I love him, my mission of teaching souls my Little Way. If God answers my requests, my heaven will be spent on earth up until the end of the world. Yes, I want to spend my heaven on earth doing good."

Finally, we can note one other characteristic of Thérèse's teaching that makes it unusual among the doctors of the church: its lack of polemics. The doctors of the church have always been concerned with correct, or orthodox, teaching, and Thérèse is no exception. However, unlike almost all of the previous doctors, controversy and attacks on error and heterodoxy have no place in her writings. Thérèse of Lisieux operates outside this framework. Spreading the message of love is so important to her that she has no room for anything else. As she put it in one of her poems:

> Love, I have experienced it,
> Knows how to use (what power!)
> The good and the bad it finds in me.
> It transforms my soul into itself.
> This fire burning in my soul
> Penetrates my heart forever.
> Thus in its delightful flame
> I am being wholly consumed by Love!
> (New Poetry no. 30)

Reading Thérèse

The best English translation of the authentic version of Thérèse's main work is *Story of a Soul: The Autobiography of St. Thérèse of Lisieux*, 3d ed., translated from the original manuscripts by John Clarke (Washington, D.C.: ICS Publications, 1996). There are a number of translations of Thérèse's letters and poems; the most complete are *The Poetry of Saint Thérèse of Lisieux*, trans. Donald Kinney (Washington, D.C.: ICS Publications, 1996); and *Saint Thérèse of Lisieux: General Correspondence*, 2 vols., trans. John Clarke (Washington, D.C.: ICS Publications, 1982–88). See also the translations of the letters between Thérèse and the young priest Maurice Bellière, by Patrick Ahearn, *Maurice and Thérèse: The Story of a Love* (New York: Doubleday, 1998). ICS Publications also has versions of Thérèse's *Plays* and *Last Conversations* (of contested authenticity).

Bibliography

A flood of literature exists about Thérèse. Here I note only a few of the most significant works.

Hans Urs von Balthasar. *Thérèse of Lisieux: The Story of a Mission.* New York: Sheed and Ward, 1954. The best theological account of Thérèse.

André Combes. *Saint Thérèse and Her Mission: The Basic Principles of Theresian Spirituality.* New York: Kenedy, 1955. Msgr. Combes, a noted scholar of mysticism, was one of the first to begin to uncover the authentic Thérèse.

Guy Gaucher. *The Story of a Life.* San Francisco: HarperCollins, 1993. A good biography.

Jean Guitton. *The Spiritual Genius of St. Thérèse.* Westminster, Md.: Newman Press, 1958.

V. Sackville-West. *The Eagle and the Dove: A Study in Contrasts: St. Teresa of Avila, St. Thérèse of Lisieux.* London: Michael Joseph, 1943. An interesting comparison of the two Carmelite women doctors.

Jean-François Six. *Light of the Night: The Last Eighteen Months in the Life of Thérèse of Lisieux.* Notre Dame, Ind.: University of Notre Dame Press, 1998.

John Sullivan, ed. *Carmelite Studies.* Vol. 5: *Experiencing St. Thérèse Today.* Washington, D.C.: ICS Publications, 1990. A good collection of essays.

Part Three

WHAT IS
THE FUTURE
OF THE DOCTORS
OF THE CHURCH?

I am not a prophet; nor am I the son of a prophet;
I am a herdsman plucking wild figs. (Amos 7:14)

AMOS DID NOT WANT to be a prophet, nor do I. He did get a divine call; I have nothing to empower this final section aside from my own musings. Nevertheless, writing this brief history of the doctors of the church has led me to think more than once about the future of the doctors as Christianity begins a new millennium. Given the important role that the doctors have played for over fifteen centuries, and especially in view of the changes that the office has undergone in the past thirty years by the naming of the first female doctors, how should we view the ongoing role of the doctors in the life of the church?

The most important future for the doctors, of course, rests in their continued impact on the lives and thought of believers of all denominations. Though Roman Catholicism, through the office of the papacy, has taken the greatest interest in promoting doctors and adding to the list, most of the patristic doctors and some of the medieval ones are part of the common patrimony of all Christians of East and West. Certainly, the sanctity of the doctors can provide an inspiration for Christians of varying persuasions. But there are many forms of sanctity. What is distinctive about the doctors as a group is the model they present of combining the intense love of God and neighbor that defines sanctity with a commitment to the intellectual work of learning, preaching, teaching, and writing. The great variety of ways in which they realized this union between love and knowledge shows us that there is no single model that defines the charism of teaching that the Holy Spirit gives to the church. In the choir of the doctors official teachers — catechists like Ephrem, bishops like Augustine, professors like Thomas Aquinas — rub shoulders with nuns and a pious lay woman.

The doctors live on not only in the veneration they receive as saints, but especially in their writings. Doctors exist to be read and studied. As I have insisted throughout this book, there is no substitute for reading the doctors themselves. However far their times and their issues are from our own, their message has a depth that renders it still full of meaning for us. In this connection it is interesting to note that many of the doctors who a generation ago were relatively inaccessible to the reader who knew no Latin, or Greek, or Syriac, today are available in good translations with helpful introductions and explanatory materials. Still, it is surprising that the major theological and spiritual writings of some doctors — Isidore of Seville, Albert the Great, Lawrence of Brindisi, Peter Canisius — are unavailable at the present time. For others, like Bede and Anthony of Padua, we have only a small part of their doctrinal works available. The fading of knowledge of Latin and Greek, however lamentable, means that the efforts of translators and historians are more necessary than ever to make this important part of the Christian tradition accessible in the new era.

The ecumenical situation in which the once warring, and still divided, Christian denominations have found themselves in the twentieth century, as well as the dialogue of world religions that becomes stronger each decade, argues for continued growth in the list of doctors, as well as for ongoing diversification. From the ecumenical perspective, there are still important fathers from the Greek and non-Greek East who have long been venerated as great teachers and seem worthy of the title of *doctor ecclesiae*. Without going back before 300 c.e. into the age of the martyrs (tradition seems to be against combining the charisms of doctor and martyr), a number of names can be identified.

The two that stand out most clearly are both figures recognized as saints in the East and West and whose works, at least in part, were available in Latin and thus helped form Western theology. The foremost name is that of St. Gregory of Nyssa (c. 335–c. 395), Basil's younger brother and the third of the great Cappadocian Fathers. Particularly today, when Gregory's dogmatic and mystical teachings have come in for so much renewed interest, it is hard to deny that he already stands among the ranks of the doctors, at least by way of universal affirmation, if not by official papal or conciliar definition (see Appendix III on how often Gregory has been cited in recent official documents). The second strong example can be found in St. Maximus the Confessor (c. 580–662). If John of Damascus in eighth-century Eastern Christianity merited declaration as a doctor in 1890, why shouldn't the same honor be given to the seventh-century monk and teacher? Maximus is one of the few later Byzantine saints who belongs equally to East and to West, although until about sixty years ago Western Christians often did not realize this. His teaching has always been central to Orthodox theology, and his years spent in North Africa and especially his collaboration with Pope Martin I in fighting against the Monothelite heresy (a struggle which cost him his life) make him an important part of the history of Western theology. It would be a fitting expression of ecumenicity if a present or future pope were to recognize Maximus as a *doctor*.

In the era before schism divided Eastern and Western Christendom, the split whose traditional commencement is in 1054 when representatives of Rome and Constantinople mutually excommunicated each other, there are other saints and teachers whose writings and influence would seem to merit consideration as doctors. One example is St. Symeon the New Theologian, monk and abbot at Constantinople (949–1022). Symeon's teaching won him the rare title of "theologian" in the Greek East; the depth of his mystical theology has also begun to be appreciated by Western readers in recent decades. Between the death of John of Damascus in 749 and Peter Damian's birth in 1007 there is a two-and-a-half century dearth of doctors. Declaring Symeon a doctor would do something to fill this hiatus.

A more difficult issue emerges when we speculate about the possibility of naming doctors drawn from Eastern Christendom in the period after the unfortunate divide that Christians still struggle to overcome. Whatever the objections that can be advanced against the advisability of a declaration of later Greek doctors, at least by the pope, such an action would be an expression of great significance — a recognition that the Holy Spirit's teaching has been present throughout the history of the church, despite its divisions. St. Gregory Palamas, for example, who lived between 1296 and 1359, can be thought of as a possible postschism *doctor ecclesiae* from the East. Gregory's defense of the mystical prayer of the Hesychasts involved him in controversy with representatives of Latin theology, especially the Calabrian monk Barlaam. But should Barlaam be taken as the voice of Latin Christianity? Whatever the merits of the controversy, it does not minimize the significance and depth of Gregory's theology. (Gregory has already been recognized as saint and doctor of the Eastern church by the Synod of Constantinople in 1368.)

Finally, and also with regard to non-Latin Christendom, we can suggest that some of the teachers of the other churches of Eastern Christendom could be considered as possible doctors. None of these figures was as prolific or as well known as Ephrem, but the history of the naming of later Latin *doctores ecclesiae* shows that neither of these criteria can be considered essential. In Syriac Christianity, for example, the extensive spiritual writings of Isaac of Nineveh (d. c. 700) were not only treasured in his own "Nestorian" church, but also translated and widely read in Arabic, Ethiopic, Greek, and Latin. In Armenian Christianity, there are the figures of St. Gregory the Illuminator (d. 332) and his descendent St. Isaac the Great (d. 440). In the Coptic church we can find monastic saints and authors like St. Shenoute (d. 466), the powerful and long-lived abbot who accompanied Cyril of Alexandria to the Council of Ephesus. Some might say that not all these figures were prolific authors and that what they wrote was not always strikingly original. But neither did Latin doctors like Peter Chrysologus write extensively. Other doctors, such as Isidore of Seville and Anthony of Padua, wrote a good deal, but cannot be said to have been original thinkers. The charism of *doctor ecclesiae,* if it has any meaning, has as much to do with the issue of representation, that is, exemplary witness to faith, as it does with theological brilliance, though most of the doctors have also been great theologians.

Pushing the ecumenical character of the doctors of the church even further, we can ask whether it is possible to envisage some of the great teachers of Protestant Christianity as candidates for the position of *doctor ecclesiae.* Such a notion would have seemed impossible — a contradiction in terms — from the sixteenth to the late twentieth century. But the action of the Holy Spirit has led to a difficult, painfully slow, sometimes interrupted, but nonetheless steady rapprochement between Roman Catholicism and many branches of Protestant Christianity. In several documents of the past decade the Catholic Church has come to recognize a common teaching with Protestant Christian churches on key issues of belief, though, of course, important differences still remain.

But how could the representatives of "heresy" ever be considered as doctors? What would Teresa of Avila, Peter Canisius, Robert Bellarmine, Lawrence of Brindisi, and the other modern doctors who expressed their antipathy to Protestant error, think of such an innovation? Surely, the declaration of a Luther, a Calvin, a Schleiermacher, and even a Karl Barth in our own century as a *doctor ecclesiae* would introduce a contradiction that would rob the title and honor of all meaning and coherence. In the present ecclesial situation this may, indeed, be the case. But is such an expansion unthinkable?

As Thomas Aquinas and the Catholic tradition always insisted, no single doctor has ever represented the fullness of truth found in the church as a whole. Almost every doctor has, at one time or another, put forward positions that were later judged insufficient, and even incorrect. Augustine's doctrine of grace is not that of the Eastern doctors. Bonaventure implicitly, and Francis de Sales explicitly, disagreed with aspects of the bishop of Hippo's teaching on grace and freedom. The Christology of Athanasius or Hilary is wanting by the standards of Chalcedonian orthodoxy. Aspects of Leo the Great's theology of redemption, especially its "rights of the devil" motif, were legitimately attacked by Anselm of Canterbury. Thomas Aquinas and Bonaventure disagreed on the issue of the eternity of the universe, the role of grace and freedom, and other questions. The list could go on. From the perspective of the fullness of "orthodox Catholicism" or "catholic Orthodoxy" no individual doctor can ever express the totality of the truth that the Holy Spirit gives to the church, a church that is essentially one despite its historical divisions. Perhaps a growing awareness of this inner unity may one day mean that the august list of the *doctores ecclesiae* will include those who have expressed important aspects of the truth of belief in all the Christian churches.

When we look to Roman Catholicism itself, there are more than a few candidates who can be suggested for the honor of *doctor ecclesiae*. Redressing the lack of balance between the thirty men and the three women doctors argues that some of the major female teachers in the history of the church should be recognized for their contributions. High on any list would be the name of Hildegard of Bingen (1098–1179), the German abbess, musician, and theologian, who has an approved cult as saint in Germany. Hildegard's teaching was recognized in her own day by popes, bishops, and theologians. The rediscovery of this "renaissance woman" in the present century has shown her to be one of the most original and varied talents of an era bursting with creativity. Hildegard's great visionary trilogy, consisting of the *Scivias* (that is, *Know the Ways of the Lord*), the *Book of the Life of Merits*, and the *Book of Divine Works*, is one of the most powerful and original theological documents of the Middle Ages. Its cosmic vision of redemption has few peers in the history of Christian thought.

In the centuries after Hildegard women were able to take on larger and larger roles in the Latin West. Catherine of Siena and Teresa of Avila are certainly outstanding representatives of this flowering of female teachers, but they were not alone. In the thirteenth century, the Cistercian nun Gertrude the Great (1256–1301), of the abbey of Helfta in Saxony, is a declared saint who left deep theological treasures to the tradition in her *Legate of Divine Love* and other writings. In the fourteenth century, the English anchoress Julian of Norwich (1342–c. 1416), although not yet canonized, has been recognized as a masterful and rich theologian in her *Showings*. Julian's long years of contemplative appropriation of the meaning of the visions God once gave to her when she was at the point of death demonstrate rare profundity and wonderful comprehensiveness of the meaning of redemption. From the era closer to Teresa there is the figure of St. Catherine of Genoa (1447–1510). Catherine's writings are brief, but her *Spiritual Dialogue* and *Purgation and Purgatory* contain significant teaching on the necessity of purgation of sin and the supremacy of pure divine love. Like Teresa, in 1473 Catherine experienced the "wound of love" that gave her insights beyond those that reason could attain. Writing of this event in the *Spiritual Dialogue* she said: "A ray of God's love wounded her heart, making her soul experience a flaming love arising from a divine fount. At that instant, she was outside of herself, beyond intellect, tongue, or feeling. Fixed in that pure and divine love, henceforth she never ceased to dwell on it."

We do not need to think that women worthy of being named doctors of the church existed only in the medieval and early modern periods, as the case of Thérèse of Lisieux demonstrates. The Little Flower was named a doctor on the centenary of her death. A twentieth-century Carmelite nun, Sister Teresa

Benedicta of the Cross, better known as Edith Stein (1891–1942), recently canonized, is also remarkable for the teaching found in her letters and her treatises, such as *The Science of the Cross*, a study of John of the Cross. In the homily he preached at her beatification in 1987, Pope John Paul II said, "Edith Stein's entire life is characterized by an incessant search for truth and is illuminated by the blessing of the cross of Christ." Not a bad definition of a doctor of the church.

While it is important to recognize the role that women have played in the history of Christian belief, there are many men of the Western Christian tradition who also can be said to be worthy candidates for the position of *doctor ecclesiae*. A few names from each of the periods into which I have divided the history of the doctors can suffice to suggest the possibilities for the future.

In the patristic age, although there are already six Latin doctors, several important teachers remain who have not been so recognized. John Cassian (c. 360–435) was almost an exact contemporary of Augustine. Born in the East, this Latin-speaking monk was trained in the best traditions of Eastern monasticism. As a deacon of John Chrysostom in Constantinople, he was sent to Pope Innocent I in 403 on a diplomatic mission and then stayed on in the West, becoming an early monastic leader in southern Gaul. Cassian's *Conferences* and *Institutes* are among the most important documents in the history of monasticism, conveying the wisdom of the desert to Latin monks and to all people interested in the higher states of prayer. Cassian is unusual in being honored as a saint in Eastern Christendom, while his Western cultus is restricted to the diocese of Marseilles.

Anicius Manlius Severinus Boethius (c. 480–524) was the descendent of one of the most ancient of Roman noble families and was a high official in the kingdom of Theodoric the Ostrogoth. As one of the last Romans and possessed of a vast knowledge of Latin and Greek thought, he sought to translate the wisdom of the Greek philosophers into Latin, showing the inner agreement of Plato and Aristotle. But Boethius was also a profound theologian, inspired by Augustine, and deeply involved in the trinitarian and christological issues that continued to percolate in the sixth century. His five *Theological Tractates*, with their concern for careful argument and exact presentation of the task of faith seeking understanding, have justly been seen as among the ancestors of the scholastic mode of theology. The doubts that once were raised about the sincerity of Boethius's Christianity on the basis of his *Consolation of Philosophy* have long since dissipated. Boethius was executed by Theodoric for political reasons, but because the German king was an Arian and Boethius a strong Catholic, medieval legend considered him a martyr. He has a local cult in Pavia, where he is buried.

In the medieval period there are a number of canonized saints among the Benedictines who might be considered as possible doctors. They are found both in the black, or traditional, Benedictines, and the white monks, the

Cistercian reformers. For example, St. Aelred of Rievaulx (1110–67), a close friend of St. Bernard, left a rich trove of mystical and historical works, among them the classic treatise *Spiritual Friendship*. Among the friars, both Dominican and Franciscan, important teachers and great preachers can be found whose impact on their age witnesses to a role of ongoing importance for the church. One good case is that of St. Bernardino of Siena (1380–1444), the Franciscan reformer and moral conscience of his age. Bernardino, like many doctors, was primarily a preacher rather than a school theologian; but his position as the great preacher of his age echoes that of John Chrysostom in the fourth century, or Anthony of Padua in the thirteenth.

The name that comes most often to my mind when I think about further male doctors from the medieval period, however, belongs not to a monk or a friar, but to a canon, i.e., a priest living under a monastic-style rule. Hugh of St. Victor (c. 1090–1142) has never been canonized, but he has been long recognized as the great master of early scholasticism, a teacher as important for his mystical works as he is for his exegesis and dogmatic acumen. Few teachers have had the breadth and balance of the great Victorine, and few have enjoyed comparable influence. It is sufficient to quote the witness of Bonaventure. In the Franciscan's treatise *The Reduction of the Arts to Theology*, chapter 5, he sets out the three forms of spiritual understanding of scripture as the basis for a triple distinction of theology into dogmatic, moral, and mystical parts. Each of these parts has its patristic doctor and contemporary proponent. "The first," Bonaventure says, "is taught especially by Augustine; the second Gregory chiefly teaches; and the third Dionysius teaches. Anselm follows Augustine, Bernard follows Gregory, Richard [of St. Victor] follows Dionysius. For Anselm excels in rational thinking, Bernard in preaching, Richard in contemplation. But Hugh excels in all three."

Finally, the modern period from 1500 on also has had thinkers and teachers who could be considered for the honor of doctor. Some of these holy men may have already had their cause introduced, though, as we saw in Part I, the exact process by which this is done remains fluid and is rarely public. This appears to be the case with St. Louis Marie Grignion de Montfort (1673–1716), the famous preacher of missions in France and the author of the *Treatise on True Devotion to the Blessed Virgin*. De Montfort's widely read work has been a major force in modern Marian piety and is said to be favorite reading of John Paul II.

The two figures that I would propose for attention are both English. Only a single doctor of the church, Hilary of Poitiers (died 367), has been married. Are we to suppose that for over seventeen centuries the Holy Spirit has been inactive in the minds and hearts of married people, even in terms of the special charism that we salute with the title *doctor ecclesiae*? St. Thomas More (1478–1535), the English chancellor and martyr for his fidelity to papal primacy, seems to provide a fine example of a married man in whom both sanctity of life and profundity of teaching came together in a remark-

able, an outstanding, way. Like the works of the other doctors of the time of
the division of Christendom, many of More's writings are polemical attacks
on Protestants. Also, eyebrows might be raised at the suggestion that *Utopia*
(1516) is the kind of book for which one is made a *doctor ecclesiae*. But the
same cannot be said for many of his other writings, such as the *Dialogue of
Comfort against Tribulation* written during his imprisonment in the Tower of
London awaiting execution. The "Man for All Seasons," as More has been
called, was also a teacher and guide for all ages.

John Henry Newman (1801–90), another English thinker, never married. After his reception into the Catholic Church in 1845, he became a
priest, joined the Oratorians, and eventually was made a cardinal in 1877
by Leo XIII in recognition of the services he had rendered to the Catholic cause, not only in England, but also around the world. Newman has not
been canonized, though his cause was introduced in Rome in 1989 with a
vast dossier of materials (thus far, however, without miracles). The diversity
of Newman's contributions to Christian teaching are remarkable, reminding
us of some of the great patristic doctors whom he studied and loved so well.
Like all of them, he was a great preacher. Newman's foremost homiletic work
is the eight volumes of the *Parochial and Plain Sermons*, delivered while he
was still an Anglican between 1834 and 1842. Like Augustine and Basil, he
was also a theorist of Christian education, as demonstrated in his *Idea of a
University* (1852). Again like Augustine, Newman was able to use his own
life as a prism through which to explore aspects of the meaning of all lives
(*Apologia pro vita sua* of 1864). Like Anselm and Thomas Aquinas, Newman
was a profound philosopher, especially interested in questions of truth and
human knowing, as can be seen in his *Grammar of Assent* of 1870. It is sometimes said that Newman was not really a theologian, but this is scarcely true.
His theology was formed more in dialogue with patristic than with scholastic thinkers, and his greatest theological work, the *Essay on the Development
of Christian Doctrine* published in 1845, shows how his consideration of the
debates over Trinity and Incarnation that had shaped the orthodox tradition
led him to the recognition that Roman Catholicism truly carried on the truth
that the fathers and doctors had struggled to clarify. In the way in which
his life and thought link the first doctors of the church with the issues of
the modern age John Henry Newman witnesses to the doctoral charism as
no other figure of recent centuries. This has been recognized in recent official Roman Catholic documents in which no modern author has been quoted
more than John Henry Cardinal Newman (see Appendix III).

Many believing Christians may think of the doctors of the church only in
terms of the distant past. For them, the doctors are those ancient thinkers
who formed Christian belief in its first stages — giants of an age that can
never be repeated. Thirteen of the thirty-three doctors did, indeed, live in
the relatively brief century and a half between 300 and 460 C.E. Their foundational role is irreplaceable. Some of these figures came to be understood as

paradigms of the divine teaching communicated to the church in a special way — a process already underway by the end of the patristic era. But the tradition of belief that created the role of the *doctores ecclesiae* already recognized that the special teaching charism of the doctors could not be restricted to a set number or to any one age. Hence, the number of doctors, whether defined in a broad or in a strict sense, remained fluid through the Middle Ages. Though the tradition of four "classic" doctors of the West and four comparable doctors of the East was a standard and oft-repeated numeration, other lists had as many as a dozen.

In the age of the fragmentation of Western Christianity in the sixteenth century, the popes began the practice of naming more recent doctors, starting with Thomas Aquinas and Bonaventure, the paragons of medieval scholasticism. Since the early eighteenth century, as we have seen in Part I, some popes have taken an interest in naming more doctors, including teachers from both the East and the West. In the past thirty years, the once unheard-of action of naming three women as doctors has emphasized the variety and the universality of the action of the Holy Spirit communicating the saving truth revealed in the God-Man to all Christians.

In closing this introduction to the doctors of the church, I would like to return to an early Christian text, one that antedates all the figures treated in this volume, but that still helps us understand the ongoing role of the Holy Spirit as the source of the "doctoral" charism. In 202 a group of Christians in Carthage was arrested, tried, imprisoned, and eventually executed for their faith. The prison diary that the young martyr Perpetua kept during this trial is unrivaled among the first-hand martyrdom documents of early Christianity. This moving text comes down to us in an editorial envelope, written by an anonymous contemporary, who apparently was responding to those who thought that all the important manifestations of the Holy Spirit had already been seen by c. 200 C.E. As we look forward to new actions of the Spirit in the next millennium, both in naming doctors of the church, as well as in raising up women and men who will continue this teaching grace to the church, these words from this ancient Christian text can serve as a source of encouragement:

> Let those who would restrict the power of the one Spirit to times and seasons look to this: the more recent times should be considered the greater, being later than those of old, and this is a consequence of the extraordinary graces promised for the last era of time. For "In these last days," God declares, "I will pour out my Spirit upon all flesh and their sons and daughters shall prophesy and on my male and female slaves I will pour out my Spirit. And the young men shall see visions and the old men shall dream dreams'" (Acts 2:17–18, citing Joel 3:1–2).
>
> (Prologue, "Vision of Perpetua and Felicitas")

Appendix I

Dictionary of Heresies

T HE DOCTORS OF THE CHURCH often wrote in reaction to "heresies," that is, what they considered to be willfully incorrect interpretations of faith. Today historians of Christian doctrine are more open to taking a less polemical view of some of these movements, seeing them as having their own role to play in the ongoing interpretation of faith that has formed the Christian churches. Since the names of these heresies often appear in these pages, a brief description of how they were used in the tradition will be helpful here.

Arianism: The followers of Arius held that the Son of God is not co-eternal and consubstantial (*homoousios*) with the Father.

> **Semi-Arianism:** This is the position of those who admitted that the Son was "like" (*homoios*) the Father, but who refused to speak of consubstantiality.

Donatism: The Donatists taught that sacraments performed by unworthy priests were invalid.

Iconoclasm: The Iconoclasts wished to ban all sacred images from Christian worship.

Jansenism: The Jansenists denied free will and the universal salvific will of God and adopted a rigorist position on all moral issues.

Macedonianism (Spirit-Fighters): This heresy denied the consubstantiality of the Holy Spirit.

Manichaeanism: This dualistic religion taught that there were two gods, the evil god who created the universe and the good god who sent Jesus to redeem fallen souls.

Monophysitism: The Monophysites held that after the Incarnation there was only one nature in Christ.

Monothelitism: The Monothelites taught that there is only one will in Christ.

Nestorianism: Nestorius taught that Mary should not be called the Mother of God. He was also accused of dividing Christ into two persons.

Origenism: Various views ascribed to Origen, especially the eventual return of all fallen spirits to God (*apokatastasis*), were condemned at the Second Council of Constantinople.

Pelagianism: Pelagius and his followers held that even after the fall humans retained the ability to avoid sin without the help of grace.

Sabellianism: Sabellius, a third-century bishop, saw the three Persons of the Trinity as merely manifestations or appearances of the one God.

Appendix 2

Ecumenical Councils

MANY OF THE DOCTORS of the church played important roles in the ecumenical councils, that is, the meetings of bishops that condemned heresies and issued the formulas of faith that are basic to orthodox Christianity. A list of the councils recognized as ecumenical by Roman Catholics follows. (Eastern Orthodox consider only the first seven as truly ecumenical.)

1. **Nicaea (325):** Condemned Arius and issued the Nicene Creed.

2. **Constantinople I (381):** Reaffirmed the Nicene Creed and condemned Apollinaris.

3. **Ephesus (431):** Condemned Nestorius and approved Cyril's letters.

4. **Chalcedon (451):** Condemned Eutyches, approved Leo's *Tome*, and issued a formula of christological faith.

5. **Constantinople II (553):** Condemned the "Three Chapters" (pro-Nestorian writings) and also rejected Origenism.

6. **Constantinople III (680–81):** Condemned Monothelitism.

7. **Nicaea II (787):** Condemned Iconoclasm.

8. **Constantinople IV (869–70):** Condemned Photius.

9. **Lateran I (1123):** Marked the end of the Investiture Controversy and the triumph of Great Reform.

10. **Lateran II (1139):** Condemned Arnold of Brescia and issued reform decrees.

11. **Lateran III (1179):** Dealt with papal election procedures.

12. **Lateran IV (1215):** Condemned Manichaeanism and issued reform decrees.

13. **Lyons I (1245):** Deposed Frederick II.

14. **Lyons II (1274):** Tried to achieve reunion of Eastern and Western churches.

15. **Vienne (1311–12):** Dealt with the Templars and Franciscan poverty.

16. **Constance (1414–17):** Ended the Great Western Schism.

17. **Ferrara-Florence (1437–39):** Tried to achieve reunion of Eastern and Western churches.

18. **Lateran V (1512–17):** Discussed issues of church reform.

19. **Trent (1545–63):** Condemned Protestantism, issued doctrinal statements and reform decrees.

20. **Vatican I (1869–70):** Declared papal infallibility.

21. **Vatican II (1962–65):** Dealt with the renewal of the church.

Appendix 3

Use of Doctors in Recent Church Teaching

O NE WAY TO MEASURE the role of the *doctores ecclesiae* in the recent teaching of Roman Catholicism is to see how often the doctors have been cited in official documents. The most representative documents are the *Decrees of the Second Vatican Council* (1962–65), as indexed in *Acta Synodalia Sacrosancti Concilii Oecumenici Vaticani II: Indices* (Vatican City: Typis Polyglottis Vaticanis, 1980); and the *Catechism of the Catholic Church* (Vatican City: Libreria Editrice Vaticana, 1994). In the list that follows, the first number (in italics) refers to the number of citations in the Vatican II documents; the second (in bold) to the number in the catechism. In addition, I have included the numbers for the teachers mentioned in Part III who are not yet official *doctores ecclesiae*.

Official Doctors of the Church
Patristic

Athanasius of Alexandria	29	3
Ephrem the Syrian	12	0
Hilary of Poitiers	20	1
Cyril of Jerusalem	19	7
Basil the Great	53	7
Gregory of Nazianzus	31	11
Ambrose of Milan	111	21
John Chrysostom	114	18
Jerome	108	3
Augustine of Hippo	522	87
Cyril of Alexandria	36	2
Peter Chrysologus	1	4
Pope Leo I	107	11

Medieval

Pope Gregory I	128	6
Isidore of Seville	12	0
Bede the Venerable	12	0
John of Damascus	32	8
Peter Damian	5	0
Anselm of Canterbury	1	1
Bernard of Clairvaux	34	2
Anthony of Padua	2	0
Albert the Great	20	0
Bonaventure of Bagnorea	46	2
Thomas Aquinas	734	61
Catherine of Siena	5	3

Modern

Teresa of Avila	14	5
Peter Canisius	9	0
John of the Cross	8	4
Robert Bellarmine	29	0
Lawrence of Brindisi	2	0
Francis de Sales	21	1
Alphonsus de Liguori	0	1
Thérèse of Lisieux	15	6

Other Teachers
Patristic

Gregory of Nyssa	15	10
John Cassian	7	1
Boethius	2	0

Medieval

Maximus the Confessor	2	3
Isaac of Nineveh	0	1
Symeon the New Theologian	0	0
Hugh of St. Victor	2	1
Hildegard of Bingen	0	1
Aelred of Rievaulx	0	0
Gertrude the Great	0	0
Gregory Palamas	1	0
Julian of Norwich	0	1
Bernardino of Siena	3	0

Modern

Catherine of Genoa	1	0
Thomas More	1	1
Grignion de Montfort	6	0
John Henry Newman	20	4
Edith Stein	1	0

Index of
Doctrines
and Themes